The Photographer
and
The Nude

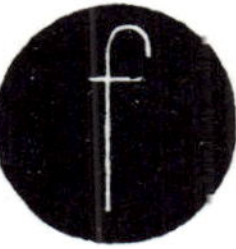

The Photographer and The Nude

HERBERT RITTLINGER

THE FOCAL PRESS
London and New York

ISBN 0 240 44971 1

This Book
was published by
WILHELM KNAPP VERLAG
Düsseldorf
under the title
DAS AKTFOTO: PROBLEM UND PRAXIS

English version by
HANS WOLFF

First published in 1961
Second Impression 1964
Third Impression 1967
Fourth Impression 1972

Plates printed in Great Britain by Maund & Irvine Ltd, Tring.
Text printed in Great Britain by Fletcher & Son Ltd, Norwich,
and bound by Richard Clay (The Chaucer Press) Ltd, Bungay, Suffolk

The Text

The Photographs

The Photographers

Expression and Endeavour

It has been said that nude photography is the most difficult field of pictorial and creative photography. In one respect this may be true, or partly true. But why should it be so much more difficult to take a photograph of a nude than a portrait, landscape or still life? Let us see.

It has also been said that landscapes are the easiest of subjects to take pictures of, and therefore the most suitable for the beginner.

Yes, but surely we are all too familiar with the seasonal spate of holiday snapshots that depict the world's finest landscapes as places desolate enough to give us the creeps! Not the author, not him. He is as pleased as Punch with his efforts and pulls out one print after another: "This is us on Lake Geneva, and that bit there is Mont Blanc."

Bad or amateurish landscape shots may be a matter for regret, but that is all. Bad or amateurish nudes are different. Intentional humour is one thing, unintentional slips are another. And, what is more important still, they may be in such doubtful taste as to be downright offensive. This is the crux of the matter and the main reason why nude photography is supposed to be difficult.

It is also the reason why the most rigorous and ruthless self-criticism is imperative for the photographer. He must throw out and destroy every negative that falls short of the idea behind the picture. He must also avoid anything that may arouse even the faintest suspicion of clumsy exhibitionism.

Above and beyond this all-important reservation, the notion that photographing the undraped human figure is extremely difficult is a myth. For good results no more and no fewer difficulties have to be overcome in this field than in any other.

Why Women Only?

Almost all nude photographs are of women. There is a psychological reason why this should be so. Traditionally the restless, driven or freely wandering male personifies dynamic force—not, it should be admitted, always to the benefit of humanity. In the dualism of the sexes he is the normally more active half while the static, receptive, maternal female represents the more passive half. That she is capable of showing more sense and circumspection than any male is also worth remembering.

Although that is a valid reason it is not the only one. There are some outstanding women photographers who are not in the least interested in male nudes and who, like their male colleagues, much prefer to seek out the shapely forms of their sisters.

A well-known art historian once disputed my belief that the female body makes a better subject than the male. He wrote that from the point of view of art (not of photography) he must contradict me: the female body was only "simpler", more relaxed in movement and therefore easier to represent photographically (and in art).

Indeed, that is the most important factor in favour of the female form, equally as important as the activity of the male. The male body—except when very young—simply does not happen to possess the charming lines and beautifully balanced curves of the normal female figure. Notwithstanding the opinion of Schopenhauer who maintained that it was "intellect befogged by instinct" that had formed this aesthetic law. Was it not rather the other way round, with instinct—but instinct guided by reason—being responsible?

It is just possible that my personal opinion of the unsuitability of men for nude photography is a little too one-sided. I have taken male nudes too, but few have pleased me. After all, we can produce a "beautiful picture" of a woman without falling into the trap of chocolate boxiness.

But a "beautiful" (should it be on a cigar box?) picture of a male nude in the act of hurling some heavy object or resting at nature's bosom can only too easily arouse a feeling of embarrassment in the beholder. Handsome men—and how significant that we are reluctant to apply the word "beautiful" to the male—are bearable only in musical comedy and some types of films. However, there are ways and means of approaching the ideal of classical times: fine nude pictures of men can now and again be had as long as they show genuine athletic or similar action.

But even when they are nothing but unobtrusive props in, for instance, a landscape, male nudes are usually impossible. It may be that there is something matriarchal about the primeval landscape. Corot put nymphs in his painting of French riversides—and modern Man is no longer a satyr but a hard-working breadwinner in factory or office—at best a football player, sailor, athlete or even an amateur photographer.

The Model Problem

Models are supposed to present another difficulty in nude photography. This is probably also correct in some circumstances. As for myself, I have never experienced any particular trouble. I have always managed to find among my friends and acquaintances girls with the necessary physical qualifications and, most important, the indispensable willingness to understand my intentions, however strange they probably appeared to the uninitiated. It is not every day, however, that Lady Luck sends two graceful and unadorned nymphs across my path. It did happen one fine day, though, on some beach or other. We were only out for an aimless stroll when we suddenly came upon two such nymphs. Though they quickly took to their heels and fled to the protecting cover of the dunes we met them again on the following day, and the chance meeting turned into a cause for rejoicing.

They were ballet dancers, unspoilt, unprejudiced and intelligent. They soon allowed me to use them as models to my heart's content, though "misuse" would be a more correct term, for modelling is very hard work. It is usual for things not to go as they should at the first try, and I always find it difficult to show my models consideration when I am straining to get the picture "just right".

Thus I have actually taken nude photographs of complete strangers. Admittedly the fact that my wife—herself my best model and faithful helpmate—was with me helped a good deal. It makes it much easier to make contact with strangers.

Professional Models

The notion that professional models are unsuitable because they are supposedly apt to strike routine poses, is another myth. Given the right kind of "raw material", it is still up to the photographer to fashion it to his liking, i.e. to teach the model what to do and what not to do. All studios engaged in magazine or advertising work use agency models exclusively. Theirs, of course, is commercial work and so the fact is mentioned only to support my argument. Our interest is in nude photography for its own sake.

No, the reason why professional models are out so far as we are concerned is an altogether different one: they are too expensive. This is specially true for outdoor photography. Good-looking and well-built art school models, on the other hand, are rarely come by. But I think a photographic society could do excellent work with professional models, arranging club evenings in a studio well equipped with artificial lighting.

Where to Look

The first place that springs to mind as a hunting ground for finding models is the nudist colony. It should be easy to convince the people who go in for nudism of our honourable intentions. And since we meet them already in the undraped state there should be few disappointments as to their physical qualifications.

But in the first place these associations and clubs refuse to act as model agencies, and rightly so. And in the second place they have become cautious as a result of abuse and are now in principle against all photography they cannot control. Finally, if you turn up in the role of a nosy guest you do not stand a chance at all.

But it is certainly not necessary to be a nudist and those who are not fond of the cult of nature should be able to find models among their close and not so close friends and acquaintances. This is quite the usual procedure, even in a good many professional circles.

To convince one's wife or close friend should not need special persuasive powers. Things are a little more difficult with the more distant acquaintances. If a prospective model has scruples about possible publication or display of the pictures in an exhibition it is better to think twice. If the scruples which may be the legitimate consequence of the model's job or background, cannot be dispersed it is better to leave well alone. Not everybody can or wants to snap their fingers at what the neighbours might say.

Incidentally, it would seem to be a fact that among some girls readiness to undress is coupled with surprising prudery. This must not be understood as any kind of recrimination. The reason for this is probably that side by side with harmless and unsuspecting naturalism many otherwise long extinct conventions seem to keep a last foothold among these same sections of society.

When the budding nude photographer comes across this type of girl he should again leave well alone. For he may well have some strange and undesirable experiences long after the event.

Photographer and Model

When all obstacles have been overcome—or, better still, if there are none to start with—the model who is not yet used to being photographed in the nude still has to get over the last and very understandable hurdle. This is embarrassment. After all there is a great difference between showing oneself in a swimsuit on the beach and being exposed to the scrutiny of masculine eyes in a state of stark nakedness, possibly indoors under ruthless artificial lighting.

He is lucky who has to wait only a second or two for the last garment to be dropped and deserves to be congratulated on his choice of model. But in this respect as throughout the session he must show sympathetic understanding. If he fails to do so he is certain to wreck all.

With the majority of models, and this is specially true indoors, the photographer will do well to allow the model to get used to her nakedness. He can easily bridge this period of waiting by looking after his preparations, setting up the camera, adjusting the lights, the tripod and attending to all the other odds and ends that need doing. One author recommends small talk and even a drink. I am no teetotaller but I prefer to have my drinks at a more suitable occasion. The small-talk is all right.

It will be found that the model quickly regains her unselfconsciousness without which no work can be done, even at the first session. She—and, of course, the photographer—are assisted by Eve's natural vanity, the pride she takes in her body and pleasant anticipation of the picture that is to be made. The most welcome but unfortunately not the most frequently met aid to success is understanding of and feeling for the work and ideas of the photographer.

On an earlier page I suggested that by the nature of her psychological make-up the female is more passive than the male. The fact that nature sometimes does the opposite of what is expected does not contradict my ideas. Nor do such active girls have any particularly masculine traits or qualities. Some models have a sparkling temperament, a quality one author considers greatly desirable. The photographer, he said, was bound to be infected and much inspired. ...

It is only too true. On one occasion, for instance, I had a girl from a ballet school for a model. She sparkled all right. It was a warm but overcast and sunless day. And since the true photographer's mood depends largely on the weather my spirits were on the low side. But the girl's vivacity really did carry me away until I sacrificed a whole length of 35 mm. film. After all, we can take pictures in any weather, with a few wise reservations.

And the results of that outing? Technically perfect and pictorially too shockingly bad to be true!

So I should say that the first and foremost requirement for good photography is that the photographer himself must feel "in the mood". And as far as the model is concerned I hold that a well balanced and equitable temperament is best. When photographer and model are good friends, when pleasure in the job, understanding, good will and fellow-feeling lend a hand, then we get our best results.

The photographer must be able to direct the model and to show her exactly how he wants her to hold her head, move her arms or turn her hips. Some hilarity will usually result but it must not lead to the photographer losing control of the situation. He must not assume that the model knows anything about posing; if she is able to make a contribution of her own, so much the better.

Ideal conditions obtain when photographer and model draw inspiration from each other in a genuine working partnership. The least satisfactory model is the girl who does not know how to move freely and unselfconsciously. The most uninhibited girls are ballet dancers and actresses because they have been trained to control their bodies.

With men the matter is both, more difficult and less complicated. Moral scruples do not arise except with people who cannot even think straight. Thinking of my own "qualifying" friends I cannot imagine that any of them would refuse. If a young man gets coy the reason is quite different—he feels he is making a fool of himself; if he is not so young he may be afraid of being thought vain.

The difficulties inherent in nude photography of men have been dealt with already. With men the idea of "space" is much more important than with girls. The more active part men play in life represents straightforward advice for the conception of the picture: Activity. Pictures of athletic, natural or spontaneous movement automatically solve the problem of space round the nude male figure and rarely bring failure. Admittedly I have seen convincing pictures of static male nudes, young athletic figures taken against a plain background in the studio, but they are few and far between. The pictures that spring to my mind are those made by a master of the twenties and thirties. Hoyningen-Huené, formerly of Paris and now in America.

As for the physical qualifications of *young* men, I have to say this: When I had my "medical" before military service I found myself in a crowd of naked young men, none of them more than 30 years old at the most. The setting, rows of desks between the bare walls of a class room, the dull grey light of early morning, matched the appearance of the boys—depressing to a degree. The procession of pot-bellied bodies, skin untouched by air, and varicose veins (under 30!) was grotesque. And, as a frequenter of public swimming baths, I had thought I had seen everything! My mistake, for at most, only half of the boys at the medical inspection ever went for a swim. They, of course, were better looking.

My ideas of the physical appearance of the average young man proved completely wrong. I had acquired them on sports grounds and in nudist colonies. Not that everybody there was a young Apollo, but at least the boys looked healthy. But then all our much praised age of sports and games gets its reputation from no more than 5 per cent of boys and men who are taking an active part. The remaining 95 per cent get their sport as spectators. They are the "fans" for whom athletic prowess exists only as far as the newspapers, pools and bookies.

The moral: finding male models is not easy either. But when a man has good proportions, is reasonably fit, and not too hairy, his age matters very little, at least up to his fortieth year or so. There are certainly many young boys between 14 and 17 with good figures, and they make the best male models. Even if their proportions fail to attain the acknowledged classical standards and when they are afflicted with teenage gaucherie their appearance is usually pleasing. After all, the body beautiful is not the only thing in our work that matters.

Children

Have I left out anything? Of course—children.

The pink, fat tummies of dimple-cheeked three-year-olds, the unfolding slenderness between the ages of 5 and 11, and the developing forms between childhood and adolescence, which comes all too soon and is characterized by an impression of things somehow not fitting properly—all this is still unfinished raw material, unmoulded shape. If children show anything at all they show all the innocence and sweetness, the beauty and sadness of the world, and the kindness of God. Taken all in all, there is no such thing as a child in the nude, only a naked child. To children the naked state is no problem but sheer happiness and freedom. A naked child is Life, amusing and charming, it is fun, heavenly fun!

From Head to Foot—Poetry and Prose

We have already seen that the theory of the inherent beauty of the human body does not prove 100 per cent correct in practice. A study of the crowds on any beach makes this fact more than clear. This does not mean that we never find sheer poetry striding right through the thick of the crowd in search of sun and water at Brighton or on Coney Island.

How old should a model be?

Youth in its often inarticulate animal beauty can be charming. But to say that the beauty of the female form can be photographed only up to the eighteenth year is an exaggeration. A body used to air and nakedness keeps its freshness and tautness, which always show up in the picture, for a surprisingly long time. The signs of *anno domini* appear first in the face.

No standard of human beauty can be set. To expect well shaped arms, hands, thighs and the rest all at the same time is to ask for a perfection that can only rarely be met with in any one person. However perfect a girl may appear at first sight, something, somewhere, is always out of harmony—to the consolation of her sisters. It may be that the breasts are too heavy, too low, or too small; or perhaps there is a somewhat baroque hipline.

But faults such as these and others need not mean that the model is unsuitable for nude photography. What they do is to make the photographer's work more exacting. He must take care to keep out those obtrusive details which only too easily creep into the picture turning it into a mere photograph of an undressed woman.

Even more than in portrait photography the photographer of nudes must be able to recognize the photogenic side of his model. However, even when he has found it he still has to work for the right pose which he will never get right at the first attempt. Its effect and expression depend on often trivial details of lighting and positioning of the body. This is the reason for our prosaic survey from head to foot.

The Head

Even in whole figure pictures the head is all-important. The fact that it can claim a wide field of its own—portrait photography—does not relegate the head to the status of a mere appendage of the body in nude photography. The head is the pivot for every turning movement of the body. This is so even when, as in ski turns, the movement begins from the hips, and in photography even when the head is turned in a different direction from the trunk.

From the tiredly drooping to the proudly erect head the gamut of expressions is richer than in the play of facial expressions alone. A model trained in a ballet school will "use her head" so naturally in perfect harmony with the shape and lines of her body that the photographer will rarely discover a flaw. Untrained or completely unmusical (I mean that) models are a different matter. Although the greatest number of pictures are spoilt by arms and hands doing things they should not, the result will be just as surely ruined if the bearing of the head fails to crown a pose or movement naturally and purposefully. Even if the facial expression is good.

The Face

The face of every human being has two unequal halves. This well known fact is worth remembering. Also, the photogenic side of the face is not always the same as the photogenic side of the body, but even this trouble can be smoothed out with suitable lighting and pose or a compromise between the two.

It is obvious that an unfitting or indifferent expression must ruin any nude picture. A face given expression by inner tension can be incredibly beautiful. A superficial or sensual expression can, in contrast to the faces of animals, degenerate into a grimace.

But if we explore the face more profoundly we trespass into the field of the subject of portraiture which, incidentally, has also failed so far to find a cure for lacking photo-suitability. Although portrait photography does not, therefore, know all the answers familiarity with its principles can help considerably. With a little extra effort anybody can be photographed.

I would suggest we keep to the basic rule of portrait photography which says that a slightly low camera position is best. But who would dare say that it is the only possible way? Even a high angle with the stark shadows of a glaring midday sun can be managed—by those who do not overlook them.

But when all is said and done it would be idle to prescribe rules for this or that head or body position or facial expression. If there is anything that needs continuous careful observation and perception of the whole, it is nude photography. But a word of warning is indicated before we go any further: whoever wants to work against the rules—and I am going to object to quite a few of the old ones—has to know them first! Only if we master the laws of photography are we in a position to flout them for the purpose of enhancing expression.

Throat and Neck

The neck is usually overlooked. True that it often seems to disappear in the overall picture but quite obviously it is entirely subservient to any movement that begins or ends with the head.

An unduly elongated neck may appear beautiful on the model and unattractive in the picture. So do taut and therefore strongly protruding throat muscles seen from a low camera angle, but sometimes they can be intentionally included in the picture. If the beauty of a throatline is to be shown it must be taken in profile.

Shoulders and Arms

In my opinion the shoulders and arms are the most beautiful parts of the female body. A model with shoulders that are neither too narrow and sloping nor too wide and masculine is a veritable gold mine of lines, planes and curves of a perfection and mobility that can only be seen in the female body. With some girls the region round the collar-bone has to be watched because with some poses deep hollows, the so-called salt cellars, may appear. Round shoulders are always preferable to square ones.

Notwithstanding the modern cult of the legs I say that well-shaped arms are a gift of the gods—and far more important for figure studies. We should not forget that human beings use their hands and arms not only for getting hold of their food and doing their work but also as a means of expression. Hands and arms express ideas from the dance of the primitive medicine man to the gesture of surrender to the enemy. The human hand can release an atom bomb or raise the conductor's baton. Compared to the arms and hands the legs have decidedly limited potentialities. The most primitive physical weapons of Man move only through an angle of 90°—but they are good enough to do half the work of driving his car.

The book of rules tells us that the arms should be slightly flexed but must never form a sharp angle. "Amputated stumps" must be watched for (as with the legs). Working against the rules means that the arms must be given specially careful consideration.

In daring intersections of lines, in the play of high or low camera angles the gestures of the arms must remain intelligible even when they are not directly visible or when the arms are intentionally or even grotesquely reduced to "stumps".

The Hands

The hands are a world in themselves. A wealth of gestures of the hands expresses a wealth of ideas important enough to find expression also in words: to lay one's hand on something, to raise a hand, to shake hands. Our hands can refute, reject, menace, throw, beckon, implore, give and take. All these and many more actions can be expressed by the hands. They are the most universal members of the human body. And in nude photography they are frequently the most superfluous.

Wanted: Model who knows what to do with her hands.

Everything and anything can happen; from shadows cast in the wrong place to well rounded gestures and a wide-angle effect without wide angle lens. The play of gestures and poses of hands and arms yield the most powerful mimic expressions in nude photography as elsewhere. To reduce the gestures to their simplest and most natural form free from bathos must be the main endeavour of the photographer.

The Breasts

Sentimental woolly thinking of a long dead past misnamed the breasts "bosom" or "bust". They are mammary glands, a secondary sex characteristic of the human female, and their name is breasts.

Unfortunately it is not often that we find perfectly shaped breasts. But imperfection is not necessarily a bar to success for pose, lighting and camera angle all play their part in covering up faults.

In any case the breasts should be considered not as separate detail but together with the whole body. Small breasts and a tall, perhaps even masculine figure may look just as unattractive as large breasts on a small figure.

Pendulous breasts are the most common fault. Full breasts that are inclined to hang low can often be included in the picture and played down by suitable lighting, arm pose and intersecting lines. Small, flapping breasts are hopeless by themselves but if the girl has an otherwise good figure there is no need to give up. The pose can be arranged so as to hide the breasts; they are usually invisible when the model takes up a prone position.

As a rule a low angle is best. A high angle combined with top lighting, for instance under the vertical sunlight of noon, can cast shadows that caricature the figure and make it appear deformed. Under artificial lighting with more than one lamp the nose as well as the breasts have to be watched with special care for double or crossing shadows. They must be eliminated at all times.

Thick or very dark areolae may also look conspicuous and unpleasing. A little vaseline can often improve matters as it will bring out good highlights in the right lighting conditions. The areolae contract in low temperatures and expand and become a little lighter when warm.

The Body

The abdomen is anything but a featureless surface. On the contrary, it is a fairly complex structure with many hills and dales, all of them controlled by the rectus muscle. The photographer has to watch out for the deep skin folds which can appear so easily in bending or sitting poses of even young and taut figures. Although quite a natural phenomenon, the characteristics of photographic reproduction, whether in colour or black and white, give them an exaggerated and highly undesirable importance.

The richly modulated surface of the back poses similar problems of lighting, outdoors as well as in the studio. Any pronounced twisting of the body forms excessively pronounced skin folds running up from the pelvis which make it impossible to get a good picture.

The pelvic girdle, another source of undesirable folds, joins the abdomen and the back. Its muscles have a great power of expression and can portray exact opposites; they can make the model look taut, joyful and proudly disciplined—or flabby, spongy or simply relaxed.

The Pelvis

The pelvis is the most self-contained part of the human skeleton. The female pelvis is as a rule broad and placed fairly low while the male pelvis is narrow and higher. Nature, however, frequently breaks its own rules, not, it must be said, to the advantage of the model. A female body with narrow hips and pelvis can look right but only if the impression is of a boyish and not a masculine figure. If a girl has an otherwise normal figure and a small pelvis it looks as if something were missing.

The backs of the thighs from the buttocks down, sometimes as far as the hollows of the knees, frequently show another unpleasing fault in the form of rolls of fat. They are usually taken to come with age but have really little to do with *anno Domini*. Even young girls with trim and slim figures may have them; they are the penalty of civilization, caused by too much sitting or standing to the exclusion of other postures. Long hours of work in office or factory reduce the blood circulation in the skin and bring out the underlying layers of fat. A natural but regular massage by air and water is the best cure.

The Legs

The legs are suspended from the rigid frame of the pelvis. In contrast to the arms whose job it is to take, pull, or push an object, the legs must carry, raise, lower and shift the centre of gravity. The legs can also point, beckon and play football. Their mime, however, is of a different kind from that of the arms; I would call it more concentrated on physical aspects and less "spiritual".

What we must pay attention to from the beginning is the difference between the leg that carries the weight of the body and the one that is, so to speak, idle. The weight-bearing leg has the most conspicuous effect on the pelvis and its muscles but as it shifts the centre of gravity it naturally influences the whole posture. An amusing experiment will prove the importance of the point; standing sideways with the right leg and right shoulder (or vice versa, of course) touching a wall it will be found impossible to raise the left leg.

"Informed opinion" still maintains quite seriously that standing with legs apart looks clumsy. But it is an opinion based on traditional ideas of beauty which fail to see the possibilities or the grace inherent in strong and determined movement.

Body Hair

Whether to hide pubic hair or include it in the picture is a moot point. In Anglo-Saxon countries the majority seems to be in favour of elimination. I am against this falsification, if only because of the balancing effect of the small dark pattern. A photograph from which the hair has been removed by retouching looks simply horrible and is just as incompatible with natural thought as a fig leaf.

It goes without saying that anything conspicuous or obtrusive is strictly out. But we have a number of ways of doing this quite naturally at the taking stage without offending good taste, from the arrangement of shadows to the angle of view.

Excessive growth of hair looks very unpleasing on bad or unhealthy skin. Thick matting on a manly chest is something even the owner usually bears with resignation. Exactly how this characteristic appears in a photograph I cannot say—I have never tried it.

The Skin

Apart from the hair, everything, i.e. the skeleton, muscles, fat and flesh is covered by skin. How to reproduce its texture effectively will be discussed on page 91. Here I will say only this: the skin is an organ that indicates without fail health, illness, and the damages caused by civilization and neglect. The skin should have a pleasant smell, good colour, strong blood circulation, and elasticity and tautness until middle age and later. A healthy skin used to open air looks natural in the photograph. In addition it also has the effect of making even those figures acceptable and pleasing to look at that may not quite stand up to the other canons of beauty. This brings us to a principle that should be remembered whenever a model is considered. The general appearance is more important than small physical defects. Second in importance is the already mentioned ability to move and behave freely and spontaneously.

Don't be discouraged, dear reader, if you can't find perfection. Here is a quotation for you, taken from a film magazine: "It is a generally known fact that a photograph is always more beautiful than reality."

Beauty and Form

In the famous Ghent altar pieces by the brothers Jan and Hubert van Eyck we discern, for the first time since antiquity, real human beings of flesh and blood. These two took such a pleasure in their newly discovered realism and natural truth that they depicted the figure of Eve in ruthless nakedness. In the caption to a modern reproduction of this Eve I read: "For the rest, this female body certainly appeared considerably more beautiful to the beholder of the time than to us."

It is said that Rubens' women and the majority of Dürer's nudes with their protruding bellies no longer appeal to our "standards of beauty". Maybe so, if we accept the criterions of show business. Yet Rembrandt's etchings of nudes are so masterly and incredibly realistic that we ask ourselves how they could possibly have been made and accepted three hundred years ago. What a good thing that Rembrandt, Rubens and Dürer were not photographers!

The ancients sought to discover the secret of form by thorough study of nature.

The artists of the renaissance were aided in understanding and representing form and the interdependence of form and function by the revolutionary discoveries of anatomy. Without their help the works of Michelangelo and Leonardo da Vinci are just as unthinkable as those of the masters of our time.

Do we have to know Anatomy?

One of the finest books on anatomy is the famous volume by Andreas Vesalius. In this old and learned work we see human beings deprived of their skins, with muscles hanging from their bodies in flaps. All this in a setting of typically southern landscapes. The muscles and pieces of muscles are neatly numbered or marked in Greek letters, and the "demolition", in this case a steady penetration of the body down to the skeleton, proceeds methodically from plate to plate.

Once the nature and function of a muscle have been thoroughly discussed, it is partly detached and made to stand away from the body. The process of removal goes on until the muscles, having been finally cut away, are stood in a corner or hung from a hook.

To the layman the medical skeletons and muscle figures, though indispensable to the artist, are now as ever nightmarish things. The question is, does the completely new approach of photography still require a knowledge of anatomy?

Since photography approaches things from outside one should think that careful observation of surface conditions, and perhaps of proportions, would be sufficient.

Well, it is sufficient for anybody who has fully grasped the fact that photography is different. If above and beyond that fact he also knows his way through anatomy, well and good. But his knowledge is valuable only in an academic way. For photographic expression it is more or less unimportant.

I am aware that what I am saying is plain heresy. But it is in no way superficial. Let me explain what I mean with an example.

A certain small lateral movement of the head causes the sterno-mastoid muscle, which runs from the jaw to the hollow of the throat, to stand out prominently. If an art student sees this during his drawing lesson without knowing the reason why, he loses his sure touch and draws an empty if "beautiful" outline. But the camera is not only an extension of the hand like a pencil or piece of charcoal, it is also an extension of the eye. And the camera says "that muscle" of its own accord. Here the inferiority of our mechanical camera has become its asset, but unless we understand its function as an extra eye the picture remains unfinished or, at best, turns out to be a sketch like an academic drawing.

The more exact knowledge of the human body acquired after the time of Michelangelo and Leonardo, though, was not able to help painters create richer or greater representation of forms. The upsurge of art during the renaissance was conditioned by that happy period of human progress when science and the arts, which to-day have no longer much in common, were essentially one. Does the secret of form then rest on the problem of proportions for us?

The classic rule of the golden section stipulates that a pictorial representation pleases when the ratio of the smaller to the larger part is 5 : 8. If the human figure were measured from top to toes, the golden section, it says, would appear at the lower ribs. This is supposed to prove the correctness of the rule when applied to the human body and also to all other proportions found in human and animal representation.

Michelangelo liked to be thought a great mathematician. In his works, however, he unconcernedly deviated from the coldly reasoned rules of the golden section. Dürer also occupied himself a great deal with the problems of proportion, and he demanded that the artist follow conscientiously in his work the calculations which the Creator embodied in His.

The photograph of our day comes to life by modern means of such optical correctness—for the objective sees objectively—that some people find all form that has not been transfigured and authorized by History, questionable. Others dive head first into metaphysical interpretations whose staleness reminds one of the smell of cold tobacco smoke in a deserted pub.

The new lenses themselves have no prejudice. They are grand and generous enough to allow the most contradictory methods to seek out the secret of form.

But it takes a lot to recognize this truth in the picture inflation of our age.

The Static Nude

Statics, the branch of the science of mechanics that deals with the laws pertaining to the equilibrium of bodies, is equally important in the aesthetic field. Verticals and horizontals are static in the pure sense of the word; so is the cross.

The interest of a static composition in figure studies lies in contrast. The beholder must be able to sense that mobile living beings have been put in a state of repose, but a repose that rests exactly on their mobility.

The tremendous substantiality of photography plays an all-important part in static composition. The muscular firmness of a thigh, the soft quality of a woman's body in light and shade—these are first of all facts that appear to insist on static expression, no matter what feelings they may evoke in us. This leads straight to the form that has been most clearly moulded by Western sculpture in the course of two and a half milleniums. No accusation of imitating can be entertained.

We are able to add the thrill of lines which play a more important part in photography than in painting without, however, attaining the sensitivity of a drawing. Line in photography is rather something between the two; in painting it has been pushed into the background and in drawing it becomes a fault, the limitation of outline and substance.

Line has great power of expression. According to the author Scheltema every vertical line is associated with the idea of masculine defiance and self-assertion, the negation of all weight, and masterful power over its environment.

The horizontal is different. It has a feminine quality, not rebellious but reasoning and calming, due to its parallelism with Mother Earth. This makes it abundantly clear what a wealth of expression the cross offers, even without reference to its meaning as the Christian symbol. Naturally, the expression will alter radically with the relative strength of the vertical or horizontal which in its turn depends on the higher or lower position of the point of intersection.

Does all this mean that in our practical work we should not picture female nudes in a standing pose? To answer in the affirmative would be misunderstanding the issue. Every human being incorporates male and female elements, and the factual idea "standing female nude" may well be more important to me than the vertical in itself.

In any case sculptors have always found it feasible to portray men in a resting and prone position, "in a feminine pose likened to the Earth", solving the problem in masterly fashion. This is different from pictorial photography where a resting or "dying warrior" has become an impossibility. It simply will not do. It is another matter, of course, when such a picture is part of a soul-shattering documentary reportage.

The prone position is very popular for female nudes and can be acceptable even when posed as a "beautiful" study, given the right conditions. The same position showing a man must have an unmistakable atmosphere of holidays and sunbathing, otherwise it is wrong. And any attempt at symbolism would be cheap trash.

When a standing figure raises both arms at right angles to the body the vertical line may be cancelled out without abruptness. If the subject is to be a detail or close-up—which must be determined in the viewfinder or on the focusing screen at the taking stage—planes are stressed and curves command attention without, however, contradicting the static idea. The static figure study offers a multitude of possibilities. It can be most impressively used to approach the laws classical art formulated with respect to the human body. Not in imitation but in free re-creation of their principles the photographer can make use of the static nude to form ever new images of human beauty, itself imperishable and essentially static.

The Dynamic Nude

One of the most popular graphic and photographic fashions of the day is the diagonal. Everybody swears by it, not least the editors of illustrated papers. They use it in make-up and lay-out if not always in the pictorial matter. For the diagonal is "dynamic".

This is true, but it is only half the truth. True in that the diagonal is the most conspicuous and most easily manipulated component of dynamics. And dynamics is the science of forces producing motion. It does not necessarily have anything to do with photographs of movement.

In a photograph of movement the moving forces are, of course, immediately obvious. A picture of a boy throwing a javelin in the middle of a jump, for instance, taken from a worm's eye view, is *ipso facto* dynamic. But only because a strong and obvious diagonal runs from top left to bottom right, supported by a weaker diagonal running in the opposite direction, does the picture gain the power of dynamic expression.

A portrait with a diagonal line running from the top of the head (the parting) via the nose to the chin can equally well show the inner force that stamps it with genuine dynamic expression. And a nude taken, say, from a low angle with feet firmly planted on the ground, legs shown in exaggerated perspective, the body diminishing towards the top to make it seem to fall into the picture, is not a compromise but an equally unobjectionable dynamic conception.

For all that the diagonal is not the only, not even the most interesting component of "inner force". From it we go on to the repeatedly broken forms (the jumping boy), to arrive finally at the curves.

Curves

Curves are mysterious shapes of a particular dynamism whose motive force originates at a point outside the curve. In geometric terms it originates at the centre of the circle. If the straight line, reduced to its essence, belongs to the world of inorganic forms such as crystals, the curve belongs to the world of organic matter, to the movement of life itself.

What this means for us is plain to see. The diagonal is cool, it has an element of demanding strictness—qualities that are, admittedly, advantageous in nude photography. But the beautiful roundness of a woman's shoulder breaking through the strict system; the young girl inclining her body towards the water without any awareness of the inner forces her round, swinging movement releases—these things are grace, warmth, life itself.

Why do we have to discuss all this in such detail—perhaps even frightening off the patient reader?

Well, if we want to get a clear idea about the technique of building up a picture, we are willy-nilly forced to visualize the abstract forms of each picture element if we are to be able to check their positions, logical relationships and possibilities within the picture area. Then, when they have ceased to be mere ideas and become usable elements of composition, imagination can have a free rein.

But to turn back to more practical matters: many other picture components can be made dynamic by the suitable use or reinforcement of photographic expression. Here are some examples:

Any momentary immediacy such as a passing facial expression. Neither diagonal lines nor movement have to be discernible;

Surprising opposites of light and shade, possible even with several static nudes. This touches on "colour in black and white";

"Pointillism"—white and black dot patterns on the body;

Strong high angles and radical low angles with deliberate distortion;

All extremes in general. Big close-ups, deliberate stressing of texture and any other exaggerated realism can always be classified as dynamic.

In the thirties the idea of candid photography became the fashion. It was intended to supply sincere pictures, true to life, and unposed. A praiseworthy intent, applicable, incidentally, to nudes as well. But it soon degenerated. Dynamism, though a perfectly true characteristic of photography, does no good when it represents an effort at any cost and the message is no longer in proportion with the effect.

Shoot faster! is the cry. But a moment is not necessarily momentous. The world of moments captured by the lens fades all too soon in the album of oblivion.

The author Benno Reiffenberg wrote:

"Nothing is to-day beyond the reach of photography and the newsreel, but much of what happens to-day seems to happen only for the level of the newsreel. ... Modern photography has been living for years through a renaissance, a reawakening of its origin. It is turning away from the instant, that unnatural section of time, and instead seeks impact. The good photograph, it is now admitted, incorporates an element of duration." And he adds in parenthesis: "It is also possible to take away the characteristic of a movement, and that is an element of static photography".

To me this seems to be the most unequivocal definition yet of the essence of a genuine dynamic photograph.

The Motivated Nude

After all that has been said before, what follows now is almost superfluous. But I certainly do not want to leave out any aspect of practical nude photography. In a fairly early book I read a complaint that nude photography allegedly suffered from a serious poverty of ideas. ...

General photography can be roughly subdivided into pictorial and documentary, portrait and character, press and feature, record and advertising, landscape and architectural, still life, aerial, sports and action, nude and nude portrait photography; micrography, black and white and colour. It is possible to carry the subdivisions further, to define still narrower categories—there are experts in all of them. Nude photography can be divided into almost as many sub-headings. Why then "poverty of ideas"?

A little earlier on I listed, starting with the one very limited subdivision of the dynamic nude, no fewer than seven additional ideas or subsections capable in practice of being permuted *ad infinitum*. Therefore, if one can speak of poverty of ideas at all, then only in the sense of the traditional "beautiful" figure study and the romantic picture of a bygone age. I do not mean to say that a nude study must not be beautiful. More than one of the illustrations selected for this book should prove the opposite.

No, what we must reject is the kind of pose that comes from woolly thinking. In this day and age we want a different approach; we have become sensitive to empty phrases. What kind of stuff was it we used to be treated to?

A gladiator posed by the watery waste possessed of a rusty sword and shield and nothing else besides, can at best produce only one reaction to-day: pathetic memories of an age when this sort of thing could be admired in photographic publications of the highest renown. Not that it is all that long ago.

Another picture showing a gentleman playing the piano on which a naked and forlorn lady was posed and called *Andante* (the picture, not the girl) must have been an advance perception of surrealism and appeared too beautiful for words! I also remember another young lady who covered her eyes modestly with her hands and was chaperoned by a stuffed owl.

Still, we ought at least to recognize the courage of those symbolizing and interpreting artists to produce such pictures. Even if we of a later generation use them as an easy target for our sarcasm. Our attitude is this:

(1) The modern nude photograph needs no motivation, no setting to produce an excuse. Not even when the setting serves a decorative purpose or is entirely incidental. For when the execution goes wrong the picture becomes an object of ridicule every time. For instance, when the connection between nude and setting is so far-fetched that even the most benevolent imagination turns schizophrenic. Or—and this happens most often with romantic nudes—when the setting for the nude is intended to appeal to cheap sentiment.

(2) The motivated nude study is the most difficult. Hajeck-Halke was the man to create a successful picture of this type—a surrealist multiple exposure of the window of some low dive, words scribbled on walls, and a female torso. He gave it the title: "Seamen's Abode". What a subject—but the kind of subject that has to be visualized long before the first exposure.

The Character Nude

Clearly the genre or character nude is also "motivated". Here the mood originates in the first place with the figure in conjunction with some typical everyday scene. It does not derive from lighting, texture, shape or form of the nude. Avoiding all obvious props such as a bed in disorder, a slipping stocking, or overflowing ashtrays, it is easy to achieve time and again quite good results without the need for experiments.

A young girl seen in morning light by the window need not have been inspired by any romantic painter, nor a girl stepping out of her bath by Degas. No picture of a beautiful nude in a marble bath or under the shower must necessarily look like a hackneyed film still, and a girl before her mirror can still be the most natural subject of all. The nakedness of women in all such pictures is real, whether conceived objectively or romantically with "mood". Thus we may say that if the picture is to satisfy and appear natural, nakedness must seem motivated only accidentally.

Difficulties arise more easily with artificial light in a room or studio than out of doors. If the picture is not built up as a "natural" character study or conceived as an abstract photograph, we get objective pictures whose interest and charm is derived from the infinitely variable play of light and pose. The more objective the better. Line and shape, beauty and distinctness of form, and the thrilling play of limbs are subjects in themselves whether in the form of sketches or as finished pictures.

Props

When props are not natural requisites of the character nude they are fairly certain to spoil the picture. The same can be said for exaggerated spotlight effects. And seductive lingerie does not necessarily belong to genuine nude photography.

One moment, though: undies are a well paying prop of advertising photography. The underwear industry is a big customer of commercial photography and naturally cannot advertise without showing its wares. Sometimes the sex angle is somewhat subdued, sometimes, in advertising smalls from nylons to bras it is cleverly exploited. In this type of photography the nude picture is a means to an end with objective motivation, but it does need the sure touch of good taste.

Out of Doors

Motivating the nude is least difficult out of doors; water, air and sun in their multiple and photographically infinitely exploitable variations are nature's gift to the photographer. If he feels like turning the panoptic view before him into a peep show with titles such as "Nymph by the Stream", "Surprised", "Innocence", or "The Huntress", he had better keep it quiet.

When a title is really necessary for exhibition or publication it should be as matter of fact as possible. Nobody with any fellow-feeling for this dilemma will object to one of the accepted utility titles like "On the Beach", "The Bath", or even "Sea and Sun".

As for myself, I quite simply try to get fresh and natural pictures free from artificiality and pose with my outdoor nudes. The fact that besides the representation of the free human being the landscape is sensibly present and mostly plays an equally important part, is not accident but design.

Nude and Landscape

In an old volume of the well-known *Photograms of the Year* which I bought in a second-hand book shop in London I found an outdoor nude photograph, a girl posed beautifully and naturally on a rocky sea-shore. Her right hand carelessly pulled some sea-weed from the water. Underneath a pleasingly matter of fact title: "Ebb-Tide". The picture showed quite recognizably that it was really low water. Strong side-rear lighting, almost back-lighting, gave pleasing modelling to the body without suppressing the least shadow detail. The negative material can only have been an ordinary dry plate, not even ortho, for the volume was published in the year 1895.

At that time bathing in the nude was quite an improper thing to do, and photography against the light had not even been officially invented. But the picture is so good that we would certainly have included it in this book if a print had been available, and for its pictorial quality, not as a period picture. For this simple photograph, taken sixty years ago and dating from a period when photography, in contrast to its beginnings, was hardly producing masterpieces, is timeless and beautiful.

It is easy to imagine what would have happened if the author, Henry A. Collins, had tried to follow the style of the period and to put his photograph "on a higher level". All that admirable spontaneity would have disappeared and the picture become impossible for us. As it is, it still enchants us because it not only solves the problems of space and expression in the most natural manner but because above and beyond that it tells us that nakedness and primitive landscape are eternal.

The girl of 1895 and the picture are beautiful because subject and setting are natural. A picture of a girl of our age photographed in a state of undress on a mountain peak will in all probability make the beholder shiver even in the year 1975. If, to crown all, the picture bears the title: "Light Prayer", the fault is not that of photography.

I am not in favour of naked people viewing the world from mountain tops. At least, I am not in favour of people pretending to do it. But if your girl friend or a fellow climber discard their rucksacks and look around, or take up a position on the hard support of their skis in order to let the hot mountain sun tan their hides, you can make more than a record snapshot of the picture. It would make a good example of a motivated landscape.

It is rarely necessary to motivate the connection between landscape and nude. Nine times out of ten it is better not attempted. For the landscape is there—big and eternal, even if spoilt by the hand of Man. It suffers and serves, it is beautiful and romantic, and Man himself is part of nature even if he has forgotten it. Fern and flower, field and forest, and the river gleaming in the shaft of morning sunlight are his no less than the telephone, the motor car, and the wrist watch. Mountains, deserts and the sea take him above himself.

There are few primitive landscapes into which Man does not seem to fit, and water suits him particularly well. Even the most desolate ground becomes attractive when it is enlivened and broken up by water, be it a spring up in the mountains, a quiet stream, a mighty river rolling through the plains, or the sea.

So no attempt should be made to turn fine landscapes into pretty-pretty pictures. On the other hand, even the nude figure must "live" in the landscape, even if she acts only as a prop without doing anything at all. She can be put in a familiar and even intimate relationship with it, or she can be made to appear lonely or overwhelmed by it. Even symbolic representation is permissible on condition that it is not forced. It must have its natural origin in the landscape, not in the model's pose. The nude must fit the landscape naturally; she can be portrayed in idle or active play, doing something ordinary—or just being there.

And we can indulge in romanticism to our heart's content without scruples. Nature cares nothing whether and how profoundly it influences our minds, whether we find it romantic or not. But when it is beautiful it fulfils our needs in a most liberal way. Sundrenched beach and shimmering sea are as rich in form and tone as the saturated green of sluggish streams and the bright leaves above a lake.

If our search of nature is sincere, what does it matter if we transform eternal subjects like trees, water, and human beings in our own way? Man suffers from a profound nostalgia for the lost paradise. And paradise has a fairly strong objection to being resolved into its factual components by a modern precision anastigmat.

Not far from the Mediterranean shore, pregnant with culture, we have often taken our sailing boat to islands to which humanity seldom finds its way. Uninhabited and unimportant, they are embedded like jewels in the blue sea that changes to a mother-of-pearl hue when the south wind blows. Rocky cliffs with pure marble showing in places at the surface rise bare and steep from the sea, populated by thousands of cormorants and the fattest seagulls in the world. But in between the rocks myrtle, laurel, figs, prickly pears and cistus roses unite to form a small and secretive wilderness in every hollow.

In their rare perfection these islands represent the absolute landscape. I mean that they are regions, already so remote from us civilized people, in which the elements, rock, water, and sky meet yet remain pure without permeating and toning down each other. For us human beings these zones can only be passages or paths. At one time they provided a path to Heaven, for their last inhabitants were hermits in the time of the Byzantine empire. Cave-like vaults, crumbling masonry and cisterns remind us of these men. Mute witnesses, surrounded by the droppings and eternal bickerings of the birds, they bake in the pitiless sunshine of a realm where only the breath of creation matters.

I am not being frivolous if I say that in such a landscape the human being, as a means of expression, can *only* appear naked. This is nothing whatever to do with so-called symbolism. It is simply that romanticism and the factual components of the scene form one great unity.

But back to practical work. In landscapes the human figure must be a complete human being. Our model must cease to be a model and detach herself at least temporarily from the urbanity in which all of us live. A picture of a fashion model who remains a fashion model even on the shore of the Atlantic is—a fashion picture, taken for a purpose. It can never be figure study.

Problems and Fascinations of Colour

Even non-photographers sense that colour photography is different from painting. The tremendous fascination and powerful impact of colour have been experienced by all. Only, it restricts the creative freedom of our work to still narrower limits and makes it anything but easier for anybody endowed with only a little sense of responsibility as a craftsman.

Colour is not just a matter of skin rendering—a problem about which we shall have to say a few words later—but requires careful attention to a number of other things. We have learned, not always easily, to take clean workmanship in black and white for granted and we must be just as exacting in colour even though it starts from quite different premises.

The majority of the illustrations to this book have been so unequivocally conceived as black and white pictures that they cannot even be imagined in colour. Black and white photography is a transformation of colour into differential and often unfamiliar grey tones; it is Life interpreted in terms of light and shade, it is writing in light. The black and white photograph is an abstraction. The technique of taking photographs is the technique of translating colour into another medium.

"With colour photographs translating is not required. You put a colour film into your camera and, if the exposure is correct, the subject appears in natural colours ..."

That is what they tell the uninitiated but it just is not so. In fact, it is about the biggest piece of nonsense imaginable. If we want to get results that are to go under the heading of good pictures, colour photography needs as much translating as black and white. Also, to say it again, we must work to narrower limits. So if anybody loads his camera with colour film in the happy illusion that he will be able to decide later whether he wants black and white or colour prints from his negative or transparency, I can only hope he will not waste too much precious material before enlightenment comes to him.

Fifty Years of Progress

Photography is about 130 years old. Colour photography can also look back on a life of fifty years, a fact that is only too often forgotten under the impact of the development of recent years. Unfortunately, even our modern methods are still rather rigid, and paper prints are not always pleasing in tone. On the other hand, the photo-mechanical processes can make perfectly good reproductions of even miniature transparencies as long as we see to it that block maker and printer do not alter the colours too arbitrarily.

Colour photography is still at the stage when it will tackle anything and everything. "It confesses," wrote Paul Fechter, "to all the wonderful chocolate box trash which it is the duty and purpose of art to avoid—trees in blossom and lilac bushes nodding over green meadows with kids and lambs. Seen from the point of view of colour photography, the relation between art and nature looks like this: nature appears much more real and right in the pictures of so-called bad painters. With their paintings of flowering heaths and young silver birches over rippling waters that mirror the blue of the sky, they approach the colourful reality of nature much more closely than the great masters of the landscape from Rubens and Ruisdael to Trübner and Van Gogh."

What we have seen of colour photography in print and at slide shows has only too often been a flood of trash, an orgy in aniline dyes. Of course there is also good work to be seen; there are excellent advertising pictures, some fine frontispieces and plates in books by a few proved masters for which not a little of the credit must go to publisher and printer. Thus the potential scope of colour photography does come to light in isolated instances, though less frequently than the advertising copy writers would have us believe. When we do find first class colour pictures they are all the finer.

Colour photography in general and nude colour photography in particular should aim at interpreting life with the same perfection as black and white, and to translate it into a genuine message in colour in the same way as, for instance, the impressionists did. Only in a manner different from either, in its own way and with its own means.

Nude Photography Outdoors

You can take nude photographs on a footpath in a park. But if you do the picture must make it quite clear that the park belongs to an establishment for training athletes.

I can think of a host of "outdoor studios": places one finds by accident, places close to nature or divorced from nature, or a roof garden high above the city streets.

A picture of the prettiest girl would make one shiver if it had been taken between the bare bushes of early spring when the rough winds of March sweep across the fields. A naked person on a bus platform may make a subject for a surrealist picture, but is more likely to be an exhibitionist who is going to be arrested at any moment. This may also happen to your model if you pose her in a flowery meadow open to the public gaze. Possibly the onlookers enjoy the view but gratitude you cannot expect. On the contrary, they "take offence". The consequences depend on where you are and to some extent on the local magistrates.

Fortunately however, it is nowhere too difficult to find a place that is not open to the public gaze, once the city streets have been left behind. Where the public does not have access it is not easy to bring a complaint of indecent exposure.

The cry of terror: "Somebody's coming!", the frantic attempts of the model at covering both top and—'er—lower half at the same time, usually without succeeding at either, spoil the mood of the moment irretrievably. It will never be the same again.

The most convenient localities are, naturally, the grounds of nudist associations which are often situated amidst attractive scenery. What else is there? Lonely beaches or river banks, lakes with or without the help of a boat, private parks and gardens, woods and copses and nature in general where it is not yet overrun by hordes of trippers and hikers. If you are keen you will soon develop a kind of sixth sense for these things.

The Background

Horizon and background are more or less interdependent in nude photography out of doors. Moving the horizon down to the bottom of the picture area or up to the top or making it disappear altogether completely changes the background from the same camera position. This is a most important fact.

A rule worth remembering is this: If an object is to stand out from its background the background must be neutral.

The experience gathered from only a few attempts that have gone wrong, teaches the background rule to the rawest beginner. In normal practical work the way to neutralize a strongly patterned background (very effective at times) is to get close to the subject and to use a wide aperture. (Differential focusing.)

With miniature cameras out of doors it is usually inadvisable to select a smaller aperture than *f*5.6 or 6.3 for this purpose; with a four inch lens the limit is about *f*8 or 9. If I stop down to *f*16 or even *f*22 (this latter only with lenses of more than 4 inches focal length) it is either in order to arrange the lines or shape of the nude as an ornamental picture component to fit in with the background; or, and this can be very important, in order to get an essential foreground sharp from the bottom of the picture to the nude.

But whether the background is neutral or not, lighting must always play an important part. More about this on later pages.

This is not a beginners' textbook on photography. The reader is assumed to be familiar with its elementary principles and a little more besides. I may therefore be allowed to limit my observations on backgrounds and settings to a reiteration of a few general rules.

However much I ponder about my own, very varied work I cannot think of more than three types of setting generally suitable for outdoor nude photography. I should like to divide them into three groups:

(1) Light and Brightness.
(2) Stone and Rock.
(3) Vegetation and Foliage.

Group (1) comprises all the scenes that are full of light. Under this heading go all open beach and sea settings, bright water scenes in the widest sense, high skies, and all wide open spaces of nature in general.

In the flood of light generally found in such settings the traditionally highly valued tone rendering may go completely by the board. Taken in the wrong direction, the most beautiful summer sky, which always has a lighter and darker side, looks inglorious and desolate. This is important because a well rendered sky with or without clouds is not only able to stress, but it may even be the only means of creating, the essential setting for the pictorial conception of the nude herself.

Since the most favourable direction for taking the sky does not always coincide with the most favourable lighting of the subject, some knowledge of filters and filter effects is needed.

Filters

Generally speaking I use filters as little as possible. For all pictures with little or no sky I hardly ever use a filter. Nevertheless I have to work with them on the all too frequent occasions when undesirable effects have to be suppressed or desirable ones obtained. I have limited my range to UV, light and medium yellow, green and medium red filters.

The red filter is used only in conjunction with ultra fast pan film with exaggerated red sensitivity, mainly by the sea and on sandy beaches where the long-wave red rays predominate, in contrast to the ultra violet rays of the mountains. In these circumstances the red filter has, as it were, a double effect and must be handled with great discretion if the results are not to disappoint. It may lead to artificial looking effects and also to completely unnatural chalky whites and a horrible skin texture under an almost black sky. On the other hand, it is possible in completely flat lighting and under a high sun to use this brightness reversal for impressive characterization and specifically graphic expression.

The filter factor, by the way, of even light red filters is never less than 8–10, not even in late afternoon. As a rule the factors given by the makers are too small.

As the red filter alters the focus the lens must be stopped down to at least *f*12 (four inch lens). On most occasions I have still been able to use 1/10 or 1/25 second with the camera hand held. This however is due to my laziness and not really to be recommended. The thing to do is to use a tripod. It does not disgrace even miniature cameras.

Colour photography with reversal film needs, at least between 11 a.m. and 3 p.m., special filters (skylight filters in various shades of pink) to eliminate the blue cast which otherwise spoils pictures taken in such conditions. They are not necessary with negative film because the cast can be corrected by an efficient printer at the printing stage, but, of course, I have also used them successfully with negative film.

As for the exposure, these wide open scenes are bright enough to allow useful fast shutter speeds with colour film as well as black and white.

In group (2) both distant background and immediate surroundings are radically different. Mountains, rocks, streams and rivers, all have a typical look of their own. Strongly broken coastlines with high cliffs also belong in this group. From the "Nude in White" for instance, taken against chalk cliffs with their strong reflecting power (marvellous in colour!) to the most abrupt chiaro-scuro effect anything can be done. All filters bar green can be used as required.

In the third group a green filter can be used to advantage with not fully green sensitive pan material. The tender light greens of early summer foliage can thus be made to yield extraordinarily beautiful silvery effects in side or back lighting, with the shimmering white of the nude matching her surroundings.

In general, however, this group is best photographed on ortho film—if you can

Page 41: *The Friends* by Herbert Rittlinger

6 × 9 cm. Plaubel Makina, *f*2.9 Anticomar, Agfa ISS film, no filter, August, 3 p.m., 1/200 second, *f*9.

Page 42: *Surf* by Herbert Rittlinger

6 × 9 cm. Plaubel Makina, *f*2.9 Anticomar, Perutz Peromnia film, no filter, noon, July, 1/100 second, *f*9-12.
This is one of the author's most successful photographs. However, the water is not surf but the bow wave of a steamer on the German river Weser.

Page 43: *Morning Bathe* by Fritz Henle

2¼-in. square Rolleiflex, Ansco Supreme film, light yellow filter, 1/25 second, *f*11.

Page 44: *The Dive* by Serge de Sazo

Page 45: *On the Sea Bed* by Serge de Sazo

2¼-in. square Rolleiflex in underwater housing, light yellow filter, 1/100 second, *f*5.6.
Serge de Sazo, who lives in Paris, has rapidly become known through his underwater photographs of nudes. He likes to work at a shallow depth in the clear waters of the Mediterranean.

Page 46: *Ebbtide* by Carl Abel

2¼-in. square camera, 8 cm. lens, 40 ASA Perutz film, light yellow filter, 1/50 second, *f*11.

Page 47: *On Holiday* by Willy Zielke

9 × 12 cm. studio camera.
Both pictures were made over a quarter of a century ago. In those days of the declining era of pictorial photography it was a bold achievement to produce work with such a natural look and unadorned with the frippery of the usual salon nudes.

Page 48: *In the Forest Stream* by Herbert Rittlinger

2¼-in. square Super Ikonta, Agfa Isopan F film, 1/50 second, *f*5.6.
This picture was taken on the Grande Leyte river which runs through France's virgin forest on the Bay of Biscay.

Page 49: *Reflections* by Yvonne Gregory

2¼-in. square Super Ikonta, Panatomic X film, 1/100 second, *f*8.

Page 50: *Against the Light* by Willi Präpst

2¼-in. square Super Ikonta, Isopan F film, October, 5 p.m., fill-in light from Blaupunkt Reporter flash, 1/50 second, *f*8, Atomal developer.

Page 51: *Souvenir of the Ardèche* by Herbert Rittlinger

2¼-in. square Super Ikonta, Isopan F film, no filter, July, noon, 1/100 second, *f*5.6.

Page 52: *Southern Sunlight* by Fritz Henle

2¼-in. square Rolleiflex, Ansco Superpan film, light yellow filter, 1/50 second, *f*16.

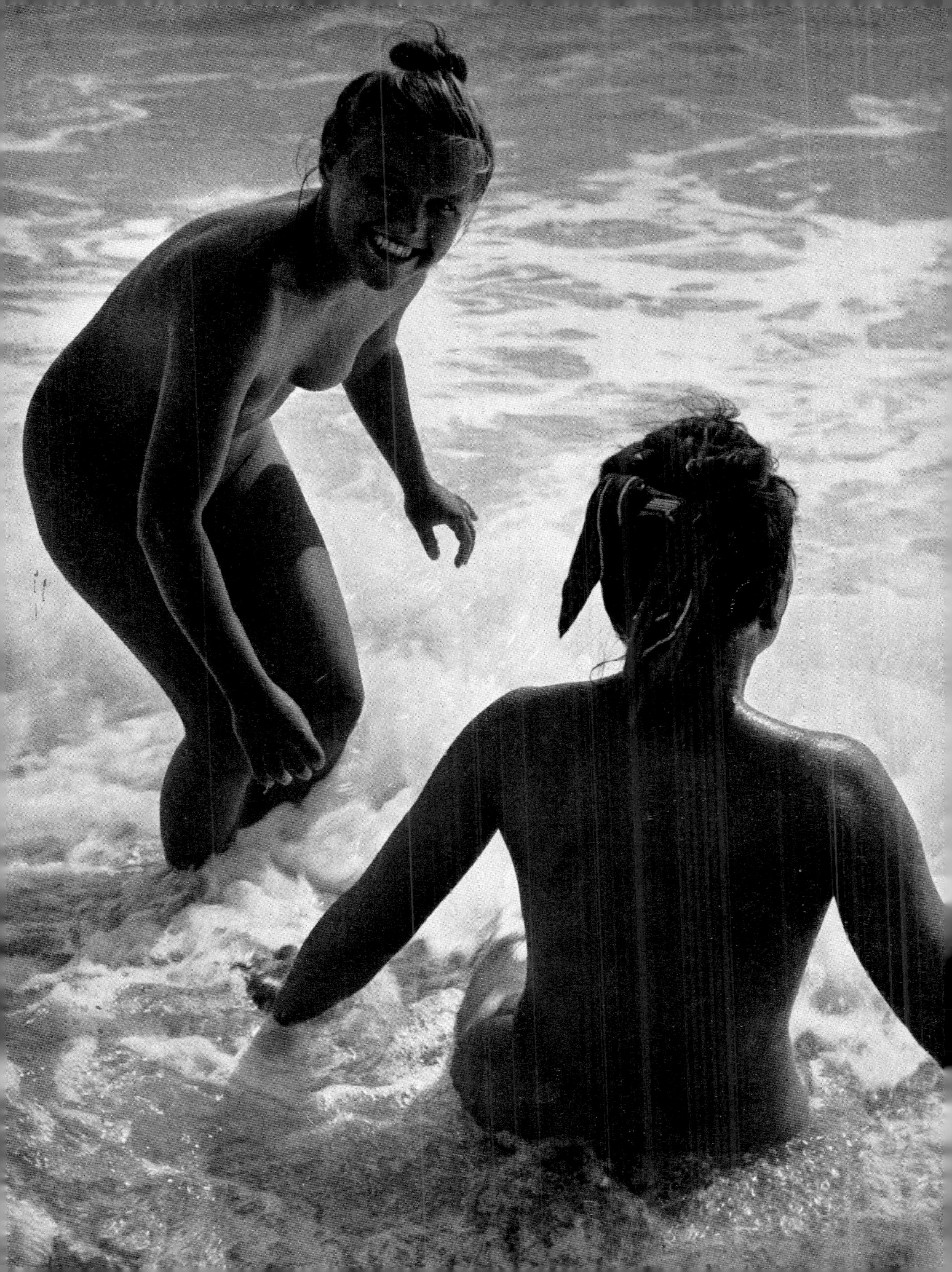

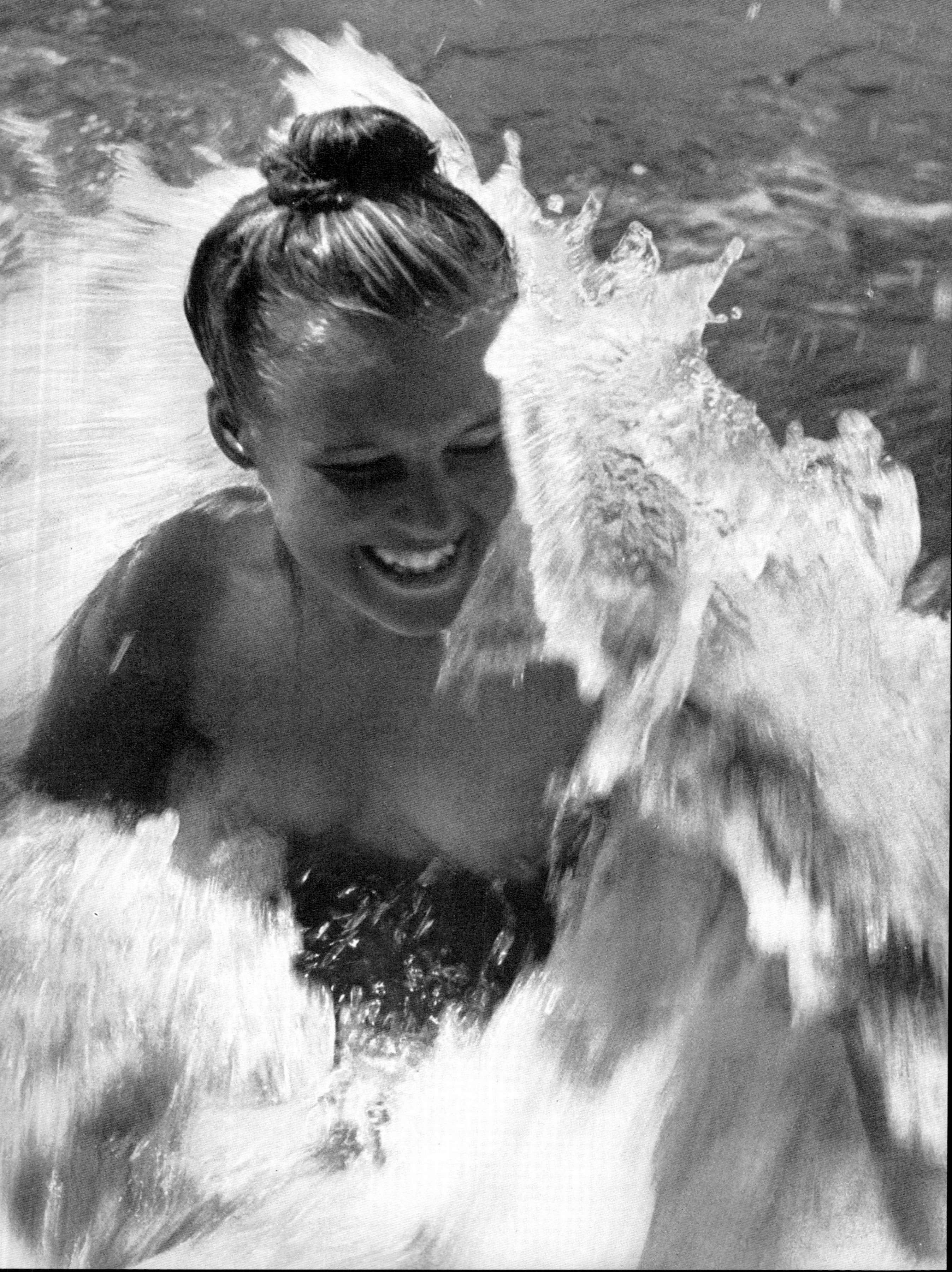

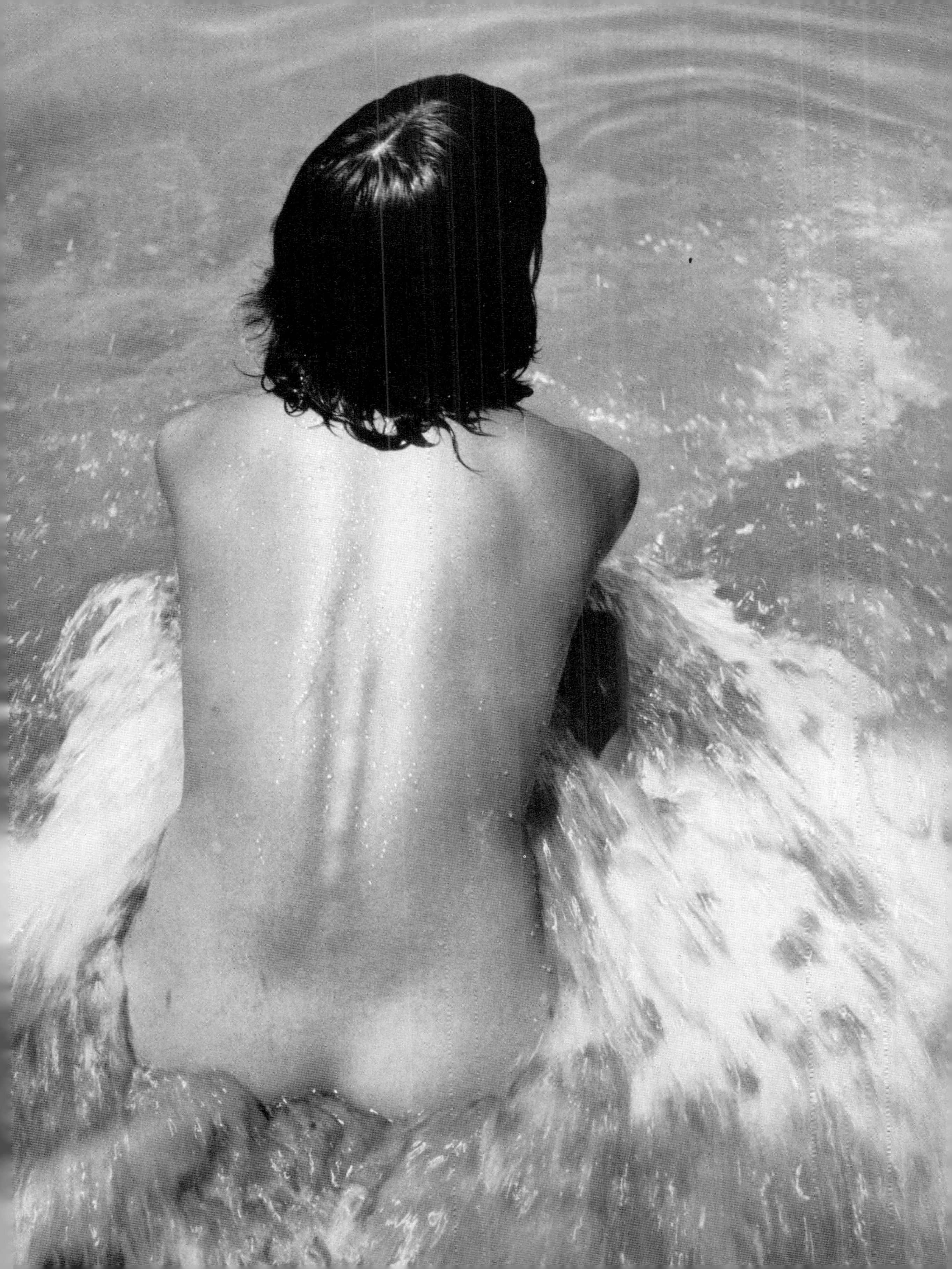

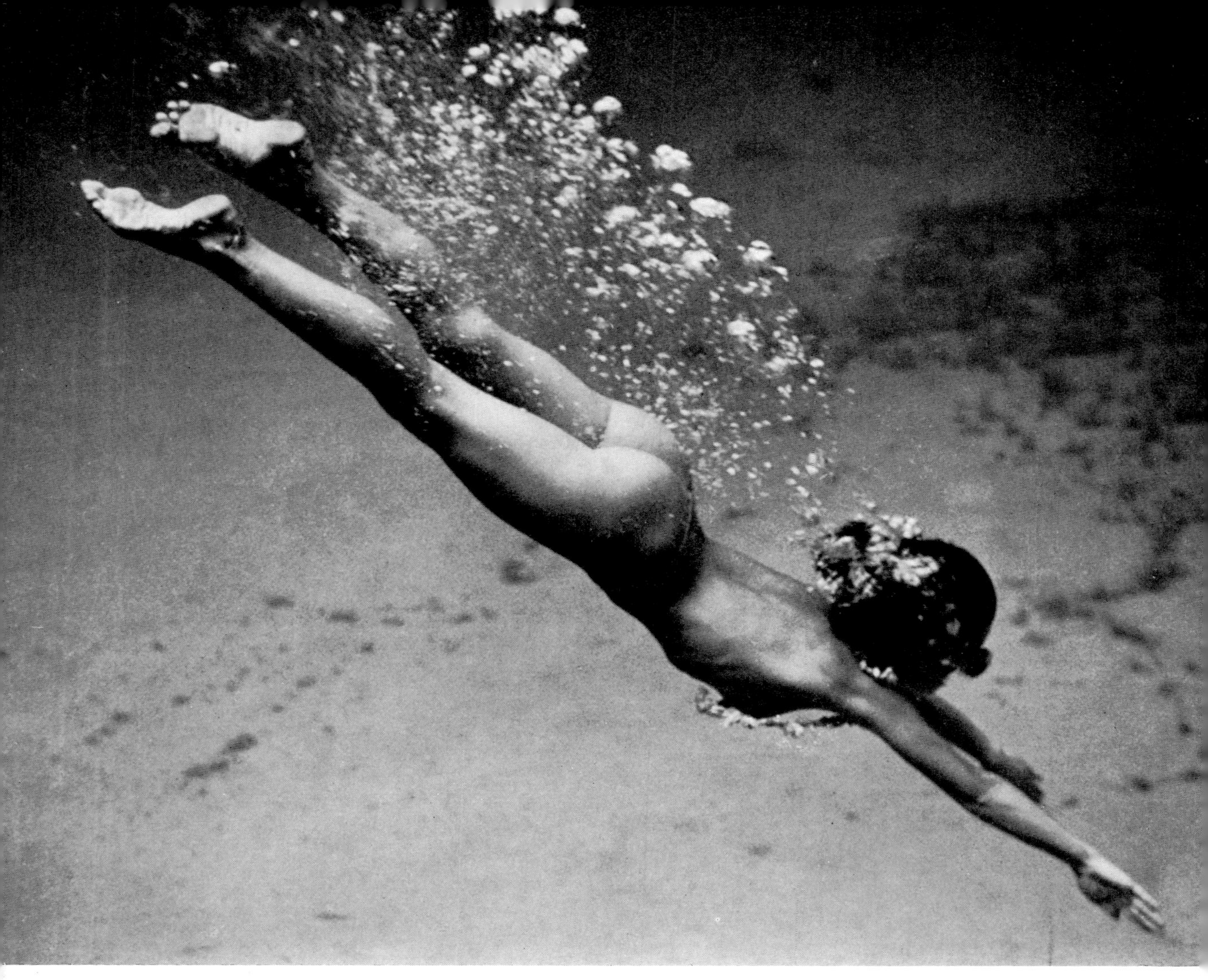

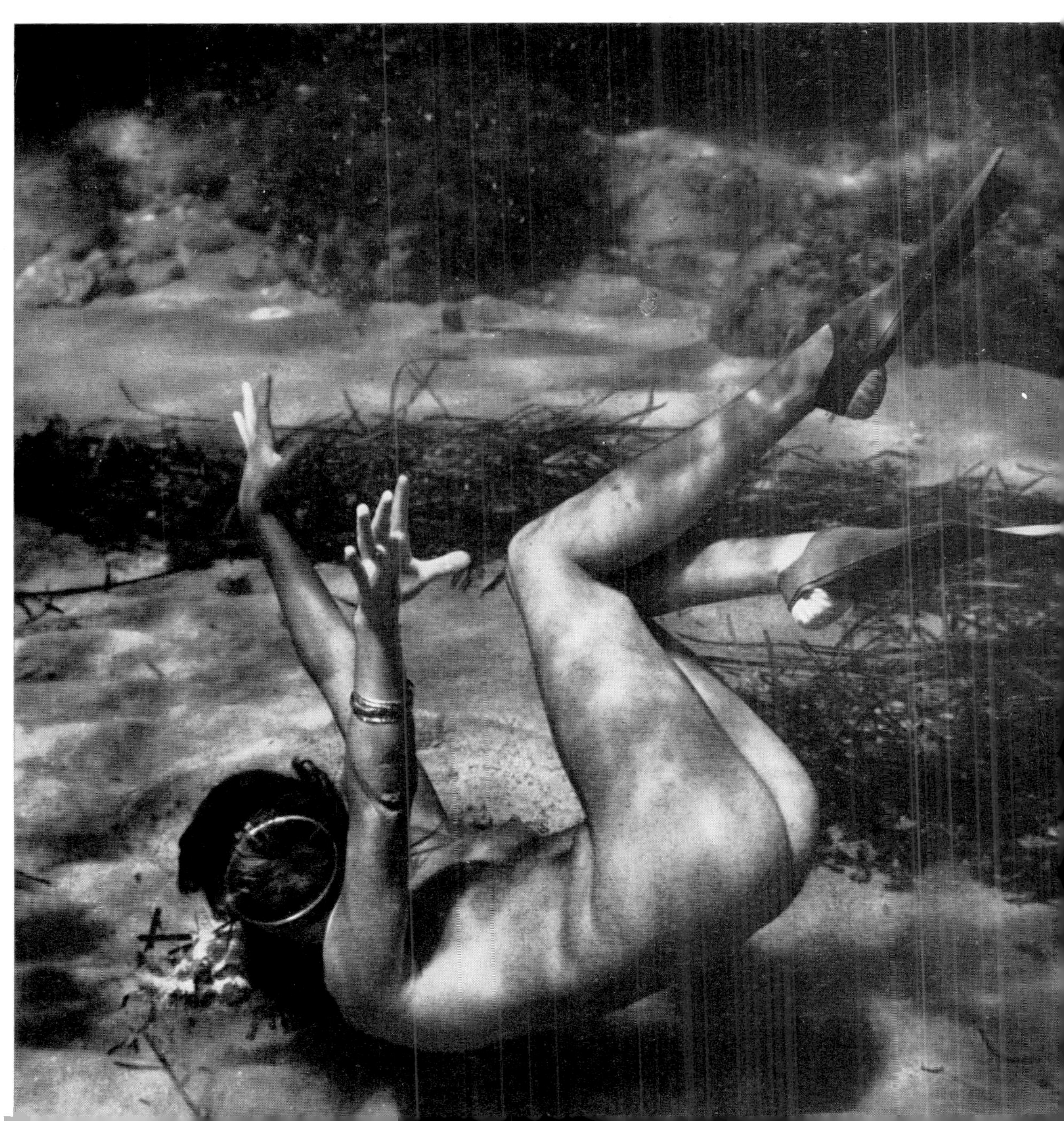

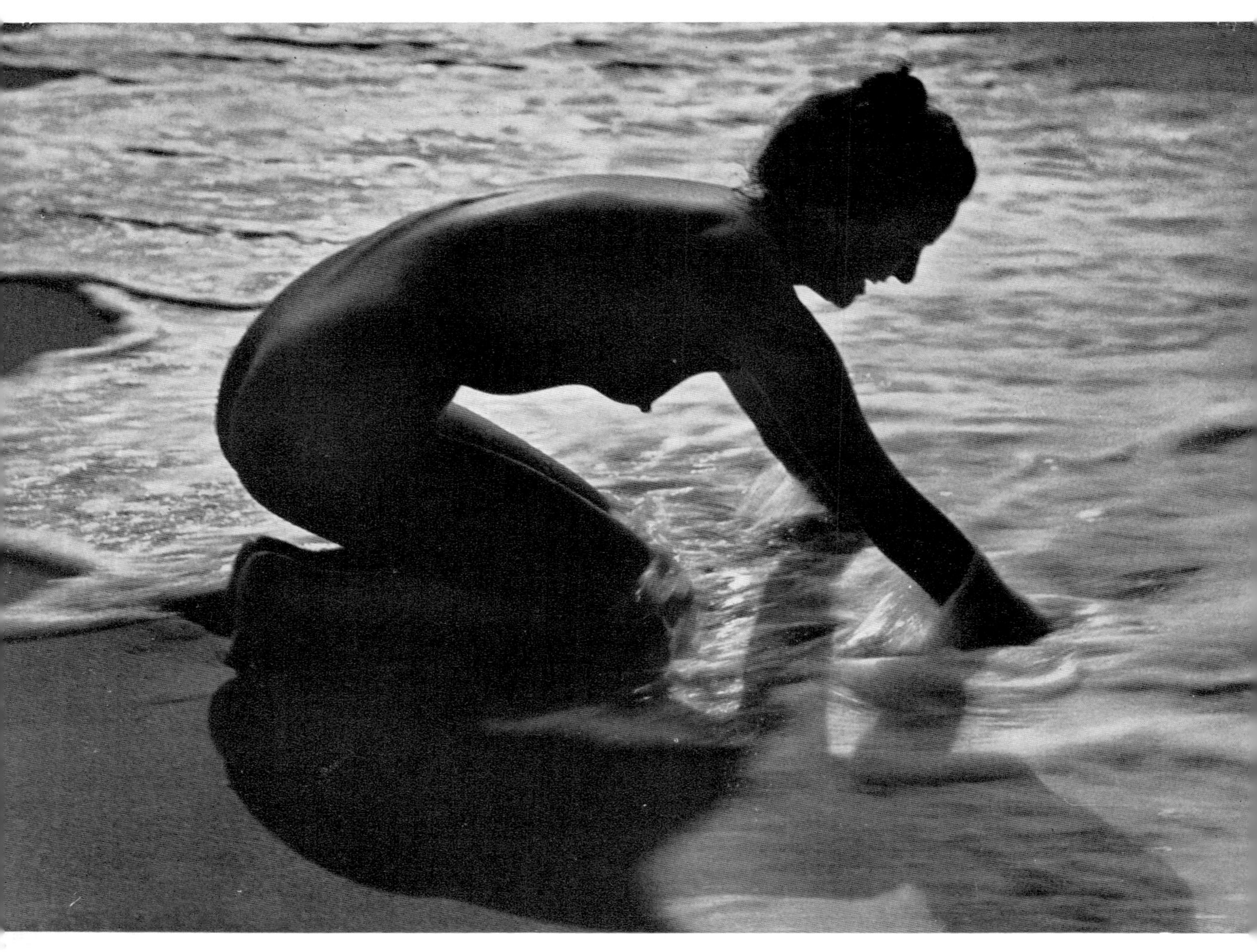

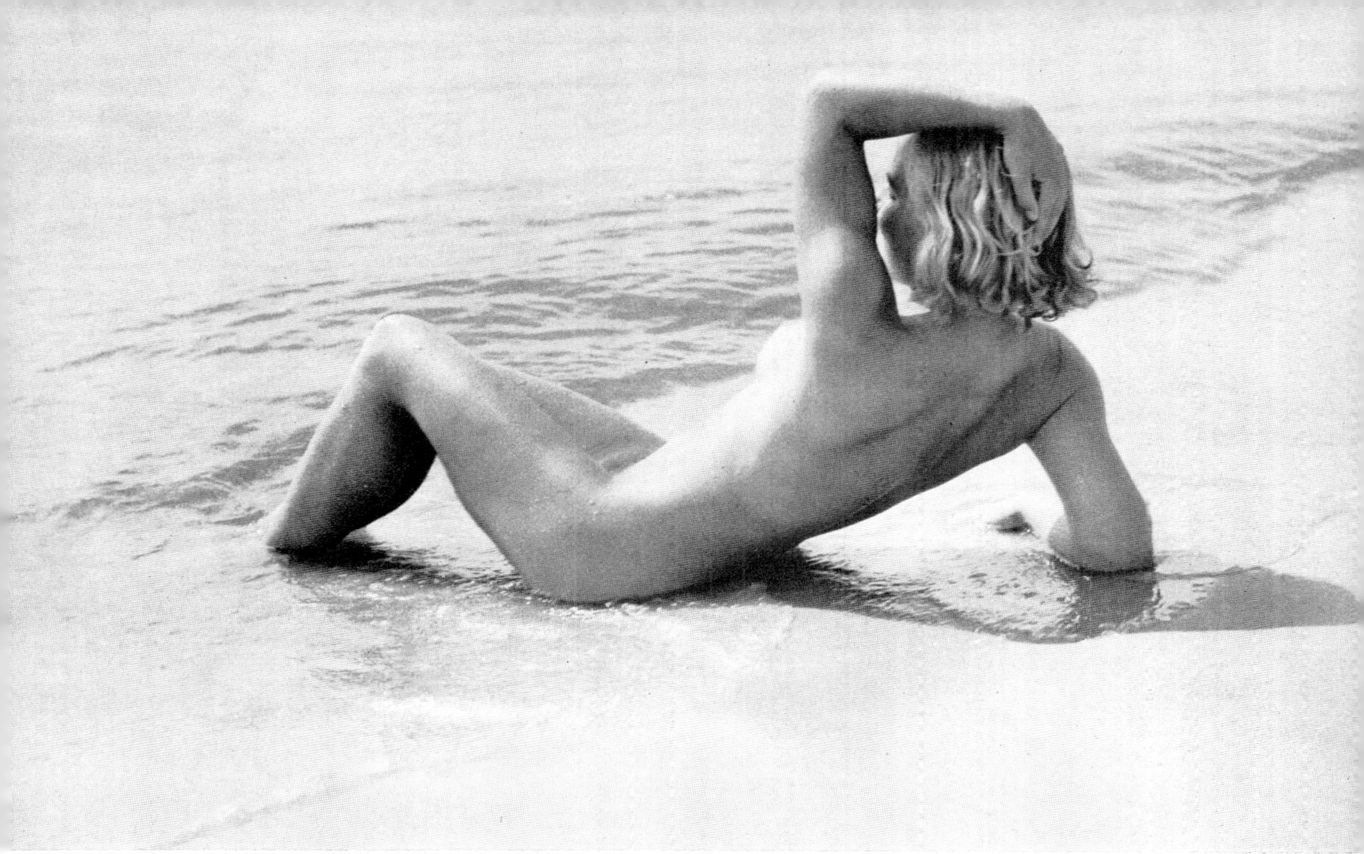

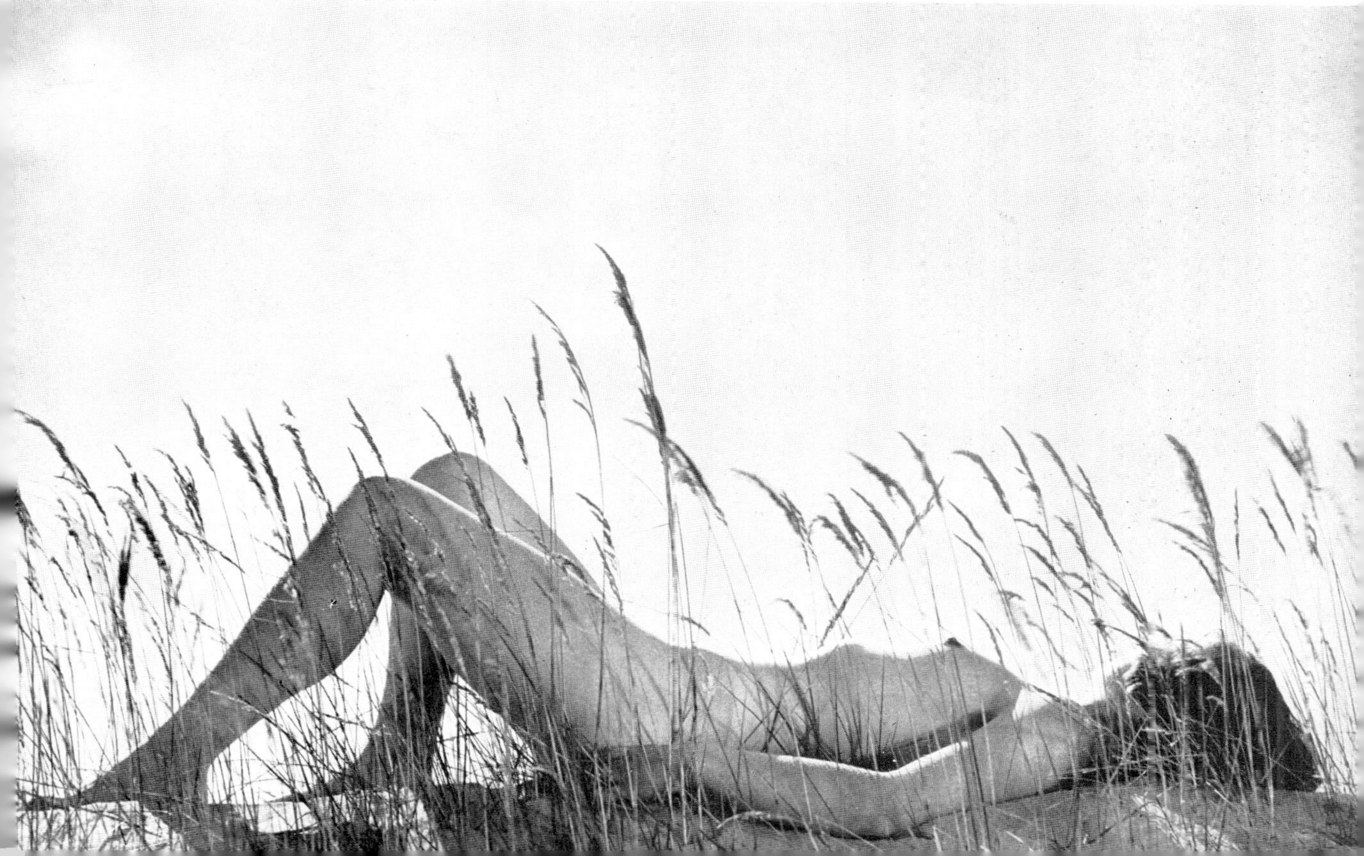

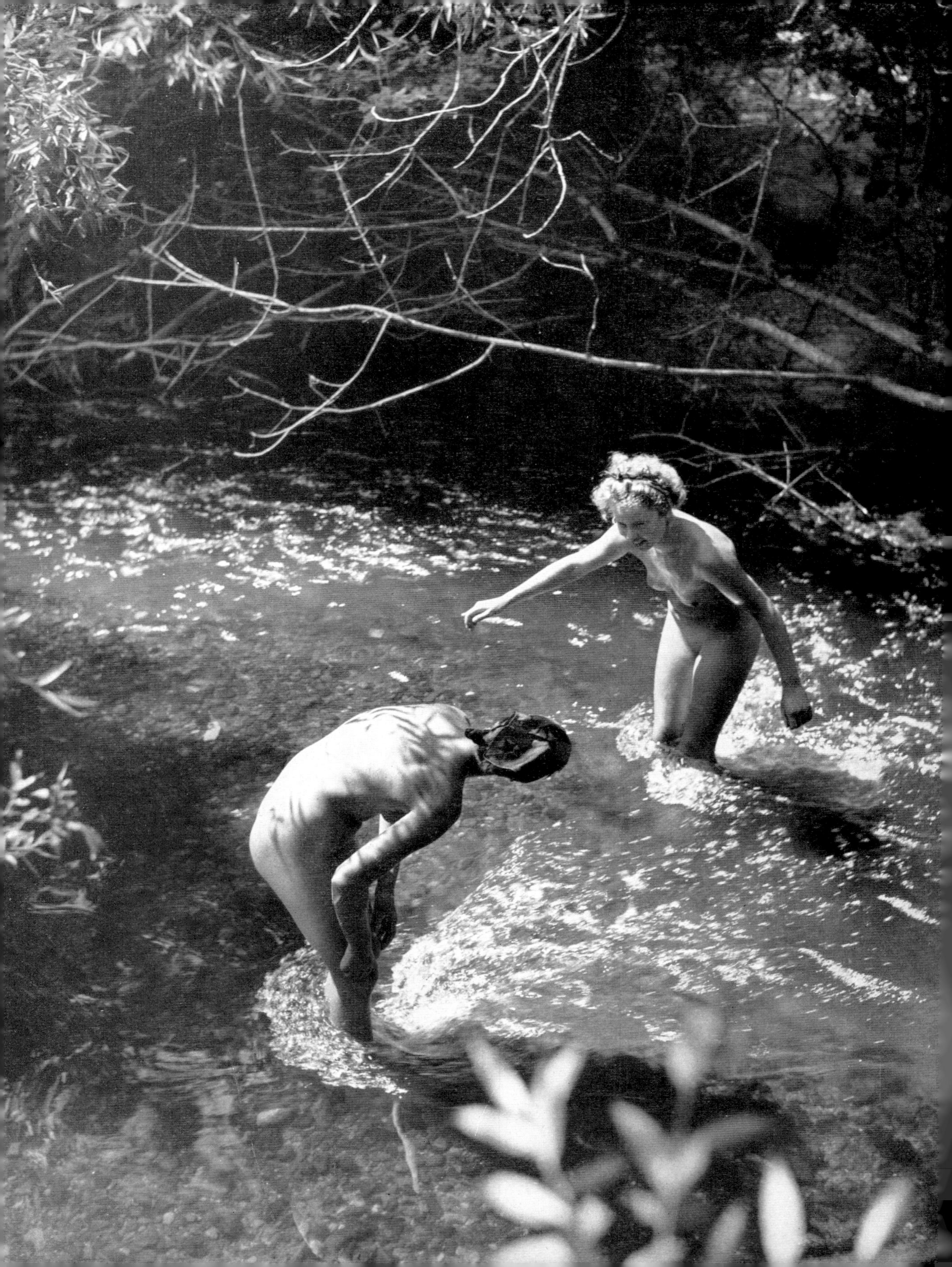

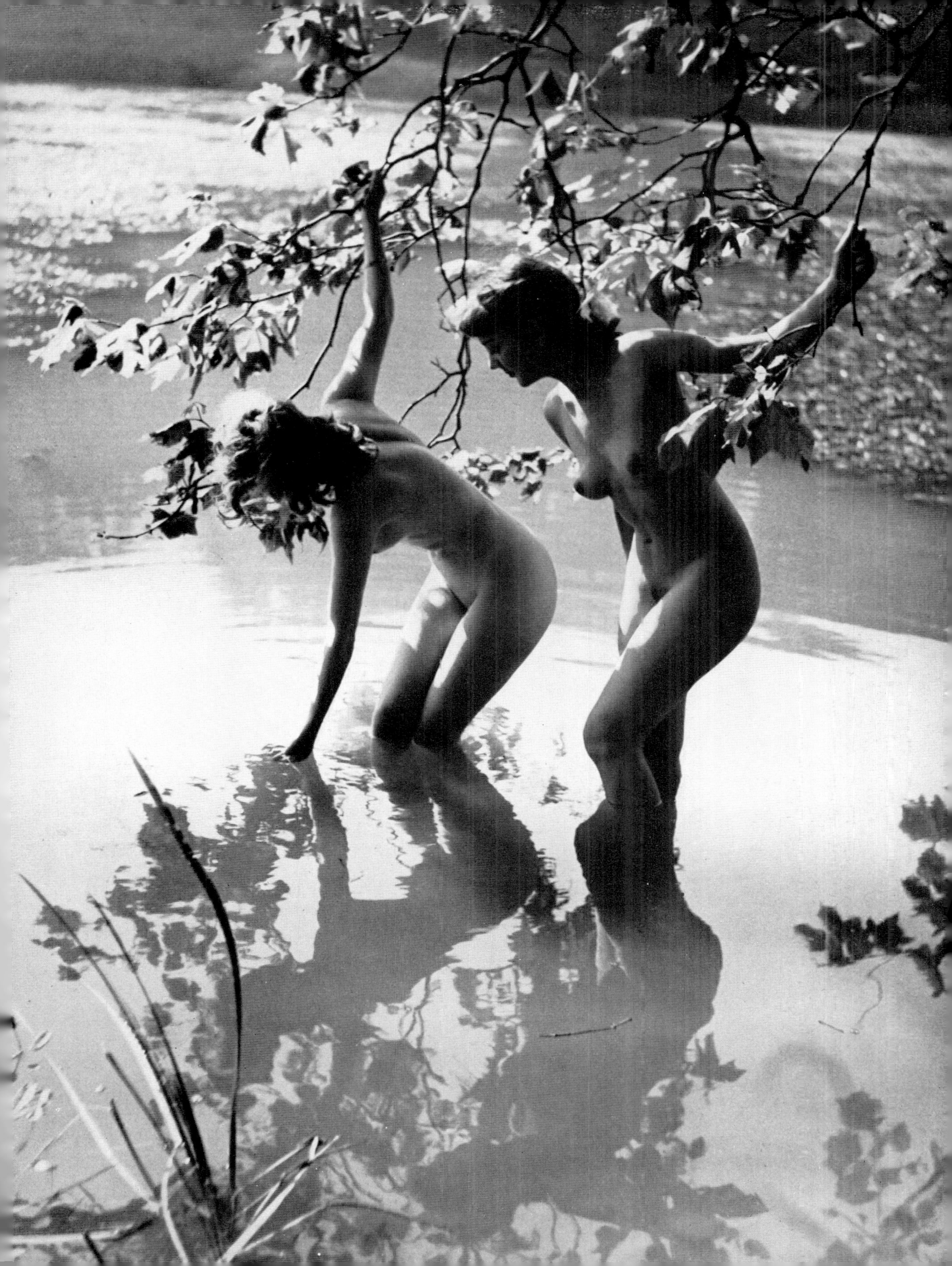

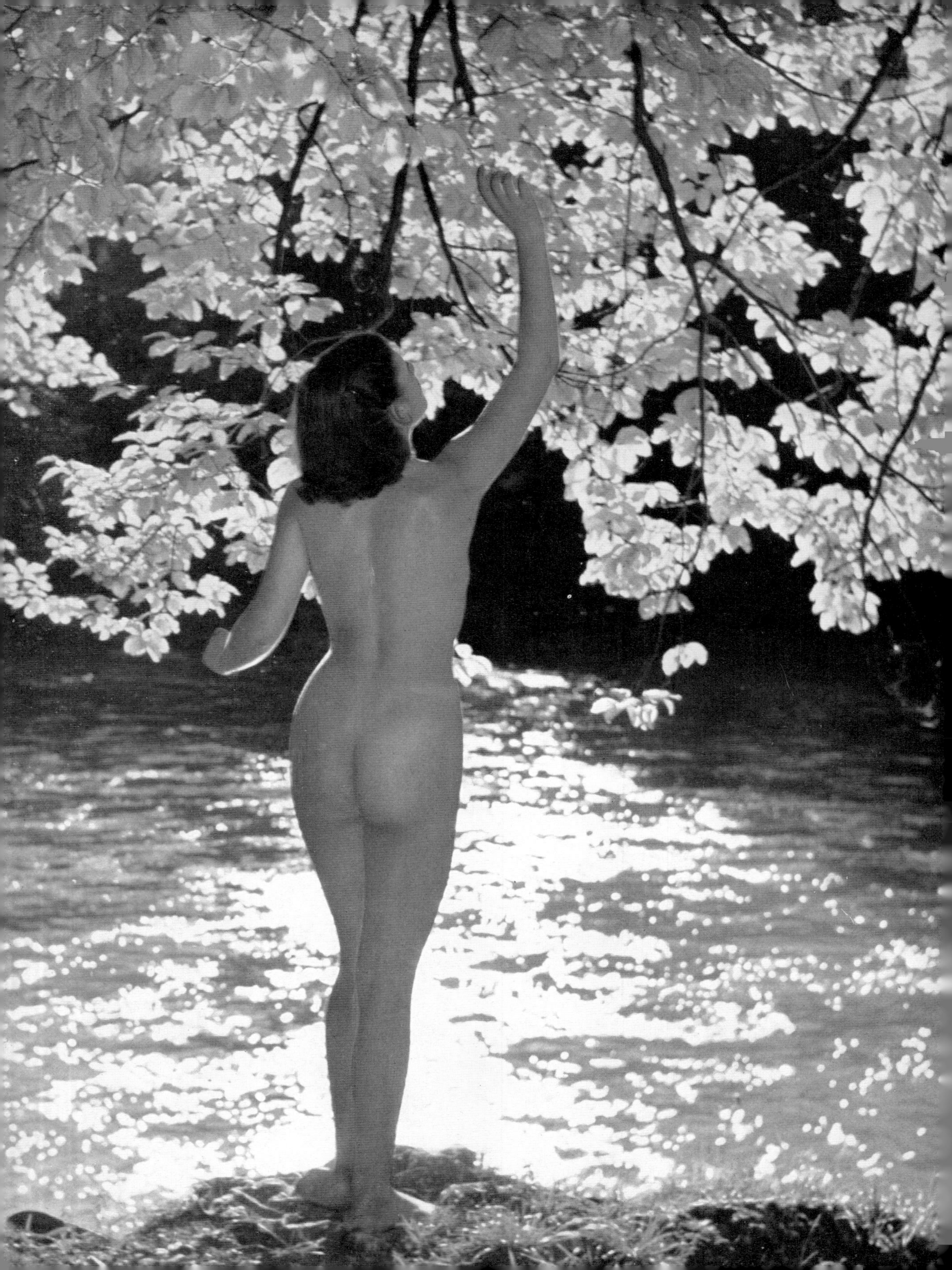

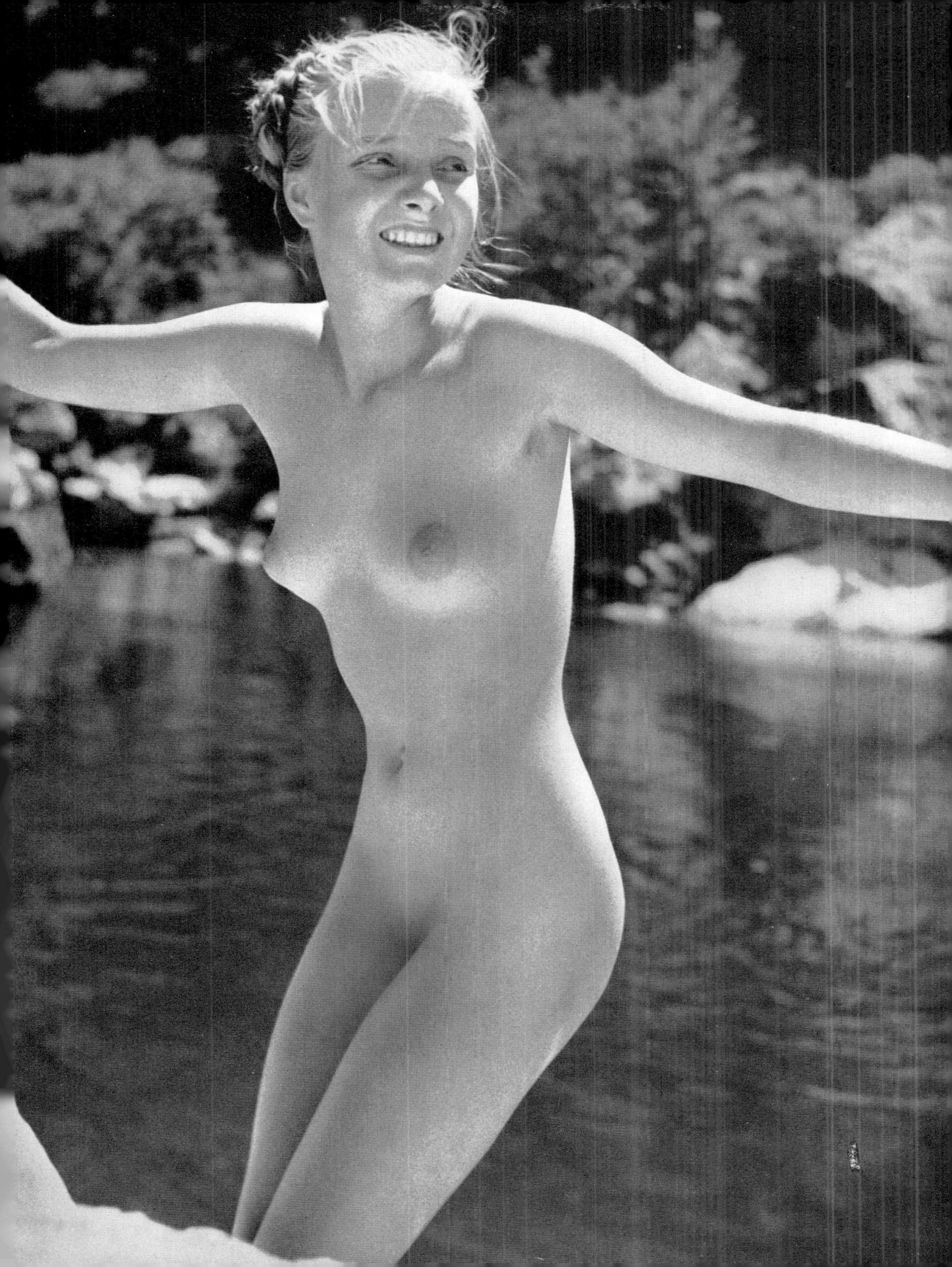

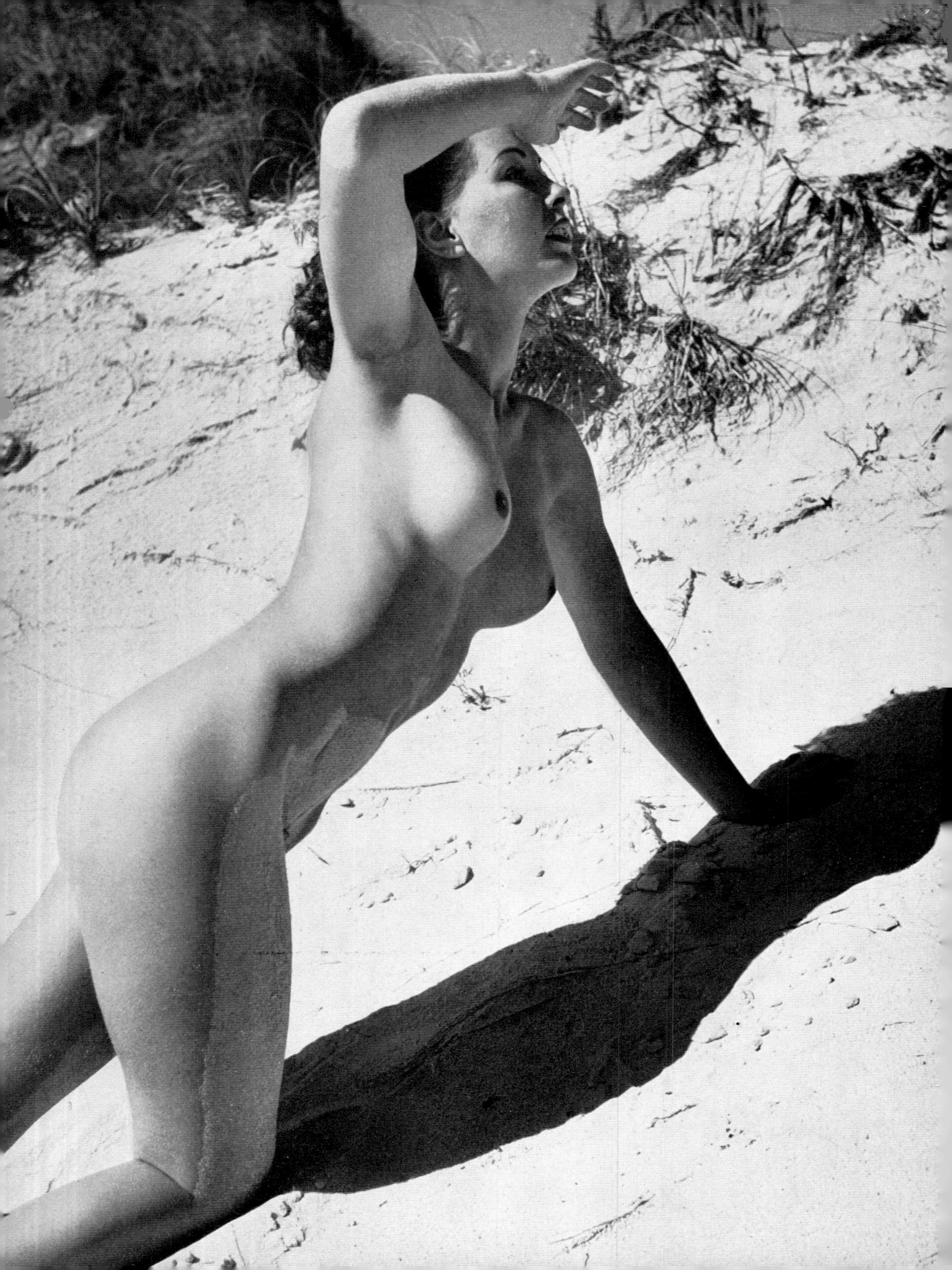

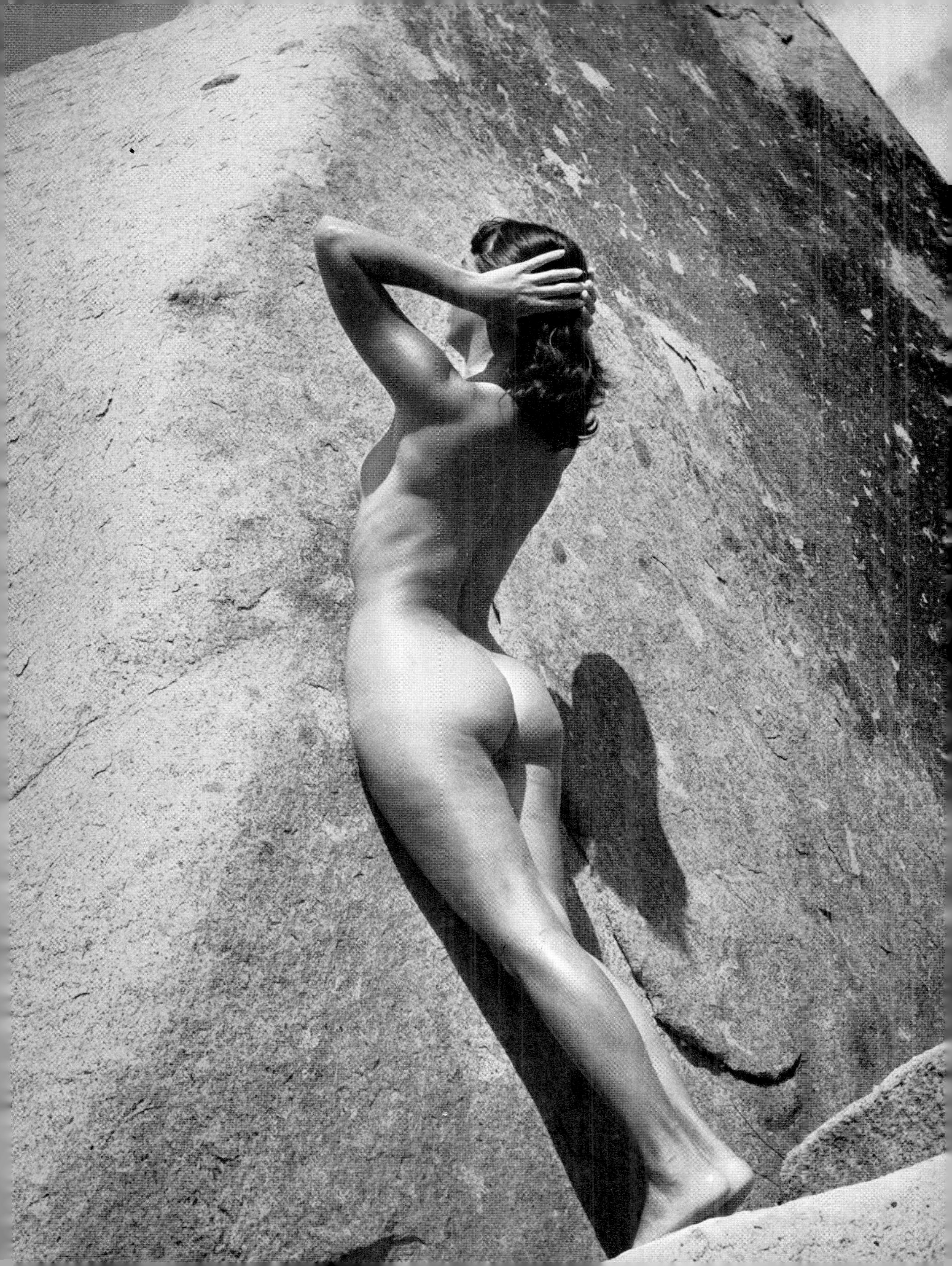

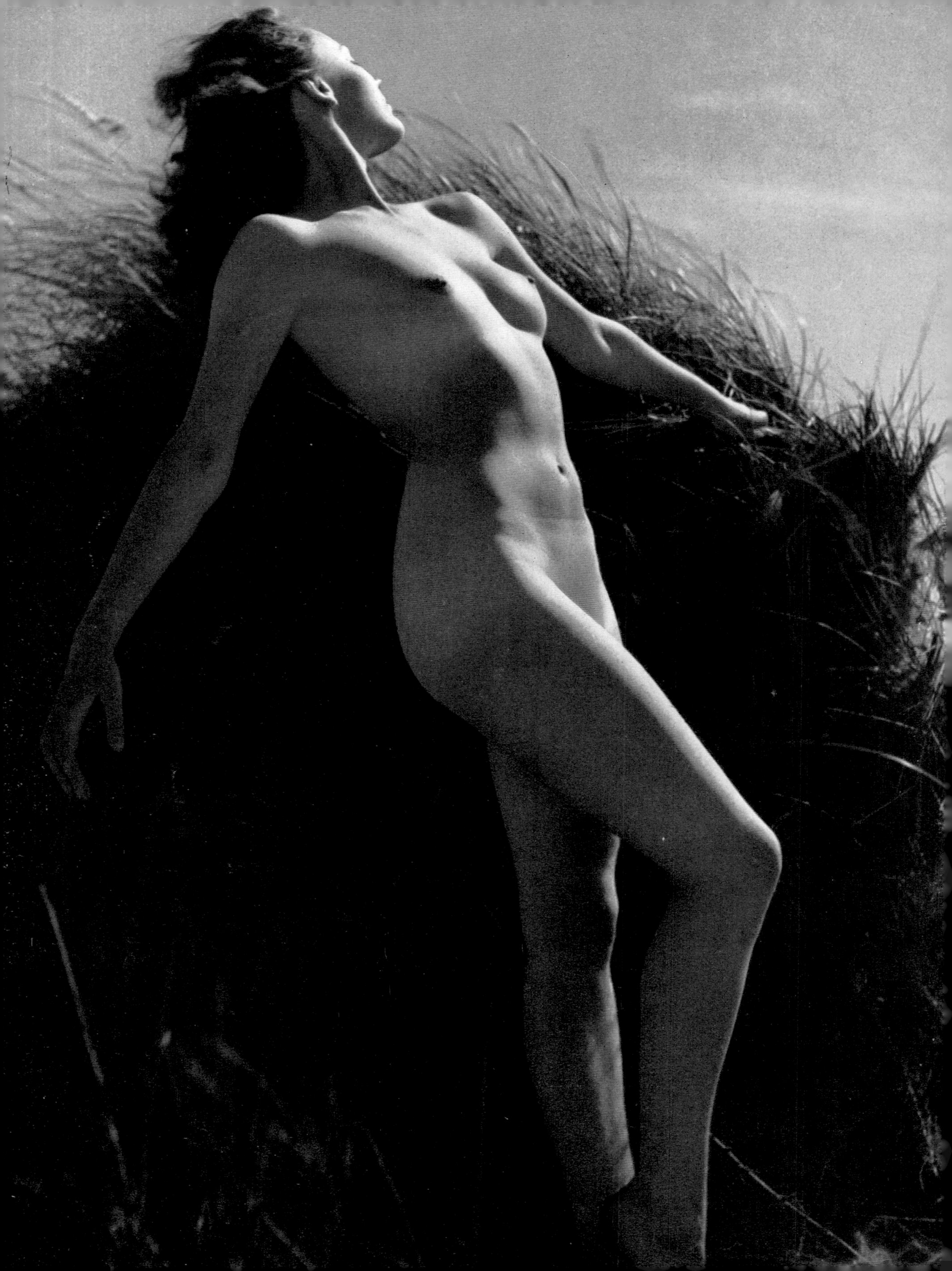

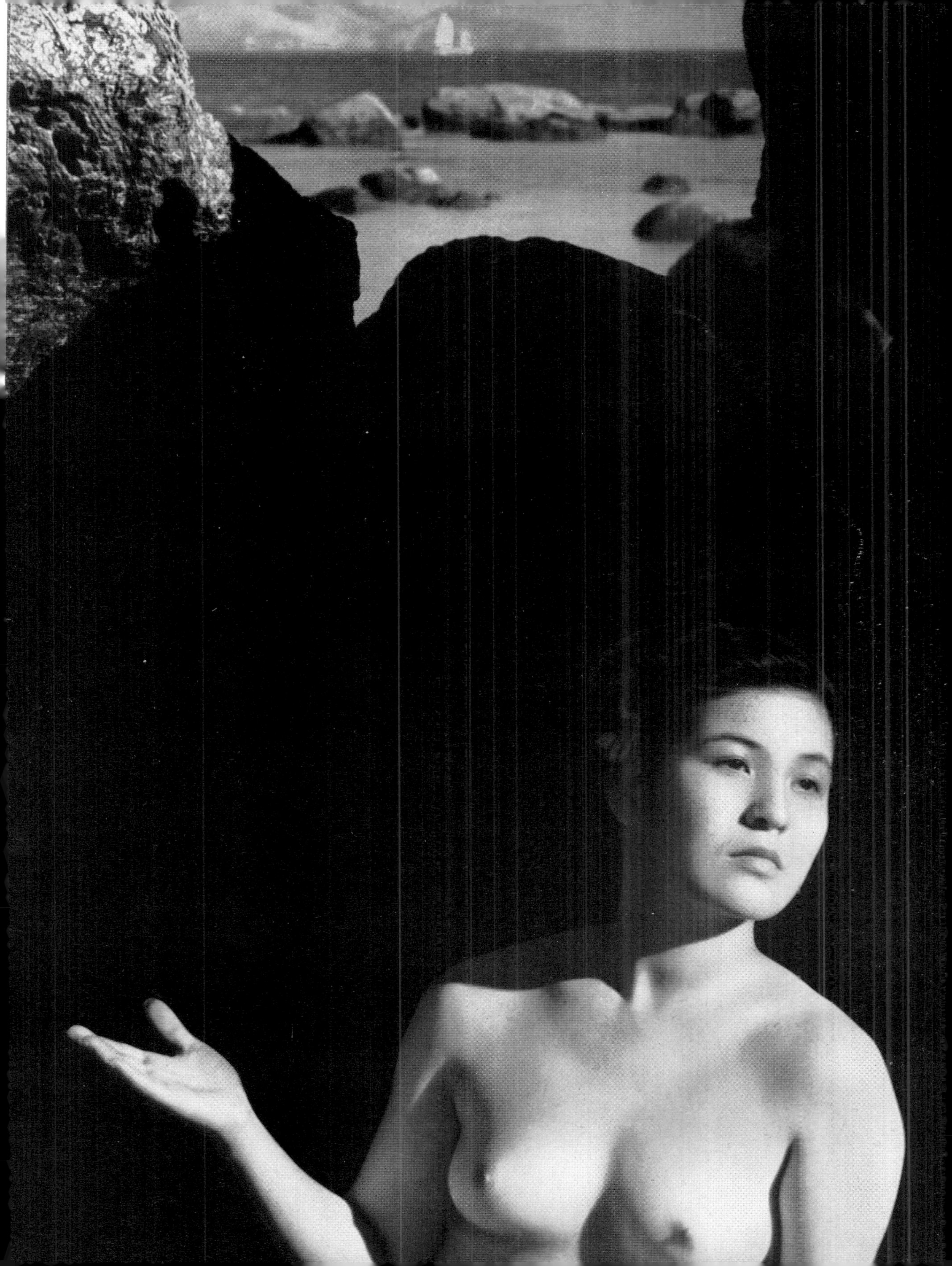

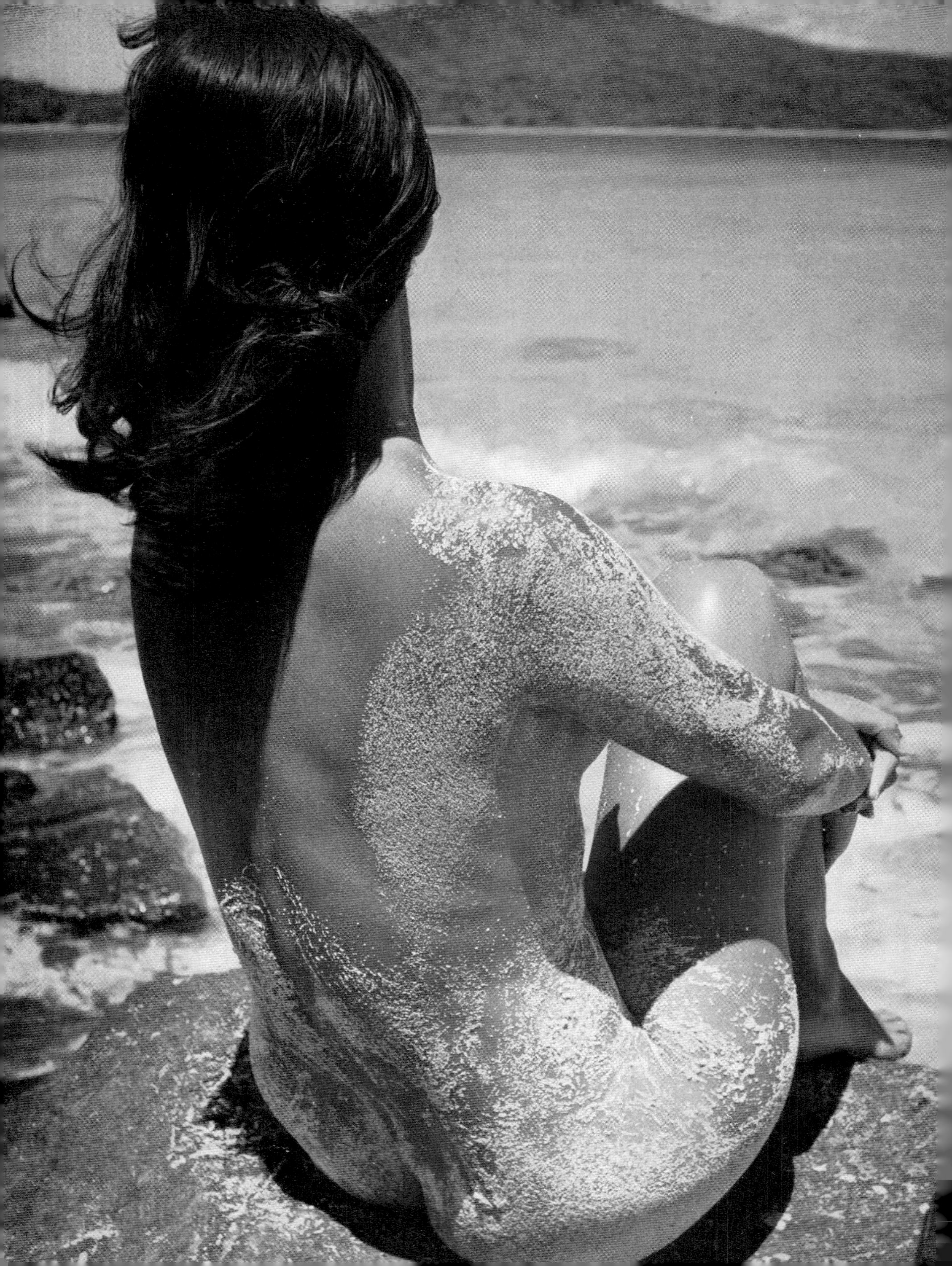

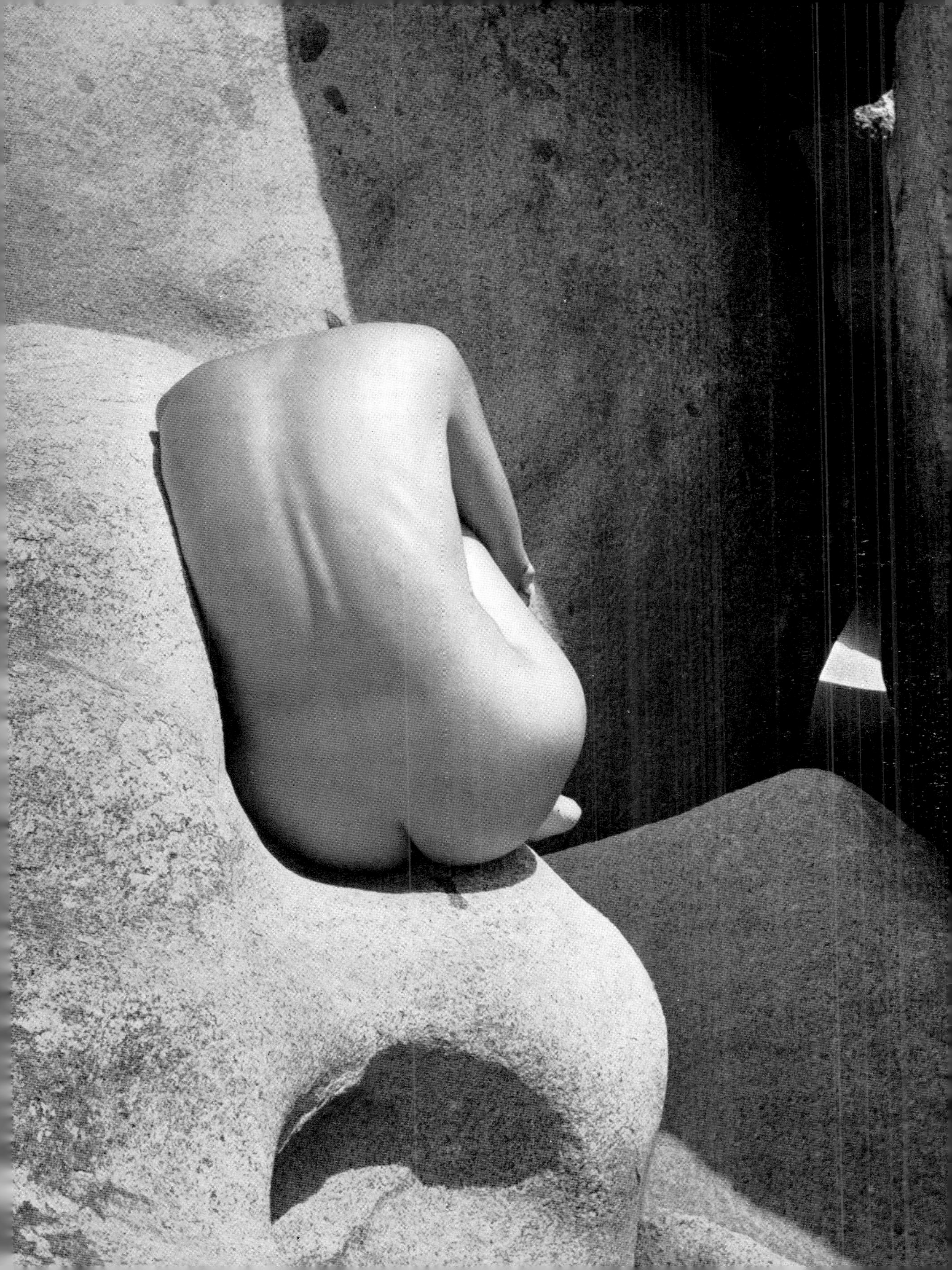

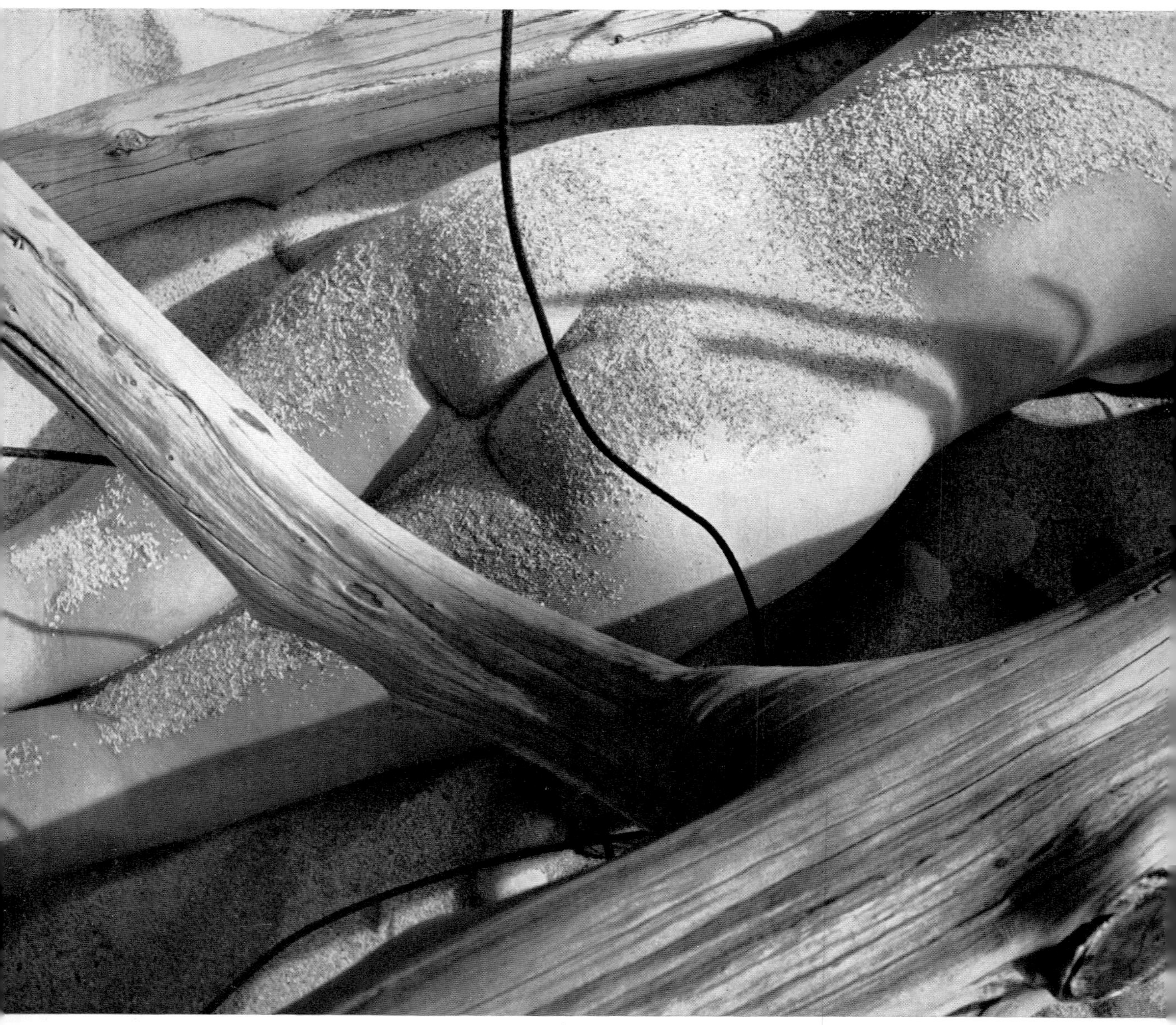

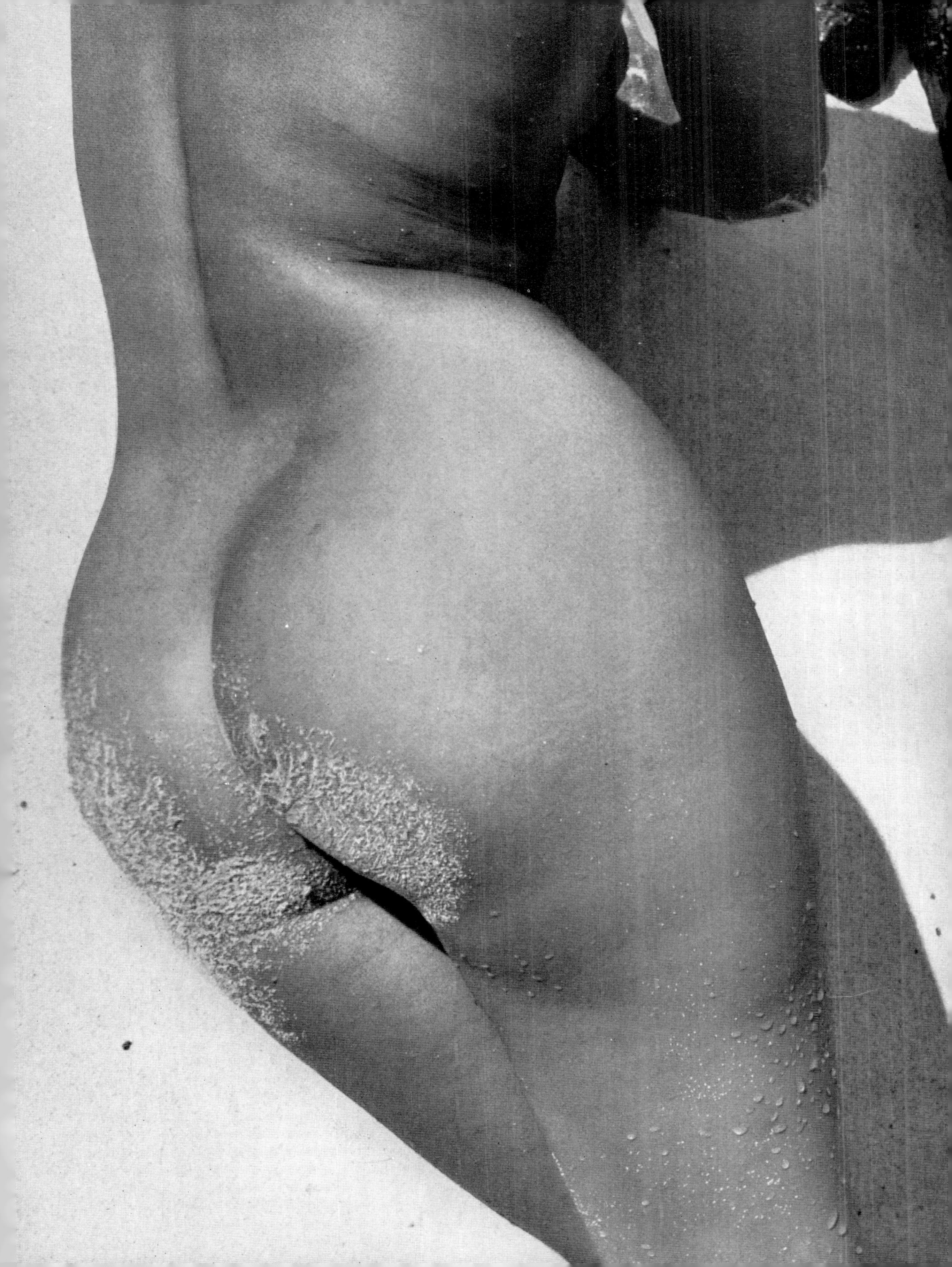

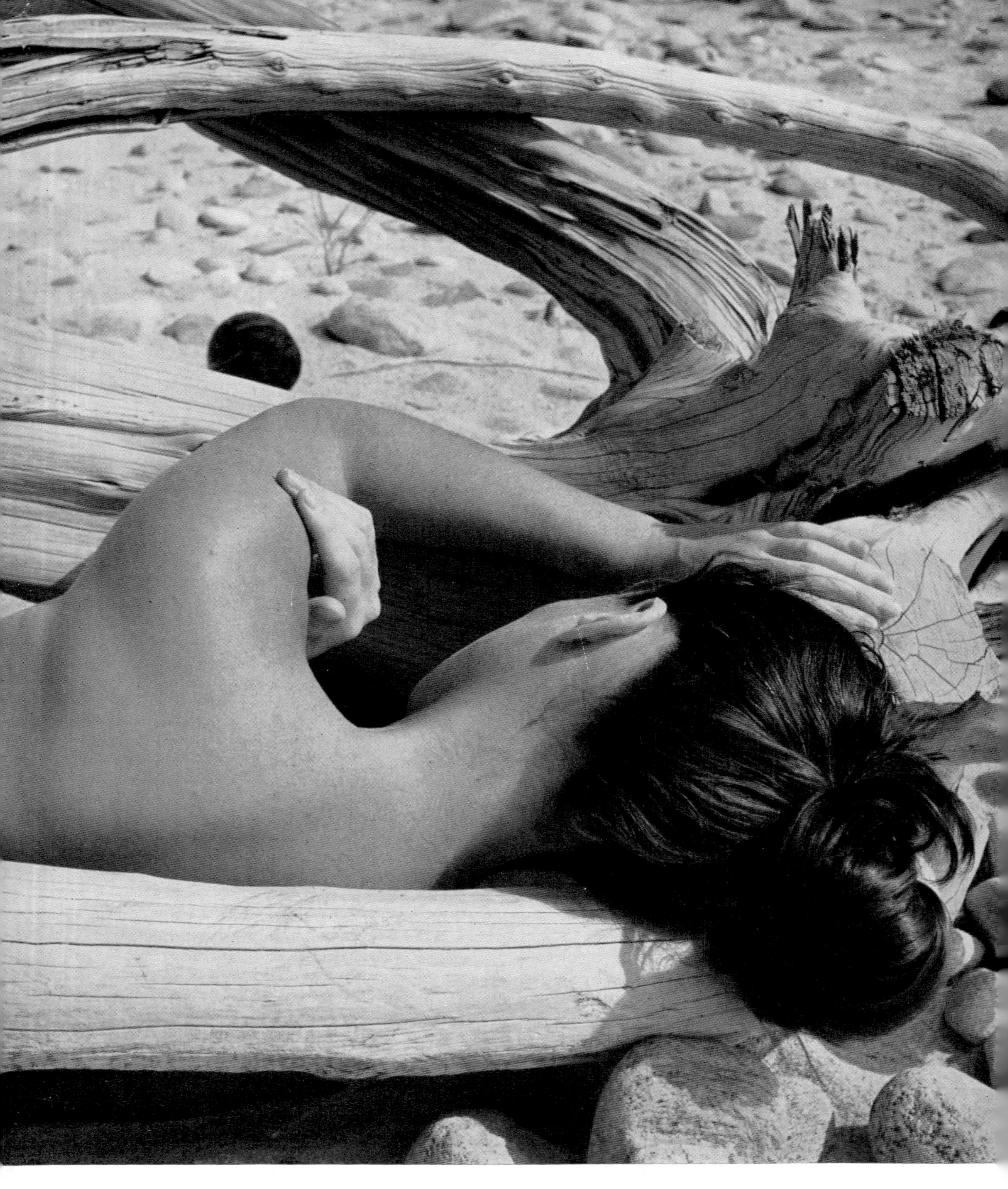

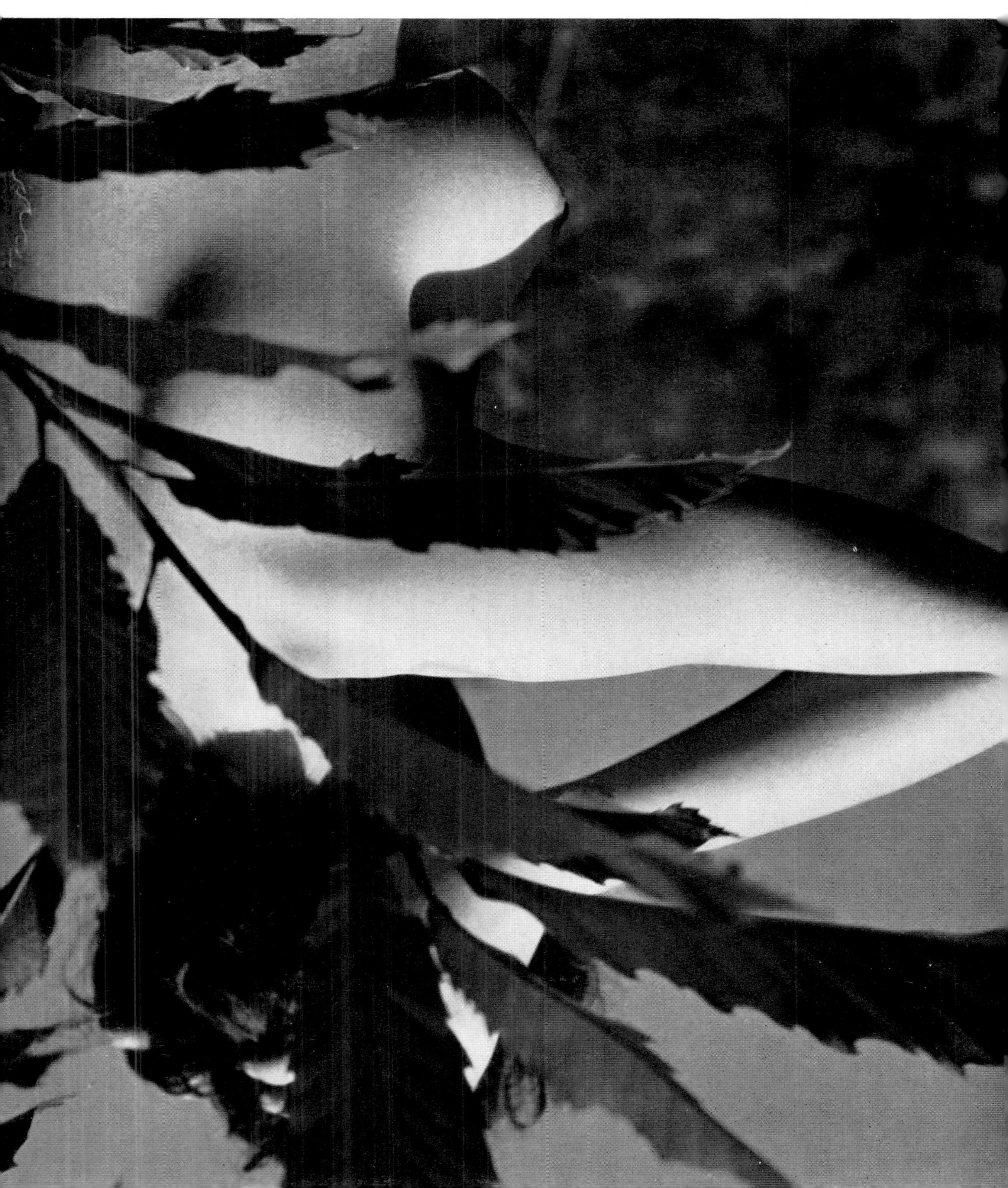

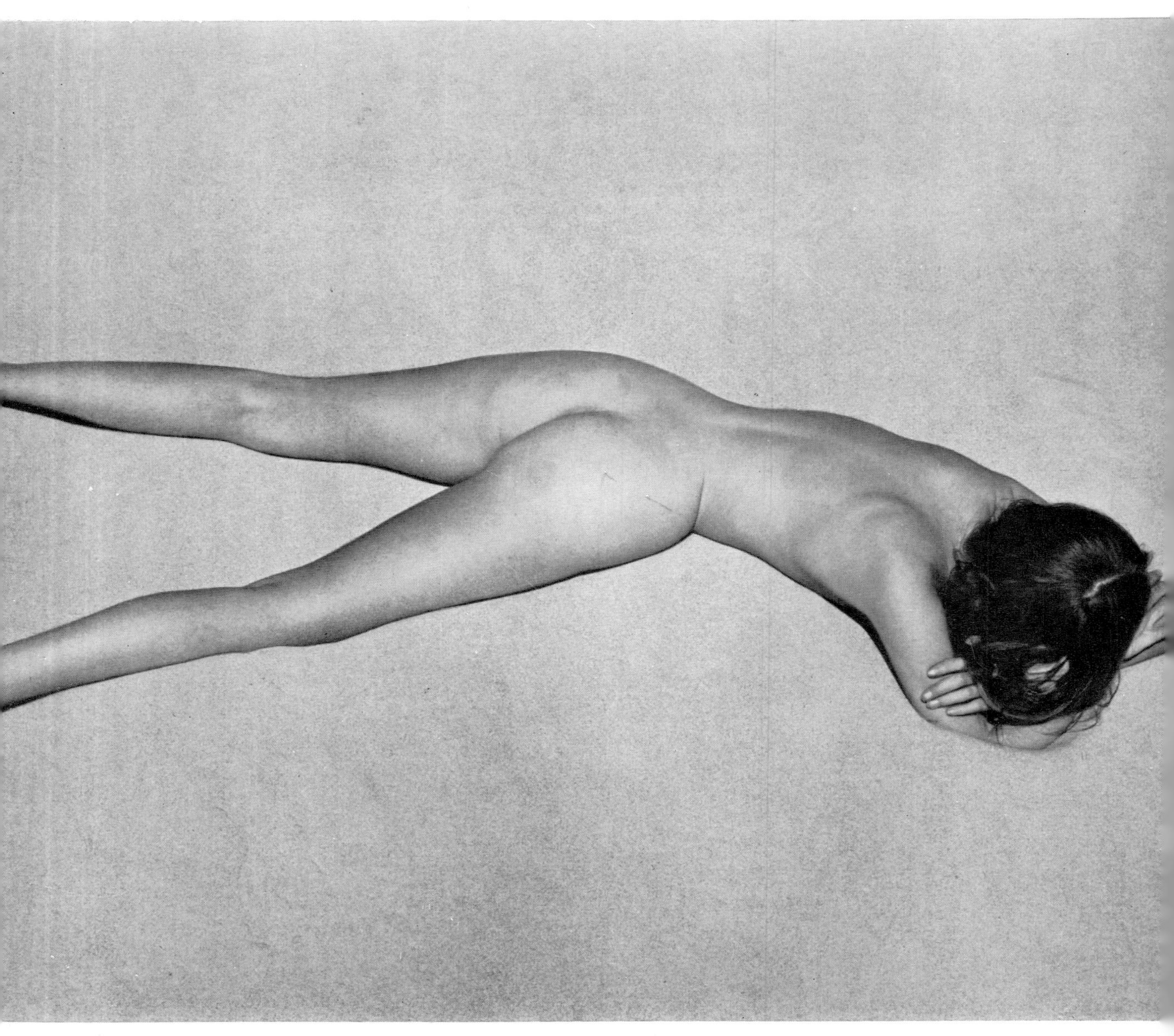

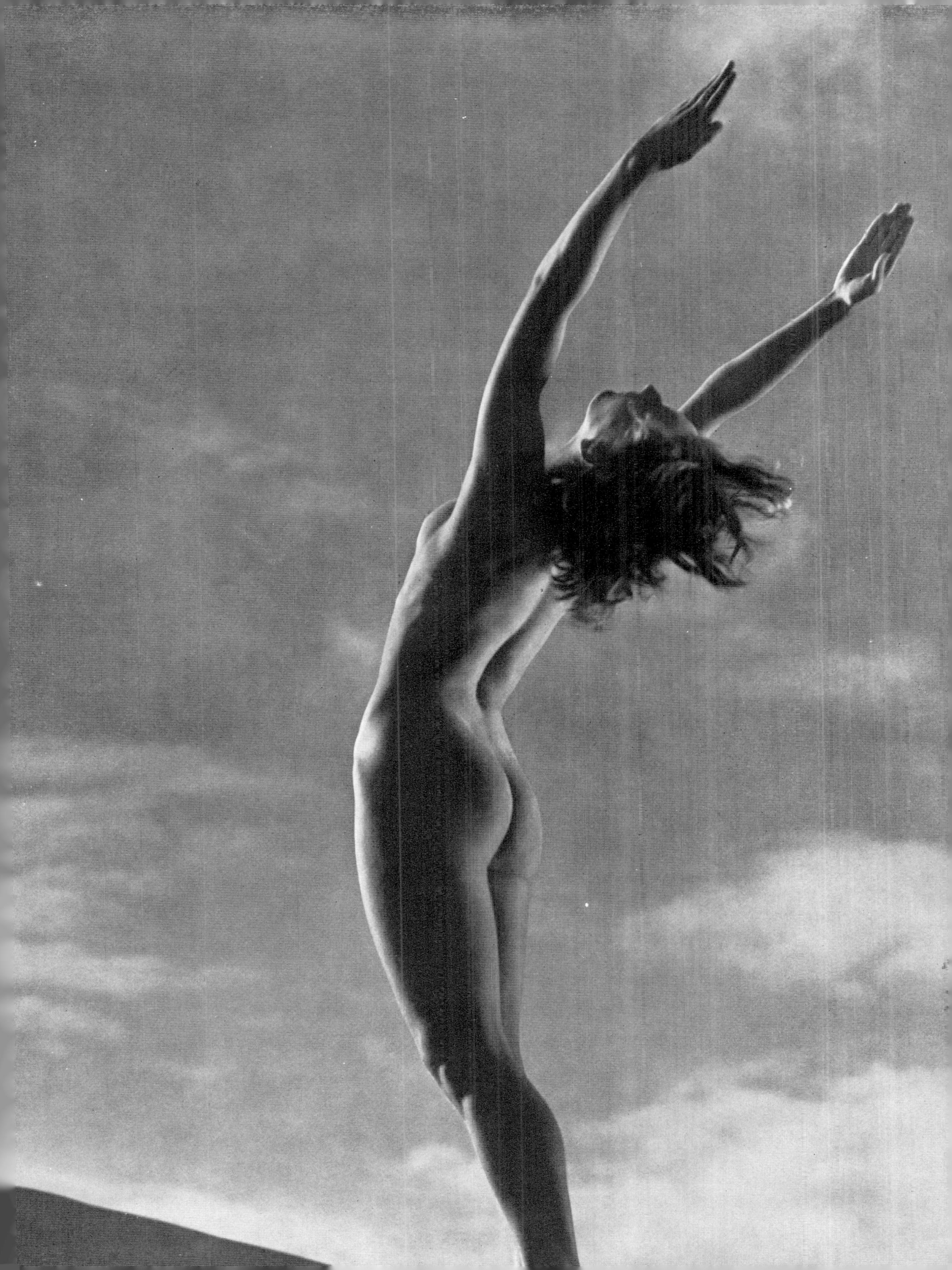

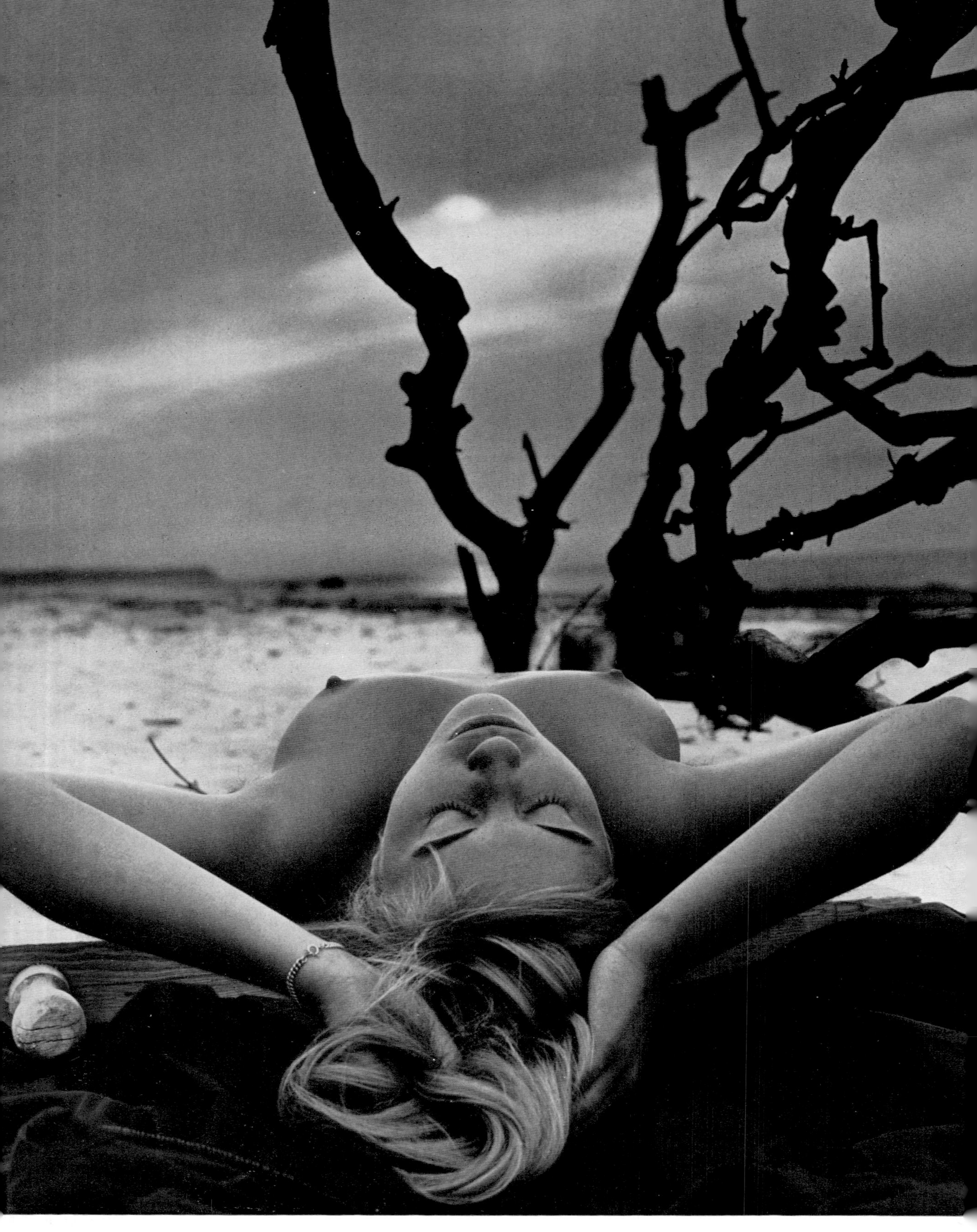

Page 53: *By the Pyramid* by Fritz Henle

2¼-in. square Rolleiflex, Super-XX film, 1/100 second, *f*16, Microdol developer.

Page 54: *Low Angle Perspective* by Reinhold Lessmann

2¼-in. square negative, 40 ASA film, light yellow filter, 1/25 second, *f*11.
The strong side lighting is particularly effective with the dark background of the sand dune in shadow. After several attempts the model was posed so that the shadows make her appear slimmer, while the low camera angle tends to make her look taller.

Page 55: *Composition* by Katsuji Fukuda

Japanese photography was greatly influenced by the progress of miniature photography in the 'thirties. German miniaturists made a strong impression on young Japanese photographers and after 1945 an equally lasting American influence became apparent. But European experimental photography also left its traces, particularly in nude photography.

Page 56: *In the Bay* by Fritz Henle

2¼-in. square Rolleiflex, Super-XX film, light yellow filter, 1/100 second, *f*16.

Page 57: *Form and Texture* by Fritze Henle

2¼-in. square Rolleiflex, Super-XX film, light yellow filter, *f*16, Microdol developer.

Pages 58 and 60: *Driftwood* by Fritz Henle

2¼-in. square Rolleiflex, Super-XX film, light yellow filter, slightly diffuse sunlight, 1/100 second, *f*11-16.

Page 59: *Sunlight* by Fritz Henle

2¼-in. square Rolleiflex, Super-XX film, light yellow filter, 1/100 second, *f*16.

Page 61: *Among the Leaves* by Fulvio Roiter

6 × 9 cm. Tenax camera, Perutz Peromnia film, 1/15 second, *f*12.5, Promicrol developer.

Page 62: *On the Sands* by Edward Weston

18 × 24 cm. camera.
Edward Weston, one of the great masters of American photography, died in 1958. His work was notable for the clarity of form and texture which he brought out in his subjects.

Page 63: *Apotheosis* by Willy Zielke

9 × 12 cm. Kühn camera.
Zielke made this still picture during the shooting of the introduction to the film of the 1936 Olympic Games in Berlin.

Page 64: *Dark Skies* by Christian Cambazard

2¼-in. square Rolleiflex, Verichrome Pan film, medium yellow filter, 1/15 second, *f*8.

still get it. The tones of body and sky can be adjusted at will with a light to medium yellow filter.

Back to pan film. If no filter is used it is possible to achieve the opposite effect from the same taking position; in particular strong contrasts of black and white seen against the heavy greens of high summer darkened by back-lighting.

Water

Every type of country has its own particular character. Water has a unifying property, and how useful it is! Generous by nature, it meets the needs of nude photography better than anything else. Broad expanses wide open to the sky reflect countless highlights. In nude photography as elsewhere pictures with reflections and mirror effects constitute a field of their own; here too they are a means of increasing the photographic effect although it is the water rather than the reflections that provides the mood.

From clear transparency to compact masses, from the almost physical permeation of the model to her complete isolation water offers everything; it is background, curtain and *raison-d'être*.

A sea of light? Not at all.

It is the sky that is bright, and so are its glittering reflections. When there are none or when only one or two shafts of light act as spotlights, the remaining unlit water absorbs much more light than is generally assumed. And if the scene is not the open sea or a lake but a small stream or even a forest brook reflecting nothing but the deep summer green of their surroundings, we arrive at surprisingly long exposures. These conditions are quite different from those obtaining where water reflects the sky.

Foreground

What part in the composition does the foreground play? Has it any importance at all since our subject is the nude? I have touched on this question when mentioning depth of field. Let me give an example of what can be done even in typically featureless country.

If we place the horizon at the top of the picture and arrange, say, the water's edge or a line of footsteps so as to run towards the nude whom we place in the upper third of the frame, we obtain a most attractive and interesting foreground with a tremendous 3D effect.

On the other hand, pictures of the tender grass of dunes or mountain meadow against the sky, with the nude posed in an attitude almost of prayer or looking out into space, have become rather too popular and now look somewhat time-worn.

But don't mind me. I am being unfair. Though what I say is true it will not worry the budding or actual master in the least. If his imagination is fired by this type of subject he will know how to see and picture it in his own way, even if it is hackneyed.

The foreground can also be a frame. The expert will not disdain framing the subject in, for instance, foliage taken against the light or in silhouette, found in abundance in the summer countryside, simply because it is also hackneyed. Flowering branches overhanging rippling water and framing the figure of a nude, softened by a diffusion disc, can hold all the "wonderful trash of life".

Only, since we are employing purely photographic means a great deal must depend on whether good or bad taste has shaped the picture. It may also happen that the model's pose and grace are so perfect and the photographer's instinct so sure, that only a natural and in no way "artistic" picture turns an everyday subject into a revelation.

Perspective

"We are used to seeing a picture, so to speak, like a view from a window, i.e., the earth is below, the sky is above, and the human figure stands upright in this frame. Thus the centre of gravity of a picture is always at the bottom, the picture rests on the baseline, and if it has no support it must invariably fall down. Also, since we are right-handed, the eye must come to a stop on the right ..."

Thus I read in a photographic magazine, not in a faded back-number but in the year 1951.

If it were expressed a little less categorically there would even be some justification for that statement, and from the aesthetic point of view nothing can be said against it. Never mind the modern manner; the studio photographer, for instance, can hardly do otherwise than keep to certain basic rules that comply with the majority taste of the public at large.

Against this must be said that such maxims have managed to put photography into a strait-jacket. Surely the essence of every new and outstanding achievement is in the fact that it breaks out of traditional bounds.

Don't let's fool ourselves. The majority of amateur photographers use the really magical and in themselves stimulating products of a highly developed optical and precision industry merely in order to snapshot away exactly as in A.D. 1900. Less well, if anything. For the large format camera of those days forced the photographer to apply at least some degree of selectivity, and the vestpocket Kodak, the first small camera, was yet to come. But certain rules dating from styles of art which artists themselves have long since discarded, are to this day passed on as laws even in amateur societies of repute.

Photography should have the courage to try anything and everything in the spirit of our "optical realism". Even the conventional, as long as it reflects solid craftsmanship. The only thing that counts is expression.

Low Viewpoint

It may well be unimportant to the final result whether the picture is taken from breast level (the conventional rule since it is supposed to make people look their best) or from a worm's eye view. In spite of conventions, people can look even better when taken from a low viewpoint, for instance at gymnastic or rhythmic exercises, jumps and in all similar action shots. The very low position of the horizon gives plastic modelling of movement and form against the sky. This is one of the rules against the rules that have long been routine practice of professional photographers, not only for nudes but above all in press and sports photography.

A warning for beginners: too low a viewpoint too close to the subject may give an effect of clumsiness unless the composition is very carefully studied beforehand. If the result promises to be nothing better than elephantiasis of the legs or—heaven forbid!—the posterior curves, it is better not attempted.

One old rule we may keep is that a sharply defined horizon running exactly through the centre of the picture is unpleasing nine times out of ten.

A close-up of a striding nude showing the body from the thighs to, perhaps, the nape of the neck, does certainly not "fall down". On the contrary, the idea of striding can be expressed more clearly and realistically in such a close-up than in a brave whole figure showing "the earth below and the sky above".

We can even go so far as to tilt the camera diagonally, thus removing any static support from the nude. The result is a simple dynamic form.

But if we do go very closely to the model in nude photography—"when taking people the camera must not approach the subject too closely since this may result in unflattering distortions"—remember? we must do it properly or not at all. Half-measures have no effect.

Wide-Angle Effects

I wonder why we see so few really high angles in nude photography? The argument of distortion does not hold water. After all, our eyes also look in every possible direction. They are just as much subject to the laws of perspective as the more one-sided though more unequivocal lens, in spite of their "variable focal length".

Frequently, however, we can make a virtue of just this fixation of the lens, even if we have to set three or more to work. With careful study of the power of expression of the parts of the body we can even obtain with the wide-angle lens effects that are far removed from clumsy caricature of the beginners' faults mentioned earlier.

Intersection of Lines

In outdoor nude photography the art of intersecting lines plays some part in obtaining three-dimensional perspective. One or more horizontal lines, e.g. water lines, mountain outlines at various levels, or simply a high horizon, are intersected by strong vertical lines, forming one unit. The verticals can be supplied by foreground props such as trees, branches, rocks, grass, bathing huts and similar objects, by framing—or by the nude herself.

I once took a photograph on a beach on the marshy Halligen region of the North Sea. It was of a girl standing between two boats. However, later analysis of this picture convinced me that the intersecting lines could have been improved. Had I placed the girl in front of the first boat instead of behind it, the horizon would have cut across her figure somewhere below the tip of the nose instead of at the nape —which would have been an improvement in the composition. And, by placing the horizon line just than little bit higher, the three-dimensional effect would have been increased.

Another ancient rule which says that all symmetric composition is dull, should also be mentioned for its curiosity value. Why dull, I wonder? Is not the human figure a symmetric composition?

It is altogether astonishing how many kinds of perspective we can find in our encyclopaedia. I must spare myself the work of enumerating their application in photography except for the following summary:

However we construct any kind of perspective in our pictures, and this is specially important with dynamic perspective, we must see the finished picture, complete in all its aspects, in the viewfinder or on the focusing screen before the exposure is made.

Part enlarging in the darkroom, after the picture has been taken, does not produce worthwhile results. It should only be done in an emergency, for instance when it is impossible to get close enough to the subject and the intention to enlarge a part exists already at the taking stage for exactly this reason. Or when it is the only way to salvage a damaged or faulty negative. Part enlarging, in my opinion, should really be restricted entirely to trimming off unimportant marginal parts of the negative!

I also think that lighting for depth, in face of the competition of line, shape, rich black and white and coloured patterns is a most beautiful aspect of photography.

Lighting

In the middle of the summer the light is unfavourable for photography between 11 a.m. and 3 p.m. It contains a disagreeably high proportion of blue rays and in the mountains an additional predominance of ultraviolet radiation. Yellow filters need a bigger factor. The high position of the sun in the sky is responsible for heavy cast shadows, leading to bizarre deformations on nose, breasts, or other parts shaded by raised arms. Because of this I try to work only in the early hours of the morning and in late afternoon. At these times the share of the desirable yellow-red light is greater, the filter factors become smaller, and nine times out of ten it is possible to manage without any filter whatever.

As I said: I try to. It is a funny thing but in actual practice things mostly happen differently. The things we haven't been doing in the burning midday sun of July at the Mediterranean and the North Sea where on some days it is hardly less brutal! It just turned out that way. And I owe the same number of successful pictures to the "unfavourable" time of day as to the morning and afternoon. The graphic black and white effects I described earlier can be obtained *only* during the unfavourable time of day, paradoxical though it may sound.

The effectiveness of oblique lighting for black and white and almost more for colour photography, and its subtle charms are so obvious and well known that further praise from me seems unnecessary. Certainly the beginner should prefer the favourable hours of the day when there really is less danger of failure because of unsuitable lighting.

The advanced worker however also appreciates the thrill of abundant high sunlight. He can permit himself the heresy of maintaining that we can also take pictures under the midday sun of high summer.

Either I *see* a picture and as an experienced photographer see it with all the advantages and disadvantages of the lighting and catch hold of my camera at once if I like it, or else I *conceive* a picture. If I have conceived the idea of a picture I have a look round the country and at the sun and, if need be, I wait until four or five o'clock. If I do press the button in spite of inner misgivings at least I know what to expect.

Some locations can relieve the harshness of high midday lighting. Among them are reflecting sheets of water seen from a fairly high viewpoint, dry sandy beaches which reflect the light from below, and light coloured cliffs and dunes which reflect it from several sides. Here is where the most perfect "Nude in White" pictures are taken.

Exposure is always short; if it is too generous the negatives will block up only too easily. These are the only conditions for which I can give an average exposure, valid from the North Sea to the Gulf of Lyons: 1/200 second at *f*9 with a light yellow filter and 17° DIN (40 ASA) pan film. This exposure is for clear sky; it is still less with brilliant white cumulus clouds reflecting the light.

Light coloured cliffs can sometimes only be taken under the midday sun while the lower ridges of dunes unfold their greatest charms only with the long and light shadows of the early morning and late afternoon.

For the rest we should really always carry three large sheets of tinfoil fitted on 5 ft. by 7 ft. frames for lightening the shadows. But then we would need a small van, and so we had better leave them to the film people.

However, a sovereign means of managing big contrasts of light and shade is available in the form of speed-synchronized flash, useful even in the brightest sunlight. Flash can lighten inconvenient shadows, tone down over-strong backlighting, and light up colour photographs. Naturally, it has to be carefully rationed lest it produce undesirable effects of its own. More about this on page 94.

Now let us proceed to the different types of lighting.

Side Lighting

I make a point of recommending strong side lighting to every friend or beginner who asks for my advice. To be precise, not the formerly greatly praised semi-side lighting but real side lighting. I have always found the most harmless of snapshotters to profit from this advice.

The reason why I like straightforward side lighting is that I am fond of good modelling. The sweep of an arm or a hip line, the slight turn of the body are beautifully stressed if the model knows how to stand.

Mostly I go a little further and change my viewpoint until I get side-rear lighting, just short of full back lighting. In this light the limbs are more sharply outlined without turning the body into a dark mass without detail, depth and warmth. Filters are usually unnecessary, specially during the favourable time of day.

Front Lighting

Flat lighting must not be confused with low sun whose rays meet the atmosphere at a low angle and, in contrast to high sunlight, take a much longer distance to traverse it. By flat lighting we mean direct front lighting which falls on model and background from the direction of the camera and at a more or less high angle, and which makes all subjects appear "flat".

What a lovely effect! At one end of the scale it gives us the high key of artificial lighting, and at the other the previously described reversal by means of a red filter. We repeat: a risky procedure. But a nude seen as a compact shape of shimmering white under a dark July sky or against a cliff that as it were radiates a curious translucency of its own, is certainly not a bad picture. Also, the flat illumination of front lighting is still best for colour.

Admittedly, the beginner who suddenly takes it in his head to take a picture of the girl friend without her swimsuit is apt to get something like a medical or ethnographical record picture with front lighting; a two-dimensional squeezed-flat nakedness such as nature herself is not cruel enough to show in such exaggerated detail.

No, properly applied flat lighting needs a strong filter!

Without Sun

Diffuse lighting also has great charm when it is derived from veiled sunlight. In such conditions we must not rest nor tarry; the occasion is unique and rare, the light still abundant and it may even be more intense when warm and humid air reflects the sunlight.

Even in a big close-up, the silvery quality of this outdoor picture, preserved by soft development, can and must be felt. And in the right conditions ranging from softly rising mist to overall haze, we can even include the veiled heavenly body of the sun in the picture.

But when the light is merely diffused by a fairly high layer of stratus cloud, when we have nothing but a light to melancholically-dark grey gloom, we had better pack up. Conditions are better under a grey-black and rather broken sky when in suitable localities many a picture can be taken even without sun. Special effects are provided by the sun breaking through the clouds or, better still, when a thunderstorm is brewing up.

Rain whipping fresh young skin should be lovely too. Not that I know but I can just imagine how it would be. For when the rain began to come down my models have so far always mutinied because they were feeling too cold.

Back Lighting

The serious worker swears by backlighting—also called *contre-jour* or against the light photography. It was invented immediately after the soft focus effect. For without backlighting soft focus pictures look simply washed out. Since then backlighting has never gone out of fashion, not even in the age of realism. Before the naked and chaste nymph rising from the waters drenched in light but modestly blacked out around the middle even the most hard-hearted of censors capitulates.

If colour should ever do away with black and white altogether, it will be seen that its finest achievements were pictures taken against the light.

The practical application of backlighting is self-evident. White is simply white, but light photographed as backlighting, crystallized as it is by the camera, *radiates.*

Suddenly a kiss of air brushes the lake—a hesitating breath under powerful light. Thousands of little suns light up, one in each curly ripple, magically glittering, strangely fleeting. Backlighting needs things to break up against; they may be tiny waves or the wonder of the human body. Hard darkness adjoins the radiant glitter—the brighter the radiance the darker the depth of the unlit tones.

Bodies are swept by light like cliffs by the surf. Backlighting condenses and creates clarity. It gives us the magic of reflections, contrasts, and long, deep shadows.

Backlighting allows the lens to capture ethereal moods as no other medium can—not even the brushes of the impressionists although they were the first to develop a feeling for atmospheric effects.

Low Sun

I have already said that water absorbs more light than is generally assumed. This phenomenon gives us a chance to introduce a variation of backlighting with a very full compression of the black and white tone scale.

When the sun is very low in the sky its rays scarcely penetrate water, and it remains black and unlit. But if they fall on a light object such as a nude in the water, those parts of her body that are out of the water (which should be as smooth as possible) stand out in stark white against the dark water when taken at the right camera angle. A slight movement of her legs below the water level refracts the backlighting and sends out long rays of reflected light floating like radiant gossamer round her limbs.

When the layman sees such a picture in print he usually assumes the effect to be due to after-treatment but it has been obtained by the purely optical medium of the camera.

The exposure must be for the light body of the nude, i.e. it will be on the short side. No filter should be used but a lens hood is indispensable with all pictures taken against the light. When the sun is very low on the horizon not even the lens hood helps. We have to ask a friend to screen the lens from the sun with his hat, coat, hand or body—without, of course, intruding into the field of view.

"Colour" in Black and White

The average amateur photographs, even those shown at exhibitions, suffer from an excess of middle tones. The old and overdone respect for the full tone range (which must on no account be lost) still haunts the salons. But preserving the tone range without regard for the subject matter can easily become a mannerism, and that is precisely what it was for a long period.

To-day the pendulum sometimes swings just as naïvely in the opposite direction. The result is pictures with sooty blacks, chalky whites and grain that stands out a mile.

"Without regard for the subject matter" is the crux of the matter and reduces what I say to the right proportions. What is right for a fogscape or the deliberate simplification of a nude with soft body sharply outlined in diffuse lighting and is not consciously felt as "grey", becomes a dish without taste or flavour on a sunlit beach, in the hard lines of mountains, and generally in the sun.

In nude photography it is the figure that dominates the picture. But we have already seen that here just as in general photography, we have light and dark subjects, line and shape, patterns and tone range and—a pronounced effect of "colour".

Since black and white photography is an abstraction—and what an abstraction!—this "colour" effect is as subtle as it is unique. In the last analysis colour photography cannot even compete, for with its direct approach it must take a different road.

Enriching black and white photography with a "colour" effect does not mean enlarging any negative chosen at random on ultra hard paper. It is something that has to be seen before the exposure is made. In the ideal case it must govern the development of the negative.

If we have taken a delicate subject and wish to preserve its delicate quality we must choose a delicately working developer. If a subject has to be compressed into a few contrasting tones it may have to be processed in metol-hydroquinone. When this individual treatment cannot be given the only means of manipulation are the various paper grades from extra soft to ultra hard. They, of course, meet nearly all our requirements, since with the subject matter as the determining factor our negatives are made for the paper!

The strongest effect of "colour" is obtained with few patterns of shapes or spots which, however, have to be arranged in an orderly relationship. The extreme pattern is made of pure black and pure white. If the subject really does express a meaning, any intermediate tones would only weaken its message. Feininger showed us two good examples of such pictures before the war, each with a nude (the same girl) on the water's edge.

One picture had broad outlines of light contrasting with a brilliant black against a blank sky. The other was taken from the front in brilliant light, with one side of the body in equally deep black, seen from a moderately oblique high viewpoint against the dark water without any sky whatever. The two pictures, taken from viewpoints only a couple of paces apart, were almost like negative and positive. In both pictures the simplified tone range modelled the figure in extreme clarity and consequential colour translation—without after treatment and fully preserving their natural quality.

Admittedly everything natural and unequivocal is difficult. From the photographic point of view, it is easier to obtain a pictorially pleasing print from a negative with rich gradation. The more half-tones between black and white the more automatically harmonious is the effect, and the more peaceful, balanced and sure of public approval its impact on the beholder. That is if we follow the rule that very harsh contrasts of tone and light make the picture look hard and should therefore be avoided.

I am, of course, far too conscious of my responsibilities to deny the fascinating beauty of a rich tone scale, as many of my pictures should prove. It is only too easy to miss the boat altogether with misconceived tone separation. We have only to think of the wealth of tones in a correctly lit setting of foliage and grass in a nude photograph.

Whether we seek flat and very delicate tones in the right place, the almost transparent play of fine middle tones, or strong contrasting tones compressed into extreme simplicity, we must always consider the whole. Applied to nude photography this means that the picture must be built round the human figure. We still keep our choice of making it a tight, loose, relaxed or subordinated arrangement.

To sum up, "colour" in black and white demands, even without suppressing the middle tones, deep blacks, rich greys, brilliant whites.

One other thing. "Deep black" must not be confused with soot and ink effects. With correct exposure during enlarging an almost clear shadow part of a good negative will show no less detail than an anaemic grey or dirty grey-brown. They have nothing to do with tone rendering but simply prove incompetence.

Correct Tone Rendering

Do I have to mention correct tone rendering as well? Our modern pan material meets all reasonable demands in this respect. One hundred per cent correct tone rendering, which may mean the merging of correctly rendered skin and correctly rendered sky, is in no way desirable. Apart from the changing spectral composition of daylight we may want to reproduce one day the velvet texture and highlights of skin in the glory of its summer tan, and another time a shimmering and mysterious white body against a dark setting. To the tune of the subject we play with film, filter, viewpoint, negative and positive processing on the keyboard of tone scales and lighting.

Pitiless Definition, Depth of Field, and Exposure

Photography is substance reproduced by optical means; it is texture and atmosphere. Lighting, controlled by the expert, introduces "mood". How does the "pitiless definition" of our lens conflict with these and other aspects touching on emotional factors, particularly in nude photography?

With its perfectly ground glass sparkling under its blue coating our lens represents a wonderful piece of craftsmanship. It would be a shame to smear grease on its spick and span surface in order to obtain a soft focus effect. The product of extremely difficult mathematical computations and highly developed craftsmanship, it wants to demonstrate, not suppress, its potentialities.

But how about the totally unsatisfactory lenses of the early days of photography and the artistically supreme achievements of a David Octavius Hill? Here our inexorable righteousness begins to waver. Thinking the matter out we arrive at something like this conclusion:

The resolving power and pitiless definition of a thoroughly corrected modern high quality anastigmat were not, of course, born of the pleasure in mathematical equations and glass polishing. They were created because Man endeavours to widen the boundaries of our world and to open up hitherto uncharted regions.

When we take a photograph of a human being in the nude we are also endeavouring to regain in uncharted regions a point of view which is only one form of expression among many others. But the principle is vitally important as the subject is Man.

Since we are the products of our times we can do justice to other human beings only with the means of our times. The world of a David Octavius Hill is of the past and so is the spectacle glass he used for his lens.

Or is it? Modern musicians also turn back at times to the Gregorian system, not to speak of the ideal of the "technically" already highly developed Bach.

Soft Focus Lenses

We do not have to go back to the pin-hole camera. But the aberrations of an uncorrected meniscus lens also represent purely optical means and may be used for expressing a specific message like any other technical invention since the beginning of photography. The effect we are concerned with is the "soft" impression obtained by spreading light into shadow areas like a halo.

Better than an obsolete lens is a modern soft focus lens or a supplementary diffusion disc of the Duto type. If anywhere, soft focus pictures are entitled to a rightful place in nude photography, even in modern days. It is essential to realize that soft focus is in no way unsharpness for it leaves the subject basically sharp and only softens the lines between light and shade.

Soft focus lenses or diffusion discs can achieve convincing pictures when used on the camera but never in the enlarger. In the thirties the Hungarians developed a gripping style of their own with soft focus pictures printed on highly glazed glossy paper. It was no romanticism. They pulled all the stops of a rich tone scale and yet remained essentially simple. Never before had Hungarian life been brought so close to an admiring world public. These pictures shone and radiated inner wealth—in glossy black and white.

The photographer Neumüller-Linz created nudes of great and radiant beauty in soft focus "as a recreation after the fatiguing sameness of anastigmatic work" with the soft working Imagon lens. In all probability people will still be looking at them long after they have grown tired of pin sharp exaggerated highlights on perfectly sharp bronzed bodies.

Blur

Now I must introduce one of the few categorical imperatives of this book: Blur obtained by deliberate incorrect focusing as a means of achieving a "pictorial effect" is out, absolutely out! This fashion of the twenties was quite naïve. Nor is severe blur due to subject movement an asset; it is something that has gone wrong. There may be a few exceptions but they have to be considered with great care. Slight or partial unsharpness due to movement is only acceptable in nude and all other photography when it stresses an otherwise clear action or idea.

With a sharply rendered nude even a very strongly patterned background can yield an excellent effect when it is made to dissolve into a blur by means of a wide aperture. That is no problem. Again there are compositions where a deliberately unsharp foreground forces the eye through gradually increasing sharpness to the main subject, the nude. This can be an excellent means of expression. The finished picture alone provides the justification.

We can try many other ways of breaking through the barriers of the usual anastigmatism. The why and wherefore can be given only with difficulty or not at all. The Hungarians too, restricted their soft focus cautiously to certain groups of subjects, and the self-same photographers simultaneously cultivated perfect sharpness with other subjects without in any way conflicting with the particular style that made them famous. This is worth remembering.

Let us allot the function of "recreation" to soft focus. It becomes us to regard the precision lens as our moblest and most "photographic" means, a means that in spite of all opinions to the contrary will always remain inexhaustible. It demands sharpness for our new realism as well as for our nude photography.

The intelligent use of the stop has already been mentioned in the chapter dealing with suitable localities. Depth of field tables are excellent but of little use when we have left them at home. This makes us grateful for the depth of field scales on lens mounts and cameras. When neither is available it is a good principle to focus on the nearest third of the desired depth of field zone, give or take a little either way according to the position of the main subject. For our purpose the main subject is nearly always the nude.

Camera Shake

When taking hand held pictures—and I dare say most of our pictures are taken in that way—it is preferable to open up a stop and use a faster shutter speed. This is specially important with miniature cameras. It is quite incredible how many pictures taken at 1/50 or 1/60 second suffer from camera shake.

The effect of camera shake is particularly annoying because as a rule it does not show until we make an 8 by 10 inch or bigger enlargement, when all the time the negative looked perfectly all right even when scrutinized with a magnifying glass. With the Makina III which I use often, I admit to risking hand held exposures up to 1/10 second, but the Makina is a rather special case. It fits specially snugly in the hands because it must be held by the front panel. I have also chanced 1/5 second holding my breath but always making at least two exposures for safety.

It is really much better to use a tripod for the slow shutter speeds. But it must be a robust one, not one of those Sunday afternoon vest-pocket affairs. However useful an emergency tripod may be on some occasions, our normal work should be done with a thoroughly rigid tripod, rock steady, easily adjustable and with a large pan-and-tilt head. The help a good tripod can give out of doors is a revelation—follow the example of the film people.

Correct Exposure

From the first the exposure should be matched to the method of development. Over-exposure with its disadvantage of loss of film speed was at one time highly recommended in the search for the finest grain. But it is useful only when followed by very delicate development in a genuine fine-grain developer, which results in artificially flat gradation.

I am all for correct exposure and for bringing out the tones in a fine grain or compensating developer which yield pleasing and not too thin negatives. With medium speed film the grain remains unobjectionable without detriment to the other characteristics of the film.

In nude photography the use of the photo-electric exposure meter is simple and straightforward. Since nine times out of ten the correct exposure of the figure is what matters, both the usual reflected light method from the camera position and the incident light method are admissible. In this method, as most readers will know, the light falling on the subject is measured by taking a reading with the meter pointing at the camera. When the reflected light method is used it is necessary with some viewpoints to take a reading close to the nude.

Pictures of fast movement such as we frequently get in the bright light of a locality we selected for exactly this reason, usually need at least 1/200 second. A shutter speed of 1/500 second will safely stop even the fastest movement normally made by a human being. In such action photography the stop has to be wholly subordinated to the all-important shutter speed and it will not usually be possible to use effect filters.

Movement and Action

The author of an early article on photographing movement recommended letting the model skip and gambol to her heart's content. The photographer had only to skip and gambol after her, camera at the ready, up the dune, down the dune, and to press the button at the right moment in order to take home a harvest of fine pictures.

That is the best way of wasting material. Don't let any outraged follower of the method protest the contrary; one breathtakingly lucky shot and thirty-five useless frames on the same film run counter to even the most liberal conception of modern miniature technique.

There is no such thing as chance snapshooting in correctly understood nude photography. It is like first-class press photography—let nobody think that the best action pictures are the result of chance shots. It may happen once in a while. But the born press photographer has a sort of sixth sense that tells him how, when and where he "presses the button".

We want fresh, natural, unselfconscious pictures. We are just as unable to manage without the action-stopping pounce of the shutter as the press photographer. But our kind of "snap" shot is the genuine kind that gives us on a film with eight, sixteen or thirty-six exposures possibly not all but certainly seven, fourteen, or twenty-five pictures exactly as we want them.

The reason why we get our pictures as we want them is that we direct them. The more movement the more careful must be our directing. In the normal run of things and with good models it may be so unobtrusive that the protagonists really do not know when exactly the picture is being taken. But directing there must be, and the "when" is what makes or breaks the picture.

Page 81: *Shadow Lines* by Christian Cambazard

2¼-in. square Rolleiflex, Verichrome Pan film, orange filter, 1/60 second, *f*8, Ethol developer. The shadows on the body of the model were lightened by the use of an aluminium reflector; the girl was kneeling beside a withered bush on the Atlantic coast near New York.

Page 82: *Torso* by Marta Hoepffner

2¼-in. square reflex camera, 6-in. Xenar, Adox R 17 film.

Page 83: *Low Angle* by Christian Cambazard

2¼-in. square Rolleiflex, Verichrome Pan film, 1/15 second, *f*8.
The curving outlines provided the attraction for this picture. Cambazard took it against the light without any fill-in lighting for the shadows. This is one of a number of nude pictures Cambazard made during a stay in New York; he normally lives in Paris.

Page 84: *Modelled by Light* by Annemarie Heinrich

A low key picture by the photographer who works in Buenos Aires.

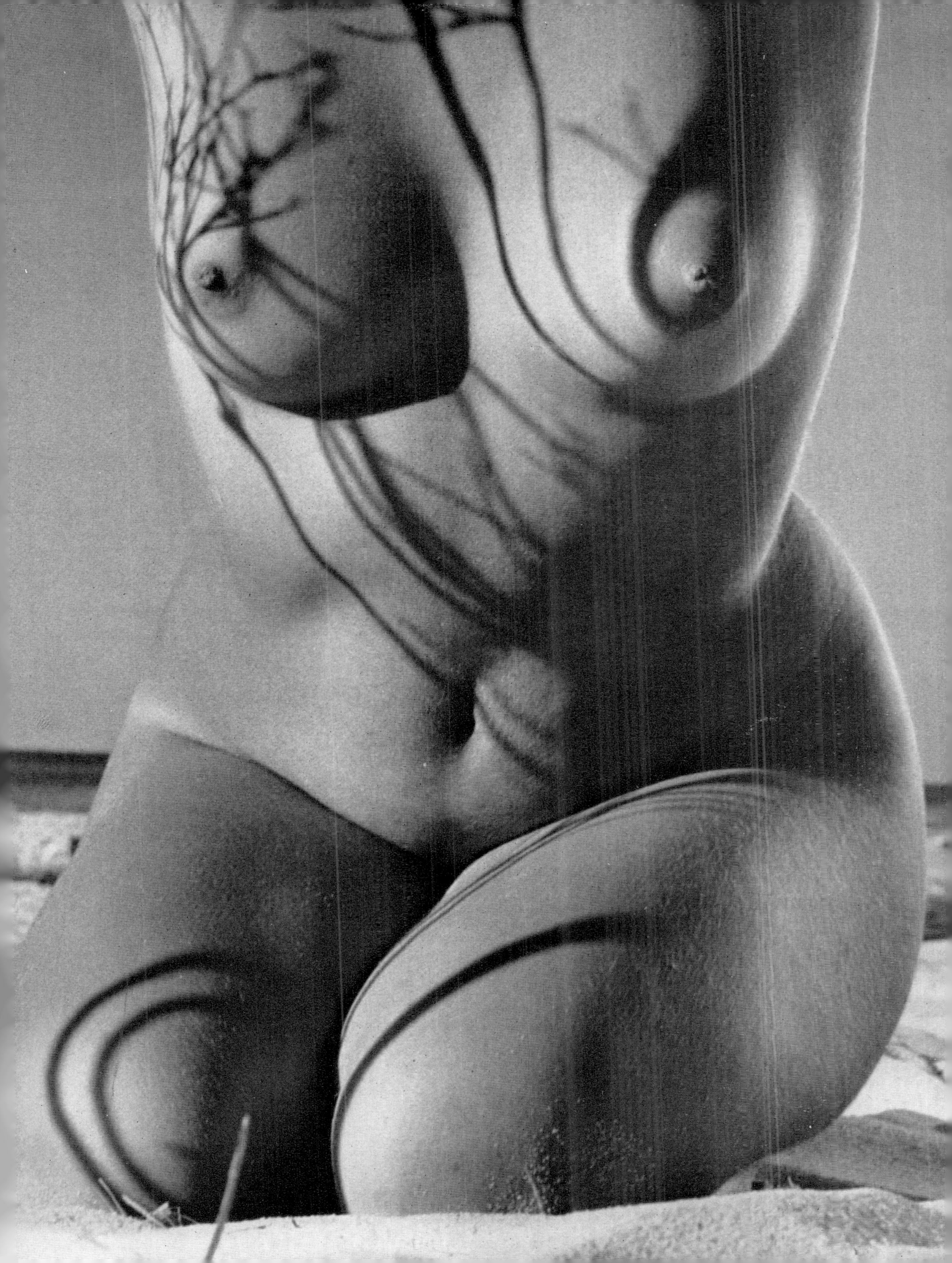

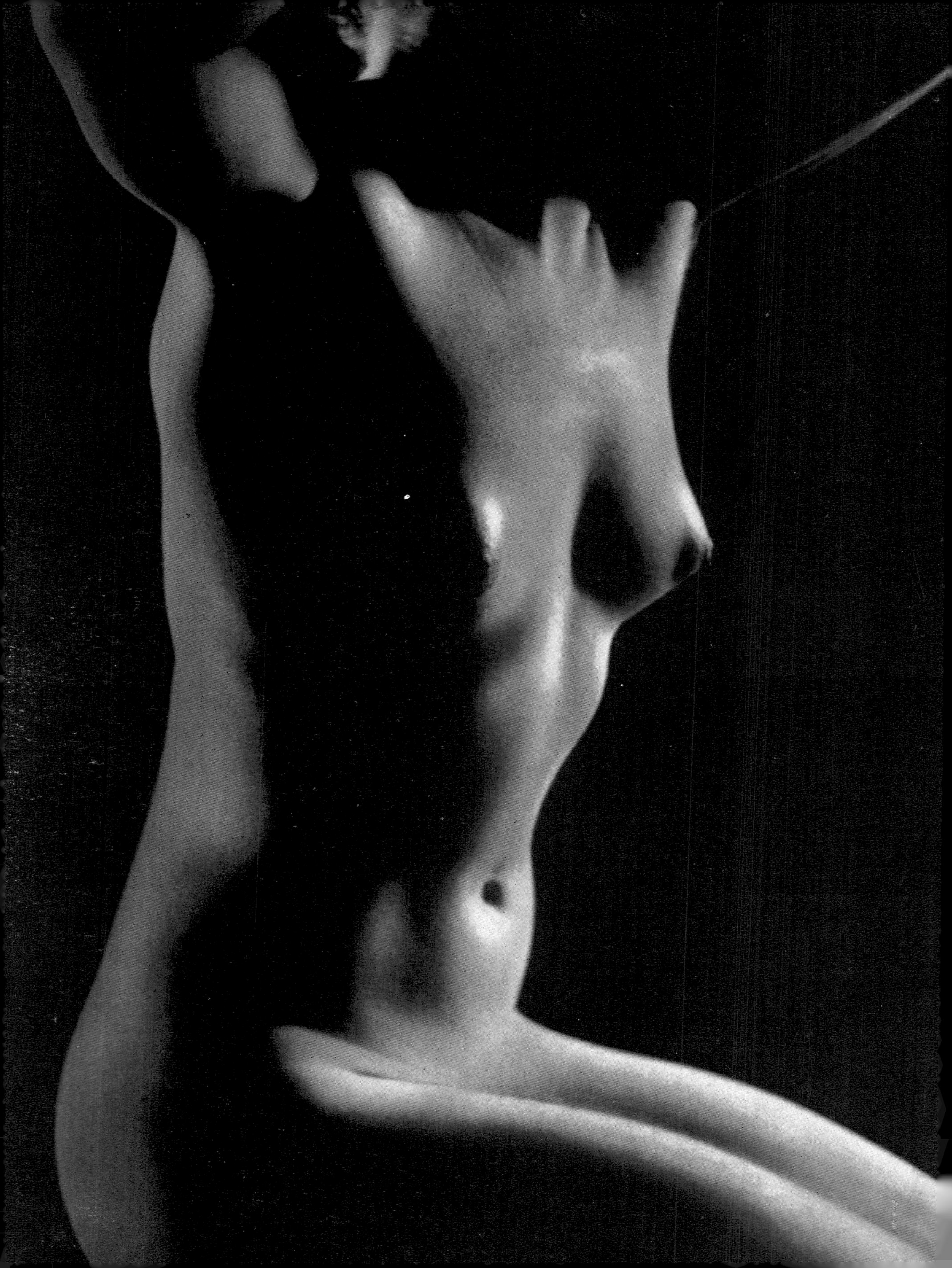

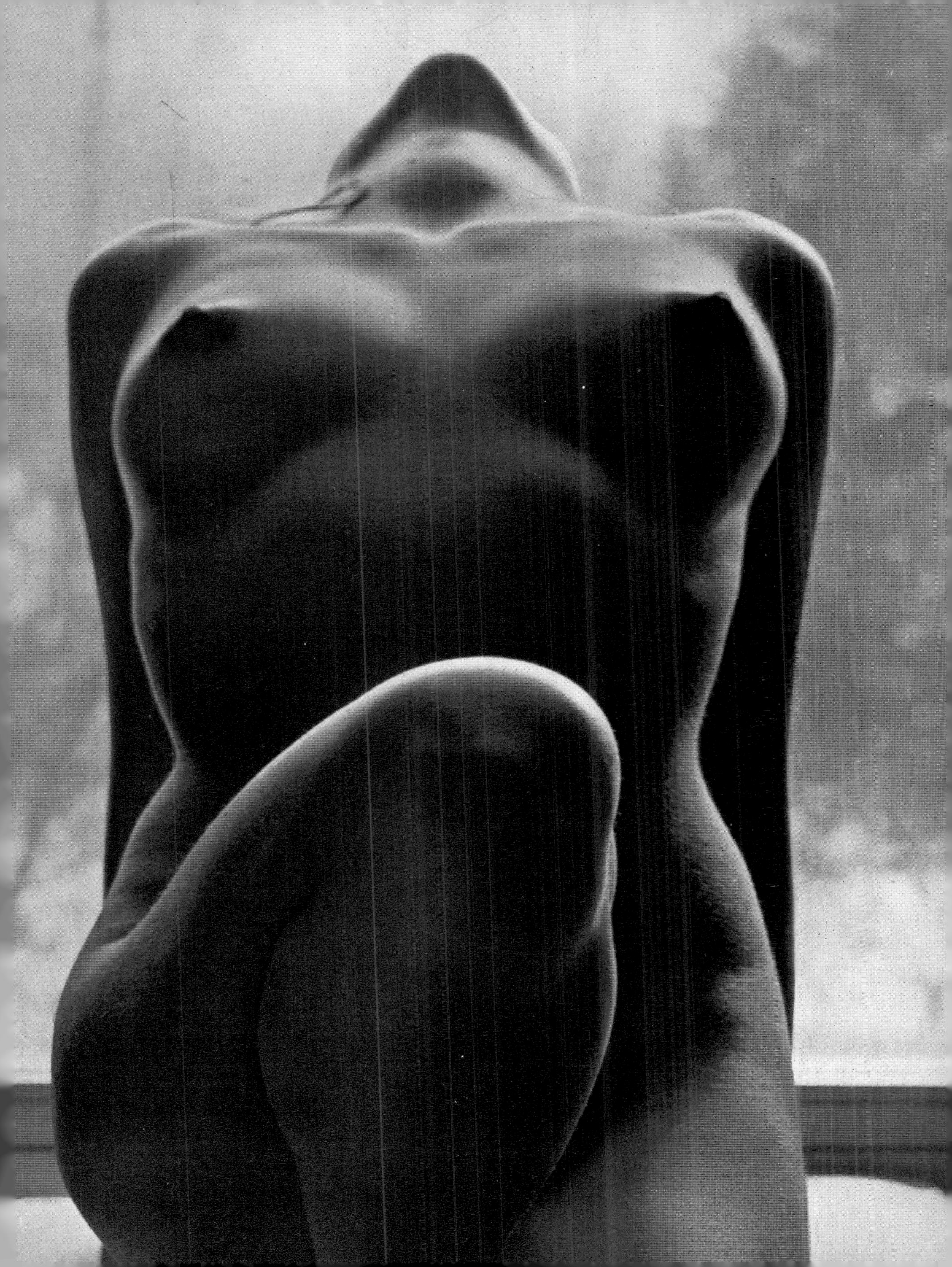

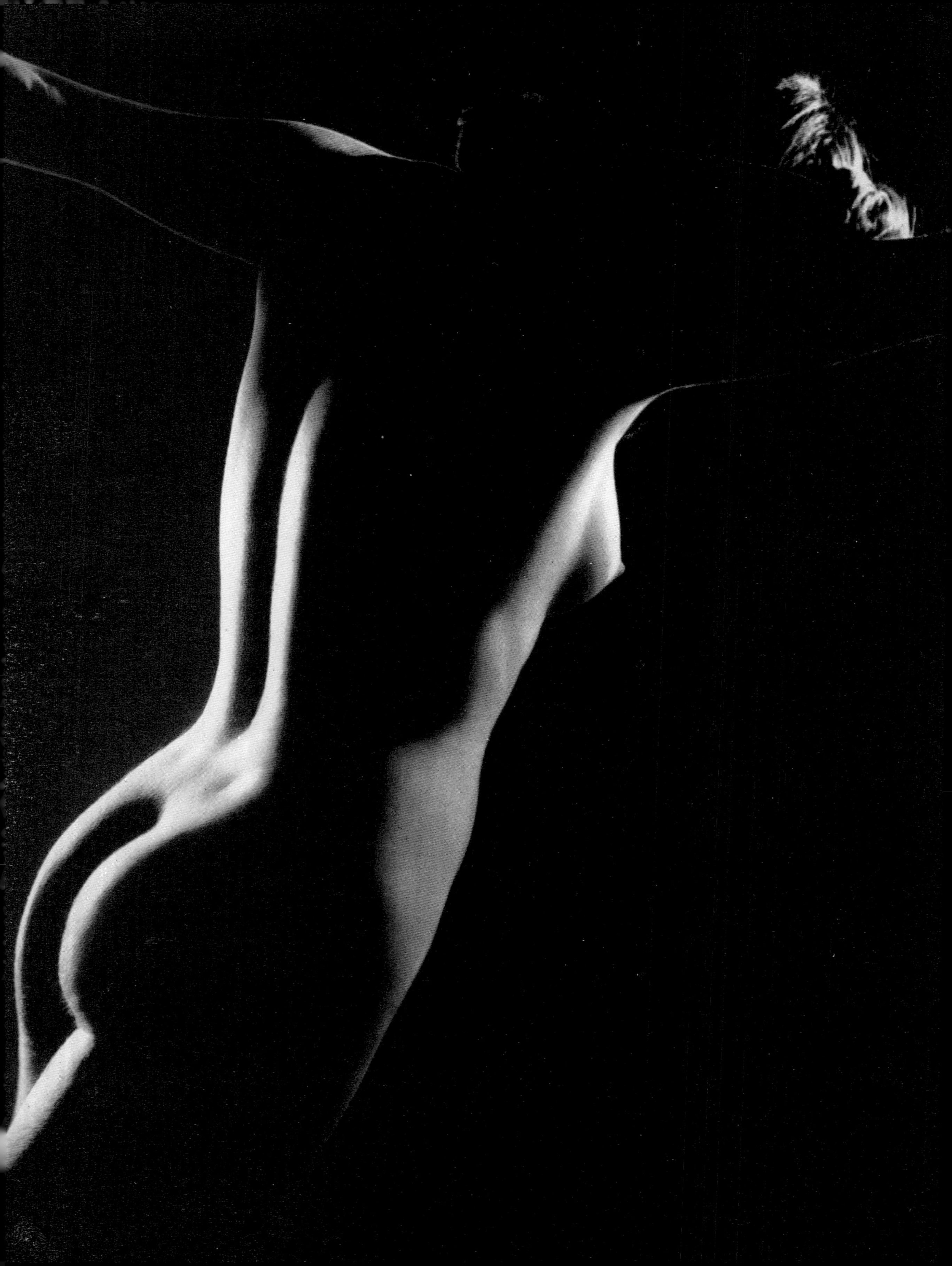

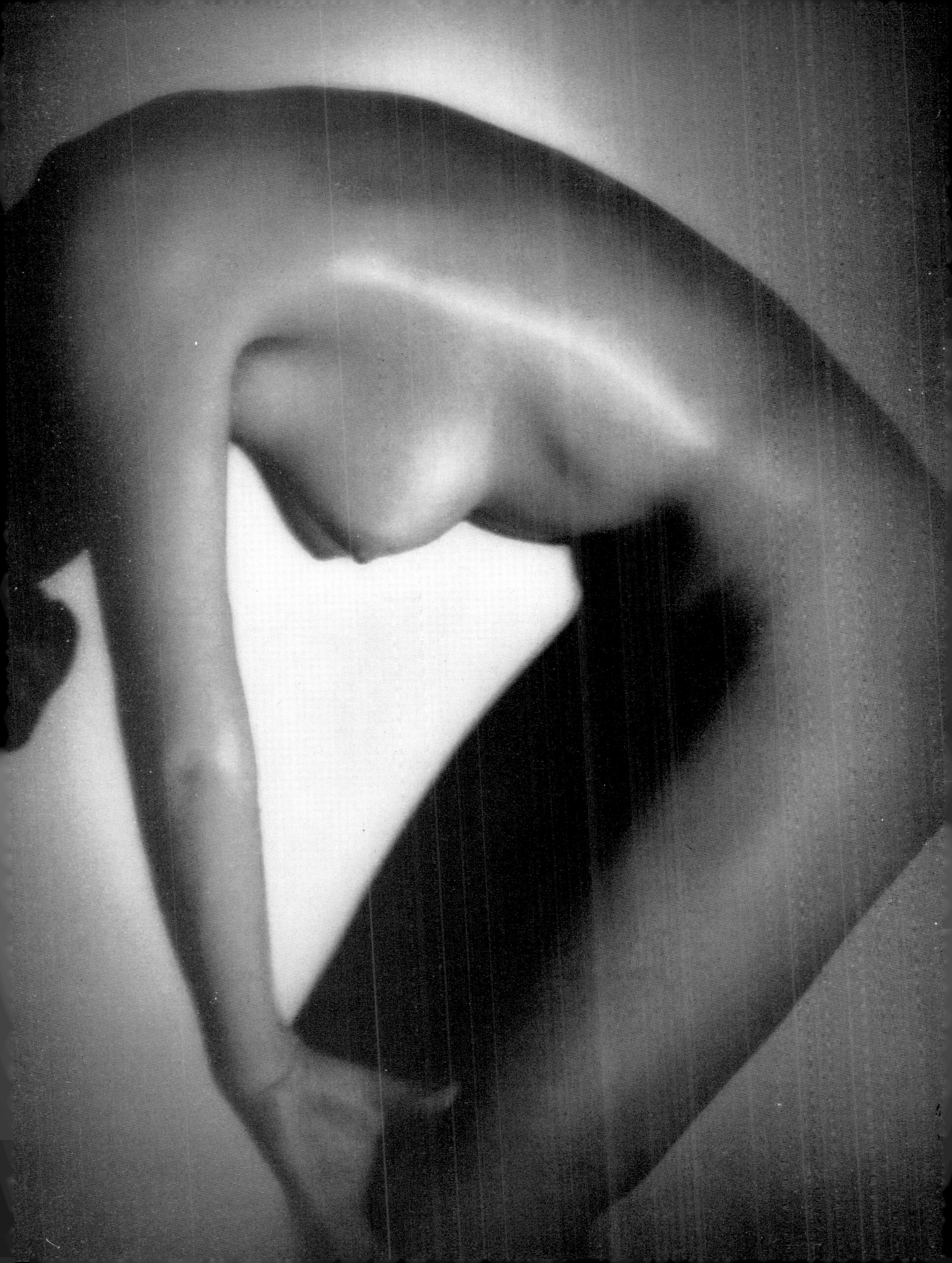

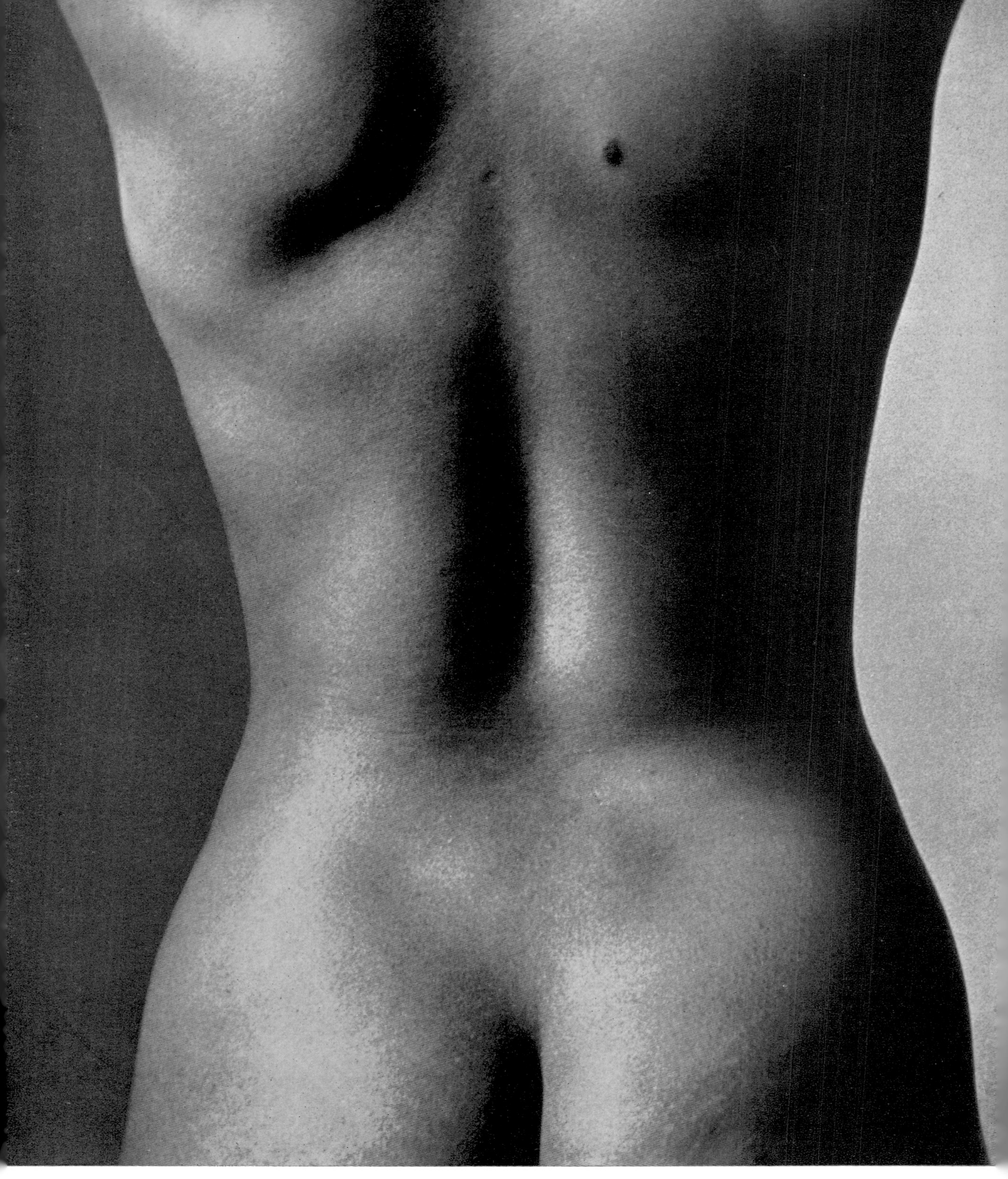

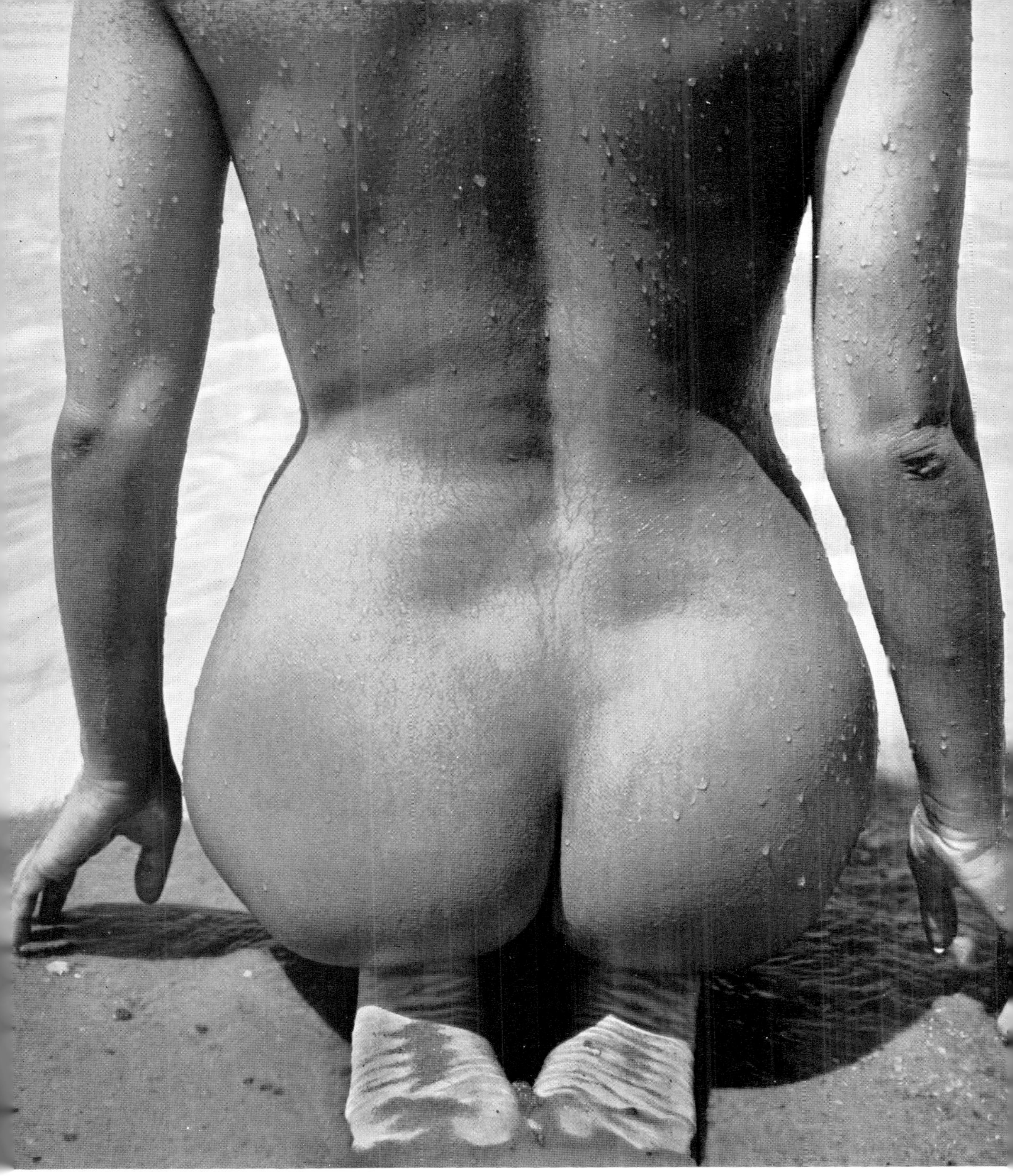

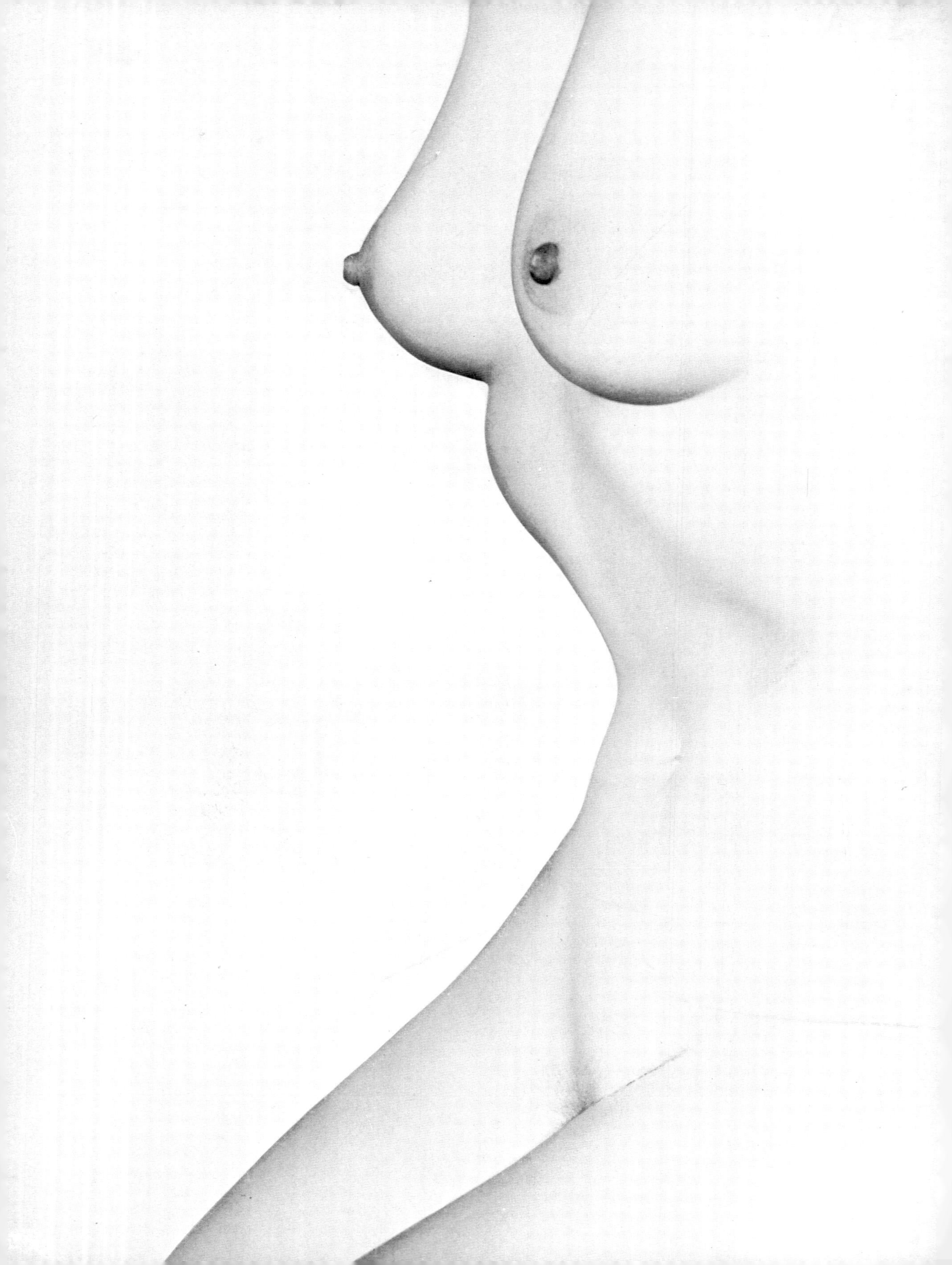

Page 85: *Study* by H. Hajek-Halke

9 × 12 cm. reflex camera, 2 seconds, *f*8.
Taken by the young Hajek-Halke in the early 'twenties.

Page 86: *Back View* by Muni Lieblein

Lieblein, like Henle with the picture on page 87, wanted to show an attractive skin texture. He is a professional photographer working in New York.

Page 87: *Drops of Water* by Fritz Henle

2¼-in. square Rolleiflex, Super-XX film, light yellow filter, 1/100 second, *f*16, Microdol developer.

Page 88: *High Key* by Ferenc Berko

4 × 5 studio camera, 29 cm. Protar, ultra-fast film, ½ second, *f*16.
Berko was one of the first to make use of the high key effect in nude photography. Requirements for this effect were completely diffuse lighting without deep shadows, ample exposure and delicate development in order to obtain bright highlights.

The "where" is easier. For instance, when taking fast movement and jumps the operator is more or less obliged to lie flat on his stomach, with the right side of the sky and the right direction of the light in his viewfinder. It does not matter if the model has to run and leap two or three times—if we were filming she would have to do it a dozen times—the picture still remains a pure action shot.

Other movements may need to be taken at eye level or even from a high viewpoint. The photographer can focus on a mark, or he can follow the model with the camera (panning). Sometimes he may have to ask the model to try again four times and expose only at the fifth attempt because he could see that the first attempts were simply not right.

If we want the best, freshness and spontaneity are not enough. The good nude photograph must have impact as well. And a good photograph, as we have already said, needs an element of duration. The pounce of the camera in action photography serves the sole purpose of bringing out the characteristic element of the movement being made.

Translated into practical terms, this means capturing the sum total of the effort, the climax of the movement. Take it from below, from above, from the front, from one side, upright or with the camera tilted, but always use the fastest available shutter speed. And always use all the sharp definition of your fine lens. After all, the human body is not a rigid structure like a motor car or aeroplane where the camera cannot distinguish between immobility and speed unless they raise a cloud of dust or trace a vapour trail in the sky.

The fact that a human body is moving is always discernible, even when stopped with a shutter speed of 1/1,000 second, and how magnificent it is when caught at the right moment!

It is very much to be doubted whether the art historian's demand that western sculpture should portray only duration and reject everything transitory and ephemeral, is to be applied to photography. Of course, the climax which is at the same time a moment of rest, must of necessity have our main attention. In actual practice watching for the infinitesimal fraction of a second when the "reversal" of a movement takes place, and reacting to it with the necessary speed, is extraordinarily difficult in spite of all directing and needs much practice. But once we have captured this phase the picture will stand up to the most critical eye.

There are also occasions, exclusive to photography, when the same can be said of a picture showing a transitory or even an unconventional phase of movement.

Blur due to subject movement or camera shake is no tool of nude photography. Its most important part is directing, laborious though it may be. Only, here as in any other achievement the labour must not show up in the result. For the rest the labour does not really amount to a great deal—how can it when it is all such fun!

Skin Rendering

The rendering of skin tones is a cardinal subject of painting. Consequently it was taken over by photography. But what applies to painting is, at most, fifty per cent valid in photography, especially in colour photography. The rendering of the sheen of silky textiles in an advertising photograph raises approximately the same problem.

The problem is one of texture and lighting. Lighting and subject treatment may relegate texture to a position of unimportance or even fail to show it altogether. But texture can never be more important than lighting. What we must attempt to achieve is a rendering of the surface that carries conviction. It may be glittering radiance taken against the light or merely an outlined shadow, or the sheen of bronze standing out from pale sand. The scale ranges from a minute speck of humanity in a landscape to a tormenting close-up of a body detail.

Since models with bad and unhealthy skin can in any case hardly be considered for serious nude photography, technical difficulties should hardly arise in the normal course of work. Spots and small irregularities have little importance; blue or other bruises resulting from the knocks of games are much more troublesome. If necessary a lightly toned powder has to be used.

Dry skin, which may be due to excessive exposure to air and the dehydrating effect of sunlight, often appears flat and textureless. Suntan oil is a perfect cure of course, for a serious degree of patchy sunburn. Sunburn, incidentally, should never arise; people who spend much time in the open air acquire a tan even though they may lack the curious ambition of week enders imprudent enough to lie in the broiling sun for hours on end.

Vaseline and glycerine last much longer than suntan oil which on hot days or under the heat of studio lights is quickly absorbed by the skin. They are specially suitable for artificial light photography indoors. Thickly laid on they yield the generally admired beautiful highlights and even reflections on bronzed bodies.

Beware of overdoing the oiling. A sun-tempered, shimmering skin is beautiful and natural. But oil idolatry easily becomes a cheap mannerism.

Oily fingers carelessly touching the lens produce unexpected soft focus effects. Prevention is better than cure: let the model do her own oiling. If the sun is so hot that the photographer must protect his own skin he should wait until he has put his camera away. For sand loves to cling to greasy hands and is no better for the camera than oil.

It must also be noted that the white marks left by straps and swimsuit tops on tanned skin make the most attractive girl useless for modelling. When taking models out in boats on the Rhône river and in the Mediterranean we always took good care not to let them wear the bra type of swimsuit top. When they had to get dressed they put on ordinary shirt type blouses.

Shivering

A shivering model is a very pretty sight. This is not a joke for—forgive me—goose flesh is a tasty morsel for the camera as well as for us. It comes out very well in low sun and hard backlighting. Have you ever admired the long, pin sharp miniature shadows cast at sundown by even the minutest fragments of gravel on the road? It is like a complete but transient microcosm of light and shade. The contracted epidermis with its more or less visible tiny hairs is a similar but still more detailed phenomenon.

However we ought to consider whether we can take the responsibility of making not only the model shiver but possibly also the people who look at her picture.

A bucket of water thrown over the girl makes the thing plausible even on a hot day. A close-up of pearls of water on a beautiful skin—but I had better not continue or I may become too lyrical.

Mastering Colour

In colour photography the skin tone is influenced not only by the extremely variable scattered daylight; it will also reflect the colour of its immediate surroundings. In fact, the reflected colour has the greater influence.

There is no need to be overmuch afraid of these reflected colours but we must learn to notice them and judge their effect on the picture. It is less distracting when the object from which the reflection originates is wholly or partially included in the picture. When the figure stands alone the reflected light may be deliberately used to give an individual note to the colour rendering.

We do not have to go quite so far as the photographer who always took pictures with a colour cast. It was an intensive green which it was impossible to overlook. Nobody could say where it came from. His films were perfectly normal, so were his camera and development. Until the day when somebody took a look at his lens hood—and found it to be green.

It is clear then that the immediate surroundings of the figure and the background have to be considered with care. The background is also important in another respect. Since colour photography deals with areas of colour whose relationship to each other is very different from that of black and white areas, an out of focus background is often rather distracting. This is the exact opposite of the normal practice of black and white photography where the same effect is accepted as desirable because it gives a pleasing atmosphere and depth. The concensus of opinion is that not many colour backgrounds can be neutralized in this manner.

Readers may remember that the late Dr Paul Wolff thought this opinion incorrect.

Since then we have seen many examples of pictures with cleverly introduced characteristic colour patterns. Again we can only say that each case will have to be considered on its merits.

Flat to semi-sidelight is not the only correct form of lighting for colour but it is certainly the safest and simplest. If we place the nude in a sufficiently neutral setting and expose correctly with front lighting we obtain beautiful and faithful colour rendering of a summer tan. Indeed, it comes out less realistically than if we used the same lighting in black and white; we might call it toned down.

Skin folds, blotches, and white marks left by swimsuits are no worse in colour than in black and white, in other words, they are exactly as ruinous. Fair pubic hair is unobtrusive but dark hair demands the same care as both do in black and white.

The fact that colour photography no less than black and white works with light is often overlooked. Still, the beginner is not advised to attempt pictures against the light, the finest effect of black and white photography, because of the restricted contrast range of all colour processes, unless he has money and material to spare.

Yet backlighting in all its variations has infinite possibilities in colour as well. Naturally there is a greater danger of undesirable reflected light effects, and partial under- or overexposure resulting in muddy colours is unavoidable. These are faults that may be acceptable in colour slides. But in paper prints which have a much shorter tone range, they cannot be accepted, nor can they be corrected by means of filtering during printing. It is obvious that each filter can only correct a very narrow sector of the colour circle.

There are two ways of getting over this difficulty:

(1) Lightening the shadows with reflectors or mixed light, and
(2) Flash.

Reflectors in this context are any reflecting surfaces, from those provided by nature to the previously mentioned tin foil sheets of the film industry. Light coloured sand, particularly the sand of dunes, water, or a white cliff can tone down the contrast of against the light pictures so much that even colour prints can accommodate them. Even a large white towel that happens to be handy can be held by a companion and bring the desired success.

Mixed Light

Mixed light, i.e. taking the picture by daylight and relieving the shadows with photofloods, can be considered only indoors or at best near a house since we do not carry power generators in the field. All manufacturers of colour materials utter specific warnings against mixed light in their instruction leaflets.

Dr Paul Wolff did not share the makers' opinion. In his book *Meine Erfahrungen —Farbig* he described how he obtained fine colour pictures with warm and good colour on daylight reversal film. He eliminated the blue cast that would normally be expected by applying the following rule from his own experience: Too little photoflood light + daylight = too cold; too much photoflood = too warm with a considerable risk of falsifying the colours towards brown.

Flash in Sunlight

An excellent method of bridging the contrast in colour and black and white is flash. For daylight type colour film the blue tinted flash bulbs are the obvious choice. In practice, however, it does not matter a great deal if the normal clear flashbulbs, whose colour temperature is between daylight and photofloods, are used instead. On the contrary, in nude photography the colour rendering of the skin inclines towards a pleasing warm tone.

Finally, electronic flash approximates daylight so closely that it presents no problem of any kind. Many photographers use it nowadays in the studio with daylight type colour film and obtain excellent skin rendering in portraits.

I must make one point quite clear: we do not want to falsify the daylight, a fault which in its most flagrant form could lead to a complete reversal of the natural lighting conditions; we want to correct it so as to meet our requirements. Therefore the flash must be correctly applied, it must counteract the vertical lighting of the midday sun or lighten the shadows in pictures taken against the light without destroying the charm of the halo effect. In flat lighting it can also be used to give a high key effect.

We must be careful therefore not to overdo the artificial lighting. The correct balance of the two light sources can be calculated, but since I have always been a poor mathematician I have developed my own (well tested) rule of thumb.

For full backlighting with heavy shadows the balance is 50 per cent daylight and 50 per cent flash.

The lower the contrast to be relieved the lower must be the share of the flash.

The exposure is adjusted by means of the stop. In outdoor nude photography I therefore close down one stop and place the flash at 1½ times the normal distance from the subject, thus reducing the flash intensity by about half. If it is not possible to place the flashhead further back the light itself must be reduced, either by hanging a thin white handkerchief in front of the reflector or by taking the reflector off the flashgun.

With electronic flash we usually have to come closer to the subject. A small portable flash of, say, 80 joules produces at the most one quarter of the light emitted by the smallest flashbulb. The light output of electronic flash is usually over-estimated. Its main advantage is the extremely short duration of the flash (1/600–1/5,000 second) and its economy in constant use.

The photographer who is able to work with speed-synchronized flash, extension cable and possibly additional flashheads away from the camera, tripod and assistant, has a real outdoor colour studio. Its scope is so wide that he can attempt anything under the sun and without the sun.

I must warn however that the use of too many artificial aids presents a real danger of artificiality. And pictures that are not worth having can be made with the most primitive equipment. ...

Overall Exposure

The fact that in colour photography the exposure must be determined with particular care and set absolutely correctly, has become common knowledge in recent years. Even a small amount of underexposure puts the colour rendering in jeopardy.

Overexposure, although it also alters the colours to some extent, leaves us a slightly bigger allowance. It is best to set the exposure by adjusting the stop since the steps between the speeds are sometimes too big, particularly with some focal plane shutters. Also the latest Compur shutters cannot be set at intermediate values between speeds in contrast to the pre-light value models which allowed this to be done.

Too Many Colours Spoil the Picture

All textbooks on colour preach limitation to a few colours in each picture. Goethe's saying that restraint proves the (budding) master is indeed true. The sparing use of colour is the most direct way to the development of both taste and skill and therefore to good pictures.

At the same time it is only right to point out that many an accomplished master may well feel like attacking the most motley of subjects—and that he may be able to "put it over".

Next I should be glad if people stopped talking about "photography in natural colours". A picture of a raspberry nude under a lovely azure sky does not show nature's colouring. It does not even have to be due to incorrect exposure, the culprit may have been the colour processing laboratory.

Aniline dyes on a celluloid base are beautiful to behold. And with correct exposure

Page 97: *By the Window* by Andre de Dienes

$2\frac{1}{4}$-in. square Rolleiflex, Super-XX film, 1/60 second, *f*5.6.
Andre de Dienes, a brilliant and prolific photographer who lives and works in Hollywood, is noted particularly for the exquisite quality of his nude studies taken only by daylight. In this arrangement he has retained modelling in the body, yet has contrasted his subject effectively against the light from the window.

Page 98: *Figures* by J. H. den Boestert

$2\frac{1}{4}$-in. square Rolleiflex, Ilford HP3 film, 1/10 second, *f*3.5, Microdol developer.
Den Boestert decided to strive for a more down-to-earth approach, after many years of trying for "artistic" poses with a battery of lights and other effects. Wishing to take his nude photographs in appropriately artistic surroundings, he chose a sculptor's studio for his setting. Here he also had the advantage of daylight falling on the scene evenly from above and from the left, allowing him to do without effect lighting. To avoid any appearance of contriving the pose he arranged the model as little as possible. In fact, the pose is one the sculptor himself might use.

Page 99: *In an Old House* by Willy Ronis

$2\frac{1}{4}$-in. square Rolleiflex, 1/5 second, *f*8, developed in D 76.
The successful French photographer took this picture in a village in Provence. Slightly diffuse sunlight of an April afternoon streamed into the room.

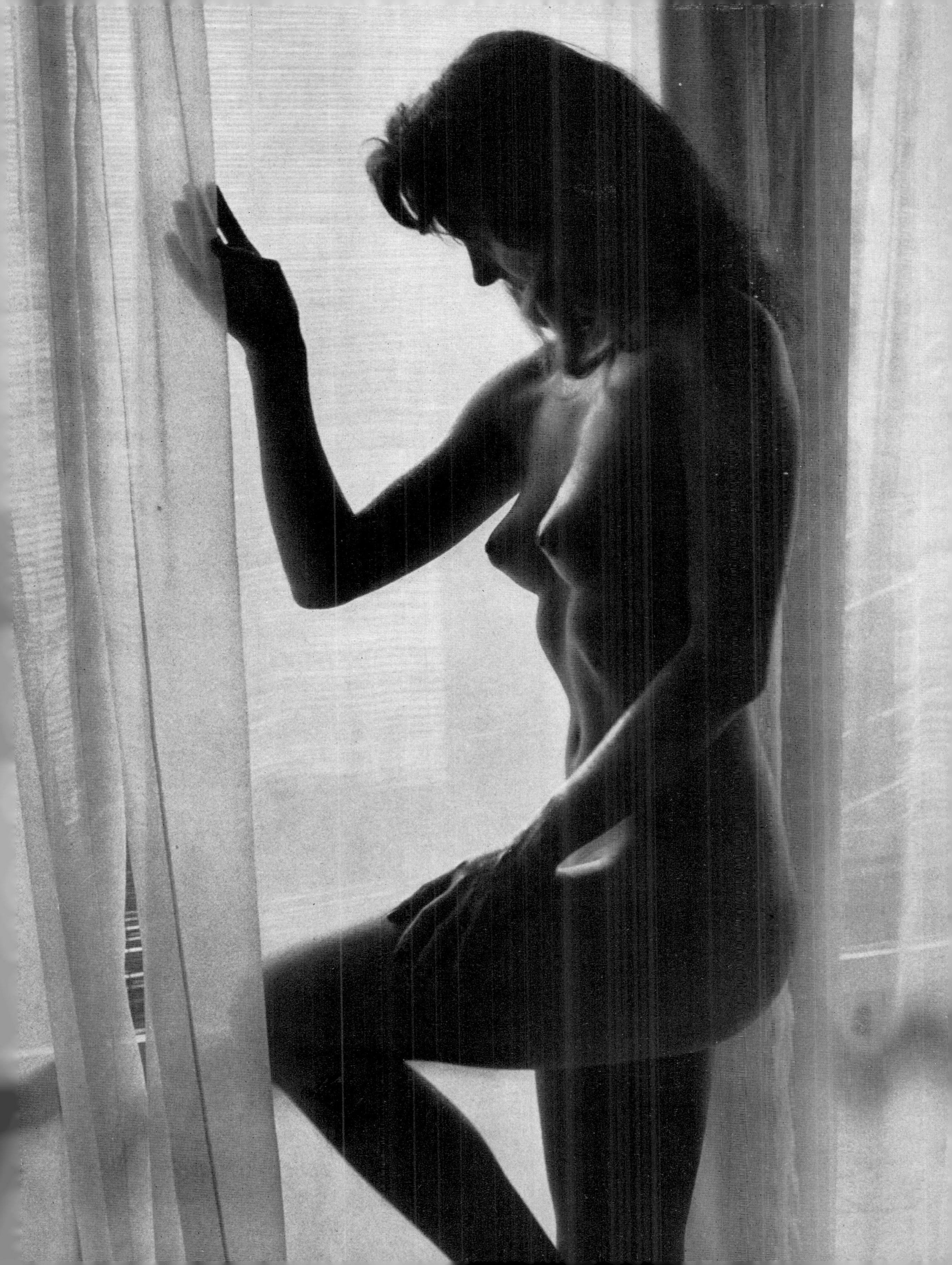

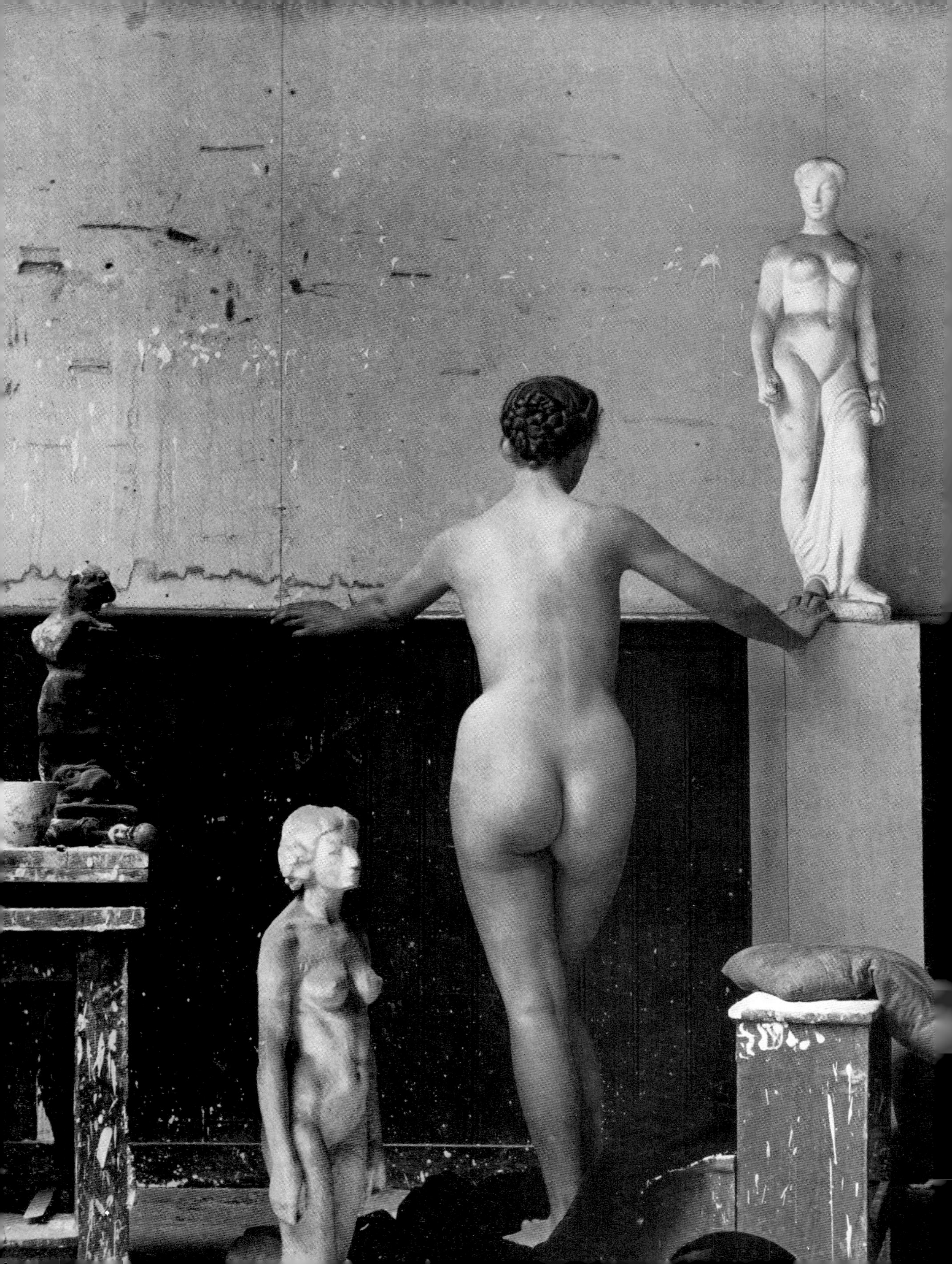

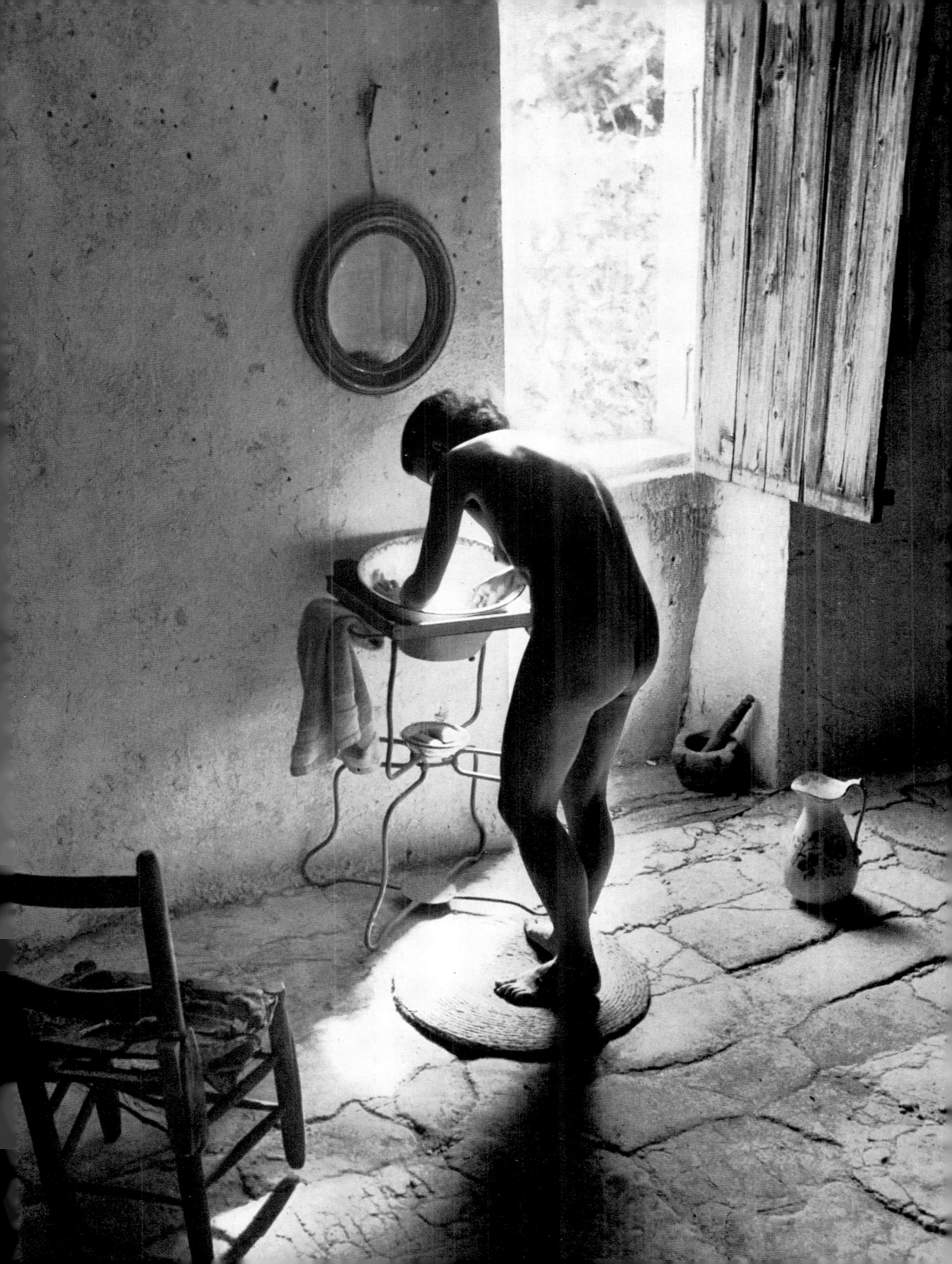

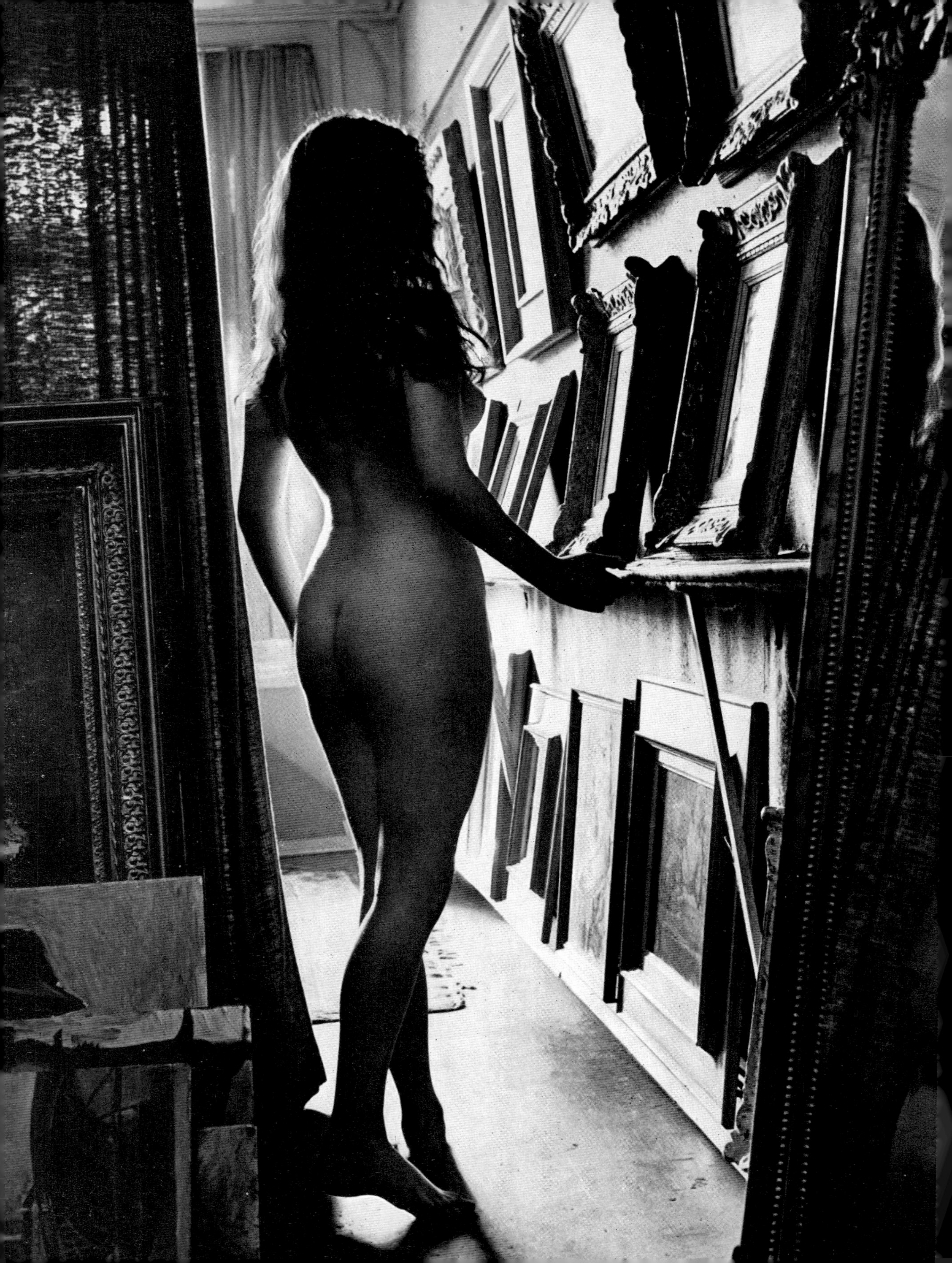

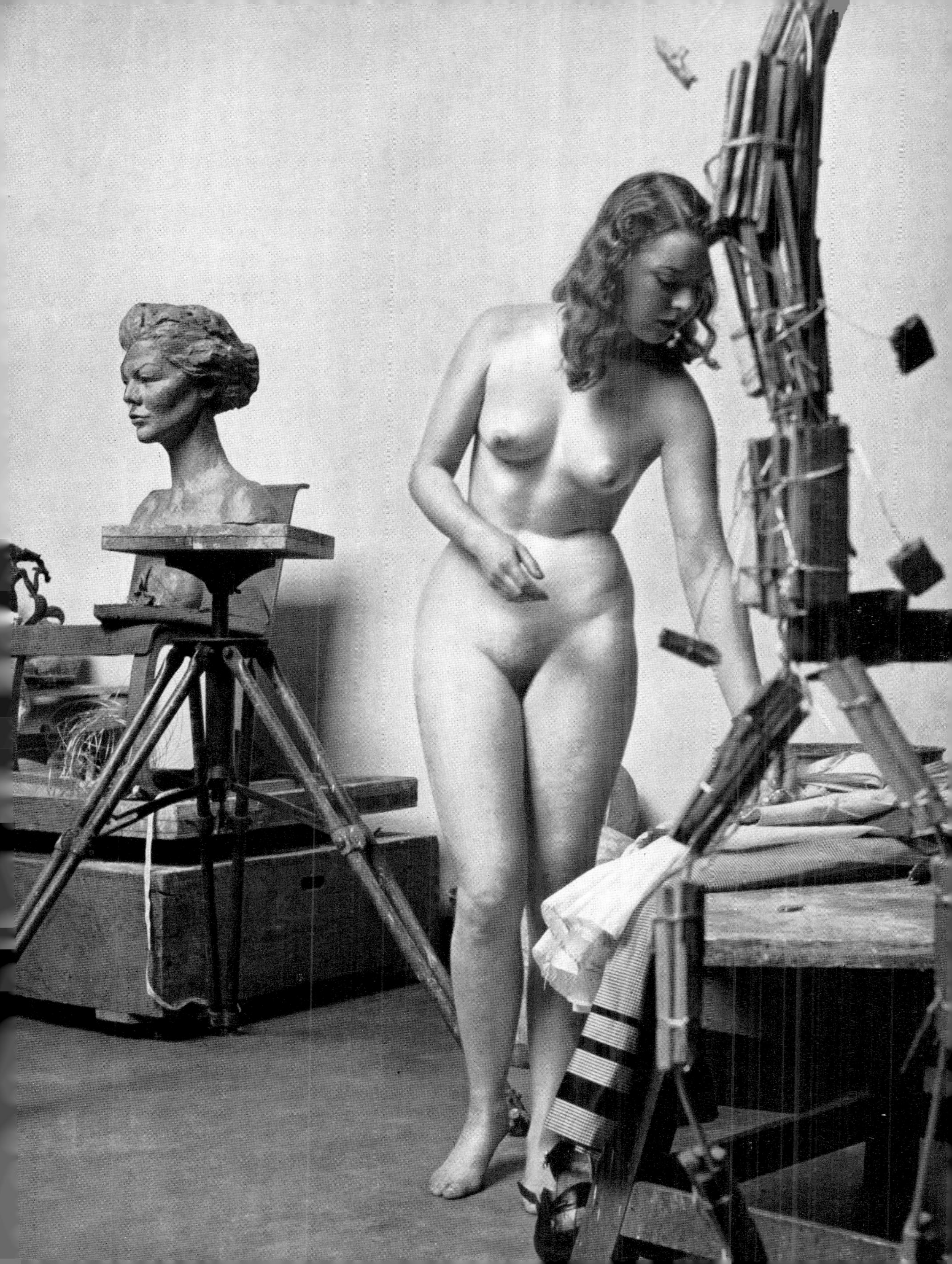

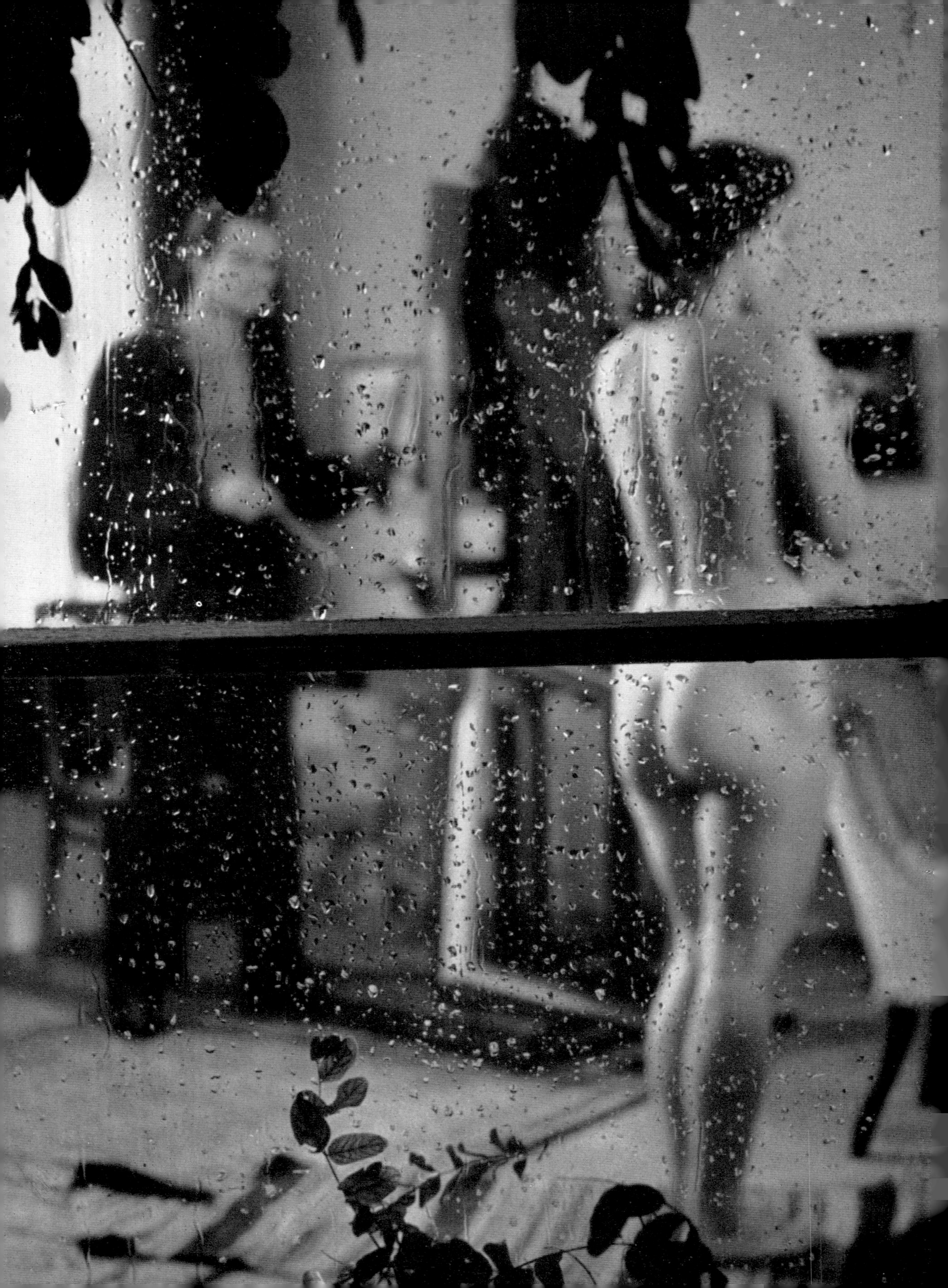

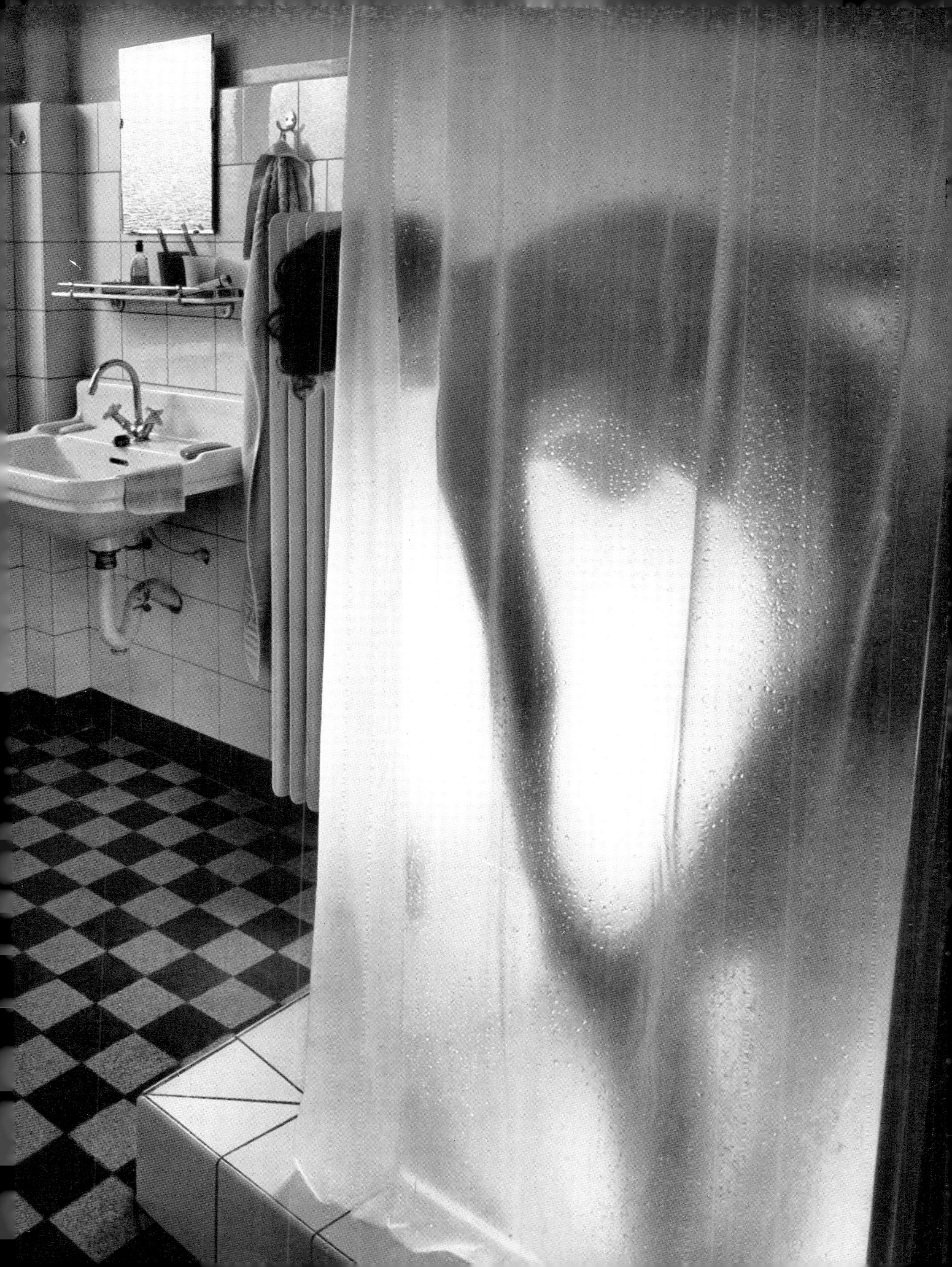

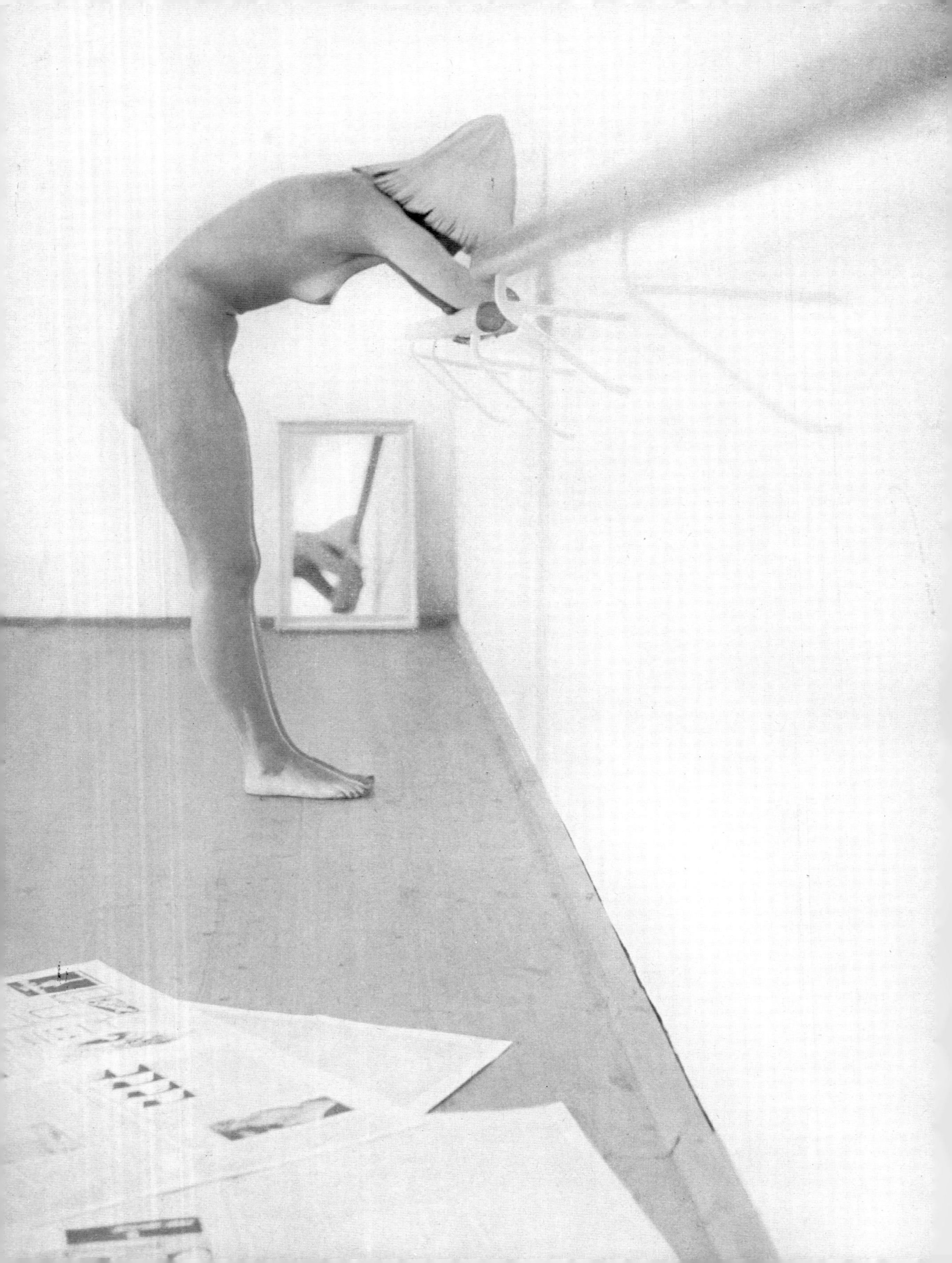

Page 100: *In the Workshop* by Albert Winkler

2¼-in. square Rolleiflex, Kodak Plus X film, 1/50 second, *f*5.6.
Taken directly against the light (sunlight through the window) with a 500-watt photoflood to brighten the shadows. Winkler is a Swiss amateur photographer.

Page 101: *The Break* by Zoltan Glass

2¼-in. square Rolleiflex, Super-XX film, 1/5 second, *f*8.
Zoltan Glass works in England and on the French Riviera. His nude photographs are featured in the international photographic press and he has published a book of nude studies. This studio picture was taken by daylight only.

Page 102: *Looking into the Studio* by Hugo Körte

Due to the large stop and focusing on the studio window the inside scene is visible only in a ghostlike aspect—an unorthodox method of veiling reality.

Page 103: *In the Bathroom* by Ludwig Windstosser

2¼-in. square Rolleiflex, Adox R 17 film, ½ second, *f*11.
This picture is from a series entitled *A Day with Ruhr Coal* which illustrated the use of all kinds of coal products in daily life. One photoflood was used to increase the overall illumination, another was placed behind the curtain and the figure as back lighting to emphasise both the figure and the water drops.

Page 104: *At the Bar* by Bernd Jansen

2¼-in. square Ikoflex, *f*5.6, Agfa ISS film.
The illumination by even daylight in the room together with the delicate printing combine to give this high key effect.

and decent processing it is quite possible to get among others also pictures with a very realistic effect closely approaching nature. It is true that our eyes register only part of the colours of the spectrum, but for all that they are by no means defective or failing.

The truth is that they are failing when they do not give the lie to the "natural colours" of all too many colour photographs. The eyes are more perfect than that. And if the mind behind them is an intelligent one it will take pleasure in colour for colour's sake in photography as well as in art. We should only be restricting the freedom of this wonderful means of expression if we thoughtlessly took over the slogan of "natural colours", a slogan invented for the broadest mass of consumers.

In nude photography colour is no more risky than black and white. On the contrary, it is rather more friendly.

But I hope you will keep an open mind about that school of thought that believes a colour picture is good merely because it is technically good. ...

Artificial Light

"While in outdoor photographs the predominating factor is the mood content of nature which has merged into one whole with the human body, in artificial light photographs another factor comes to the fore: form and line of the body. Its substance becomes the dominating feature of the picture. For this reason there is more room here for the problematical which shows itself in selection, lighting and contrasts. Here the photographer too becomes the wilful creator of the picture."

Thus another quotation from a magazine, and for the most part it is true although it seems to me that the genuinely creative photographer is not tied to any technical-accidental limits but brings the best out in every field. This is also the reason why in this book the two fields, technically so different, have been conceived as one single medium of expression.

Artificial light photography is possible with a 40W lamp and even by the light of a match. But in nude photography pictures taken with such primitive aids can hardly ever give us pleasing results.

Among amateurs artificial light photography to this day encounters much prejudice. The most commonly found notions are these:

(1) Out of doors I give 1/50 second at *f*8. With artificial light I don't know what to give.

(2) With artificial light I always get the same known light values. With only a little experience I can't go wrong. (This is a half-truth.)

(3) With artificial light I must have a studio and a battery of lamps.

Basic Requirements

What is really needed in the way of both equipment and skill is this:

(1) More than average photographic experience;

(2) A fairly spacious room that can be turned into a make-shift studio.

(3) At least three lights with accessories, reflectors, stands, diffusing screens, reflecting screens, nigger boards, backgrounds.

The first requirement is really a matter of course.

No. (2): We should have about 220 square feet of floor space or at least an open door through which we can point the camera at a smaller room.

No. (3): If need be two photofloods and one ordinary 100W pearl bulb will do. If you want to take artificial light photographs often and enjoy it it is best not to start with the small amateur lights which one never knows how to arrange.

Better start from the beginning with proper lights, one flood with matt reflector and two with polished reflectors. Better still, replace one of these with a small focusing spotlight with Fresnel lens.

Diffusing screens made of fine white cambric or gauze which can be placed at varying distances from the lights, soften the hard lighting as required. Even the directional light of the spot can be adjusted within limits with diffusing screens and by altering the focus.

Rigid stands fitted with casters and extending to a considerable height are available for the lights; they are extremely mobile despite their not inconsiderable weight. A boom for top lighting will prove its usefulness time and again. If necessary this can be improvised by fitting a lamp with reflector to a wire strung along the ceiling. Good equipment is not cheap but it pays for itself in the long run.

Reflecting screens however present no financial problems and can easily be made at home. They should consist of two square yards of hardboard which can be mounted on a wooden frame if necessary, painted over with washable matt white paint. A folding support to hold the screen up at an angle of about 45° can be most useful.

Shiny and even matt tin foil needs more cautious handling in the studio than out of doors because its effect is somewhat conspicuous. It is most suitable for lightening the background.

A niggerboard is a screen, painted black on one side and a light colour on the other, fitted with feet and measuring about 2 by 5 feet. Placed between camera and the source of backlighting a niggerboard will often render better service than even an adjustable lenshood in screening the lens from the light. Some against-the-light effects are manageable only with the help of a niggerboard.

Light Sources

Photoflood lamps are the usual light source indoors. As readers may know, these lamps are considerably overrun (they burn with a higher voltage than normal) and this raises their colour temperature to about 3,500°K. The 250W lamps burn for only two hours when used at the full voltage while the life of the 500W lamps is given as 100 hours.

Photoflood bulbs incorporating an internal reflector are also available. Although they make it possible to work without the usual lamp reflectors—except for special light effects—they are only conditionally recommended where artificial light is used often and weight not a primary consideration.

If we like to work economically and prolong the life of the lamps considerably, we should invest in a dimmer. This is a device incorporating a resistance and switch similar to those used in electric cookers. During focusing and arranging the subject the lamps receive only a part of the current and are switched on to full power only for the exposure. This is also preferable for the model, not only because she is not exposed to the dazzle for such a long time, but also for psychological reasons.

The Fundamentals of Lighting

"... our arrangements do not depend on the position of the sun but the lighting is adjusted to our own requirements. Front lighting, side lighting and backlighting can be varied at will at the touch of a finger."

True enough. In practice however arranging the lighting time and again proves to be a battle with contrast, particularly in colour. Except, of course, when the photographer has a great deal of experience.

Beginners as a rule produce blocked out highlights and yawning emptiness in the shadows. They hope to increase the overall brightness by placing the lights too close to the model. But if this is done the light intensity falls off so rapidly that the negatives become unprintably hard. If this and other faults are to be avoided from the very beginning, the following rules should be adhered to.

(1) *Light normally comes from above.* Therefore top lighting looks always more natural than even the best placed low level lighting.

(2) *The lamps must not be placed too close to the model.* For instance, if one light is $3\frac{1}{2}$ feet from the head of a standing nude but 8 feet from her feet, even lighting cannot be expected. The best way is to place a second light under and parallel with the first light, or

(3) *Use greater lamp-to-subject distances altogether,* and

(4) *Keep the subject as far as possible in one plane.*

(5) *When the nude is well lit by two lamps* a third light usually does more harm than good. We can find a better use for it since

(6) *The background puts the finishing touch to the picture.* It is always useful to keep at least one light specially for lighting the background.

(7) *Switch off before rearranging the lights.* Electric light bulbs are sensitive things while they are burning. They reward considerate treatment with longer life.

Beginners will derive considerable benefit from a study of Walter Nurnberg's book *Lighting for Photography* (Focal Press).

There are two methods of obtaining good lighting. The first method is safe for the beginner while the second leads to more pronounced lighting effects.

For method No. 1, first arrange the overall lighting. That is, illuminate the whole subject area evenly and uniformly so that every detail gets all the light necessary for correct exposure. It can be done with one light directly above the lens (at varying distances) with a cambric diffuser before the reflector. The diffusing screen is not necessary with an already diffuse light source. It can also be done by pointing the light at the (white) ceiling. This produces a soft indirect lighting.

Daylight can also be used to provide the overall illumination. When colour is used the film has to be of the daylight type.

Only now are the effect lights arranged. They give the subject modelling and depth. The basis of correct lighting is the correct balance of the two lights. It can be adjusted not only by using differently powered lights but also by varying the lamp-to-subject distance.

With Method No. 2 the first step is to position the main light. It is the function of the main light to deliver the subject from darkness, make its substance visible to the eye, and to put the light where it matters.

The term "main light" does not describe a type of light but a function of lighting which is to stress the picture idea. The beam or cone of light must include all the important elements of the subject matter, if necessary softened by a cambric or gauze diffusing screen. A soft or indirect flood placed at some distance from the subject can also act as main light, and so can daylight be it front, side or backlighting.

Next position the supplementary light. The supplementary light has the function indicated by its better known name of "fill-in light", it is to fill in the shadows. The simplest way to achieve this is by positioning a diffuse flood near the lens, parallel with its axis.

Some professionals even take the picture through a ring of lights placed round the lens. This is the best way of making sure that all shadows facing the camera are properly filled in.

We can fill in the shadows either with a second lamp placed opposite the main light, or with one or two reflecting screens. The screens are turned and tilted until they reflect some of the main light into those shadow parts that have to show more detail.

It is important to acquire at an early stage a sense of the "correct", i.e. pictorially pleasing contrast ratio. An overdose of supplementary lighting will tear even the finest picture idea to shreds.

If we have a focusing screen or are working with a single lens reflex camera (without pre-selected stops) it can be very helpful to view the scene occasionally through a small stop. This shows better than a wide aperture if the shadow illumination is well balanced.

A very useful form of fill-in lighting can be provided by bounce flash (pointing the flashgun at the ceiling for indirect "bounced" light) but we must be perfectly familiar with its intensity and effect.

Finally, light the background. Let us hope there is a lamp left to give the finishing touch to the picture by stressing the idea of the main light with a corresponding illumination of the background. It may be placed on the floor immediately behind the nude or slightly to one side or at such an acute angle that the light is almost parallel with the background. By varying the intensity of the background lighting we can make it come away from the nude or deliberately bring it into the picture idea (cast shadows for instance).

It is the background treatment that shows if the photographer has thought out his picture to the last detail. The further the background is from the nude the more easily can it be made to play a part of its own. Ways and means are plentiful, from light patches and patterns projected with mirrors and all kinds of shadow designs to background projection which, however, requires a very powerful projector.

A strictly directional spot of concentrated light is supplied by a small focusing spotlight fitted with a projection lamp. Where a miniature slide projector is available it can be used to fulfil the function of the spot; many slide projectors are fitted with a tripod bush. The projector can also be used to lighten or illuminate the background.

A two inch square piece of fine netting (tulle, cheese-cloth, nylon) inserted between the cover glasses of a slide frame, can project magical and decorative patterns on the background or the nude.

High Key

Artificial light is the most certain aid to procuring the previously mentioned high key effect in colour as well as in black and white. High key requires a light coloured, if possible white background and walls, and widely diffused direct or indirect lighting of the nude. However, no amount of light will tone down the South Sea tan of a sun worshipper.

All shadows on curves and limbs must be completely suppressed. Only the outlines of the body are allowed to stand out in narrow lines of light and shade. The background should be hardly discernible in the picture and must therefore be evenly and fully lit.

In black and white photography high key yields intriguing pictures of great graphic charm. In colour it represents the most effective expression of the principle of the sparing use of colour. But there is an equally great risk of getting an icing sugar effect.

Low Key

Low key describes a manner of photographic representation which in its most extreme form renders the subject mysterious rather than clearly recognizable in the gloom of its surroundings. Rembrandt understood low key, his picture of the man in the gold helmet is a useful example for us. Thus, the background should be dark (dark grey for preference), the setting dull with low reflecting power, and the lighting of the skin economical and soft rather than hard.

Low key is a medium that requires a skilled craftsman. Underexposure is not enough.

Exposure

After a brief period of amassing experience including a once-for-all calibration of the exposure meter, the correct exposure with artificial light is soon determined at every sitting.

If the reflected light method is used the reading should be taken closer to the subject than out of doors. The incident light method also yields good results. The prudent worker will compare the results obtained with both methods. The newcomer can also consult the tables supplied with the lamps. They can give him a starting point but they do not make the exposure meter and making notes of well tested exposures superfluous.

The rapid falling off of the light intensity is the real problem of artificial light photography. We know it very well from enlarging where twice the magnification needs much more than twice the exposure. If we tilt the baseboard with a sheet of hard paper and expose it briefly through the lens, we obtain a grey scale whose gradation is the steeper the closer it is to the lens.

The same problem arises in taking our pictures. It should be remembered that the falling-off is much less noticeable when the lamp-to-subject distance is increased. With sunlight which comes from infinity it is nil.

The narrower the beam of light we use the less we are exposed to the troubles

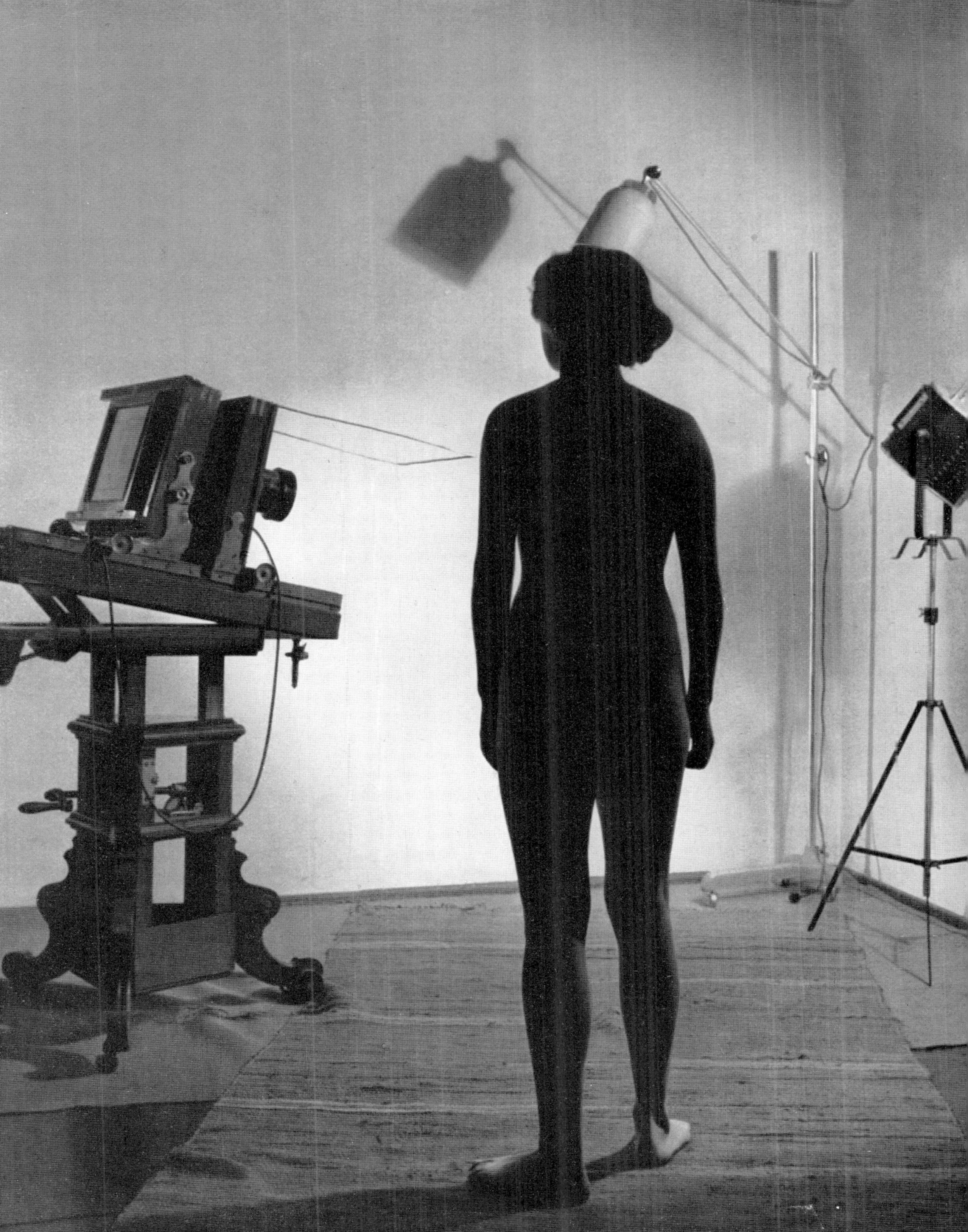

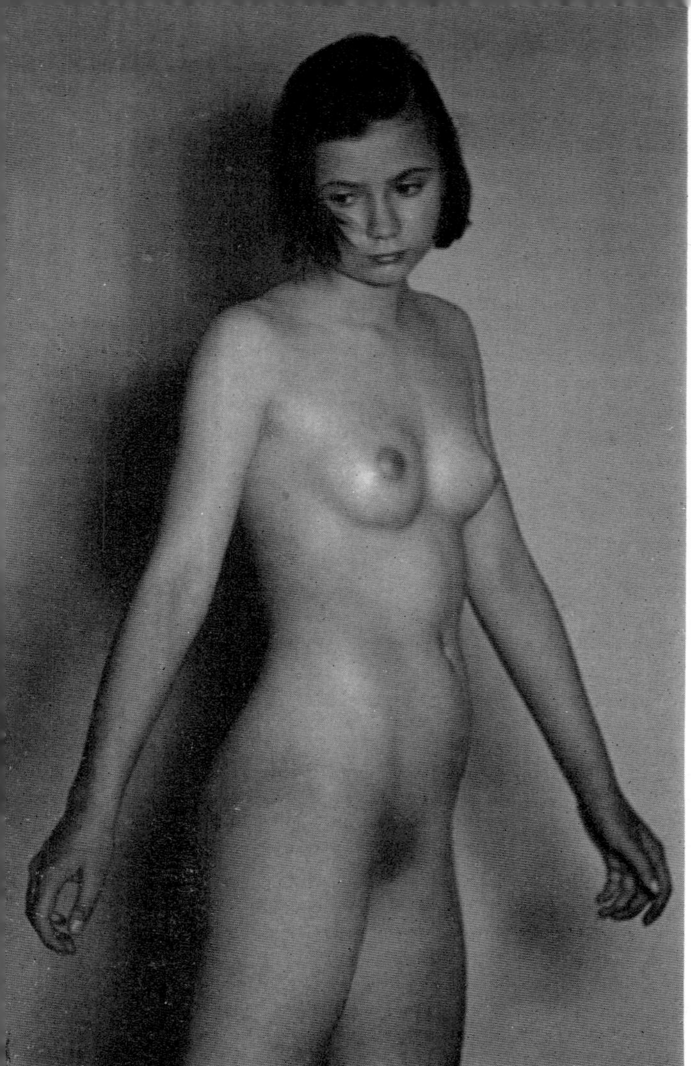

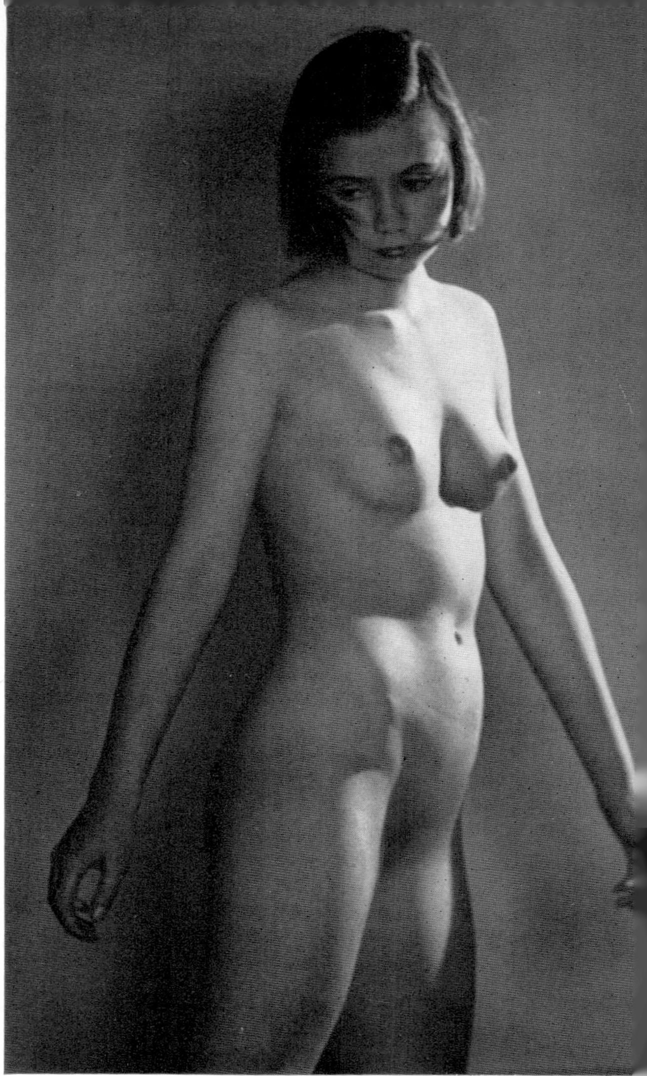

p. 113—*In the Studio* by Hans Toppler.

Building up the light

The illustrations on this and the following pages show how it is possible to build up lighting and pose by stages in order to create an effective photograph of the nude model.

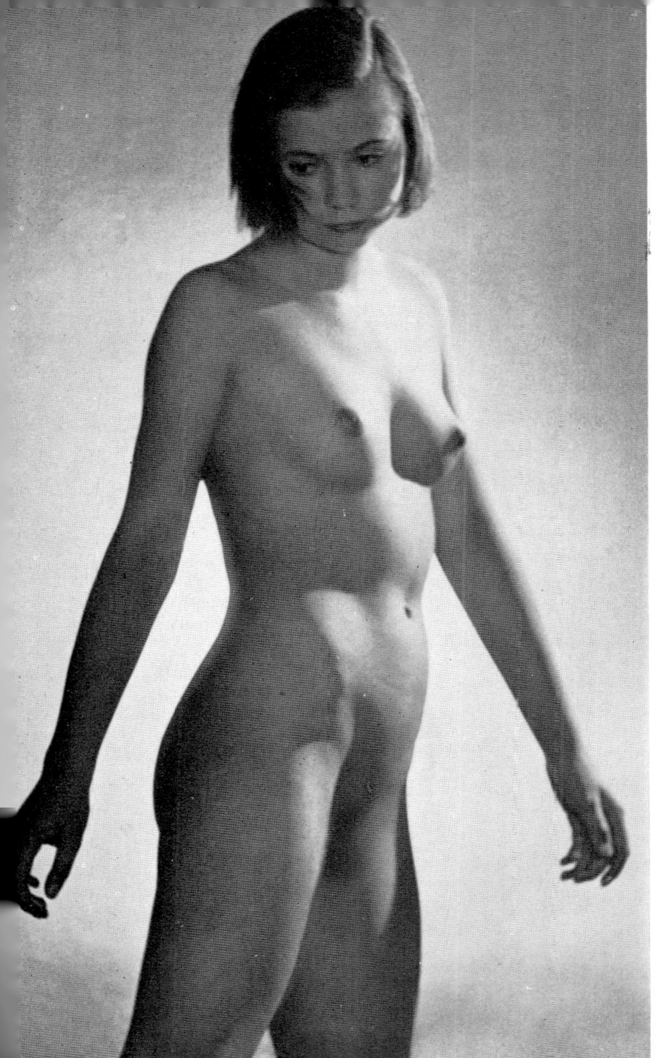

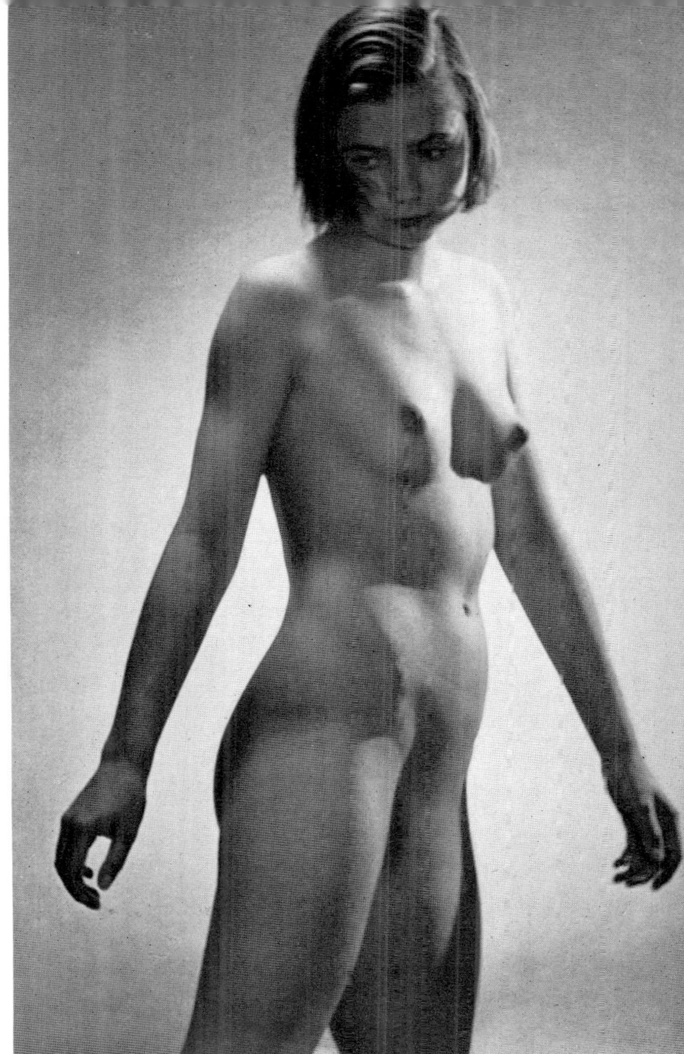

p. 114 *(left)*—Position the overall light. This is a diffused light placed near the camera.

p. 114 *(right)*—Switch on the effect light. This shows its characteristic highlights. The light source is a 500-watt spot with Fresnel lens about 7 ft. from the subject.

Above left—Light the background to match. This was done with a 250-watt photoflood in a shallow reflector, slightly dimmed by the use of a resistance.

Above right—Make the final adjustments. In fig. 4 in this illustration top lighting was added. It has brought out additional detail in the hair as well as in the extensive shadow areas of the body.

The choice of whether to make the background dark, closely matching the subject, or light in tone, depends on the intended overall effect of the picture and is largely a matter of personal taste. If the intention is to show space round the model, the middle picture on the right is to be preferred.

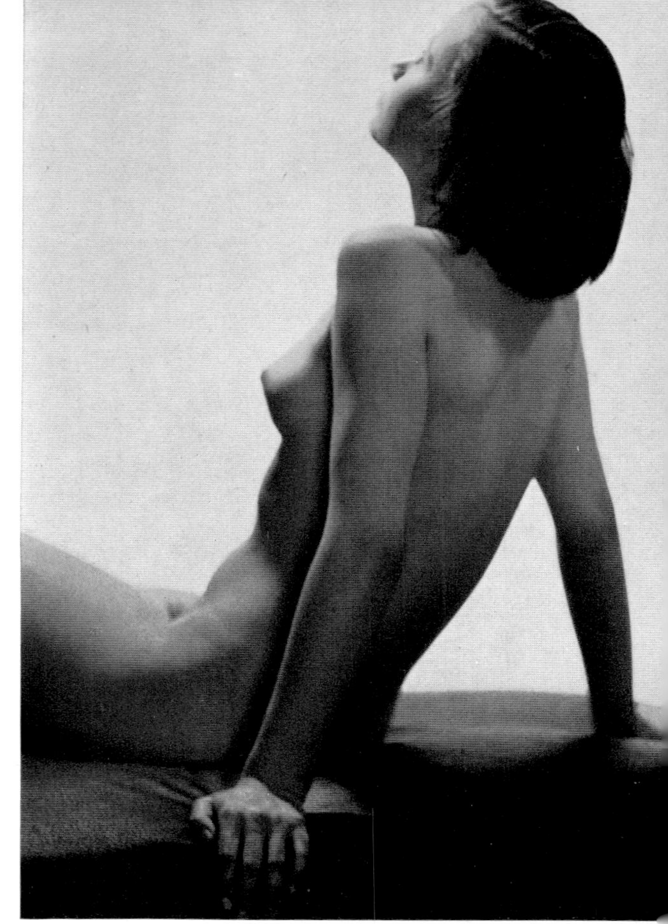

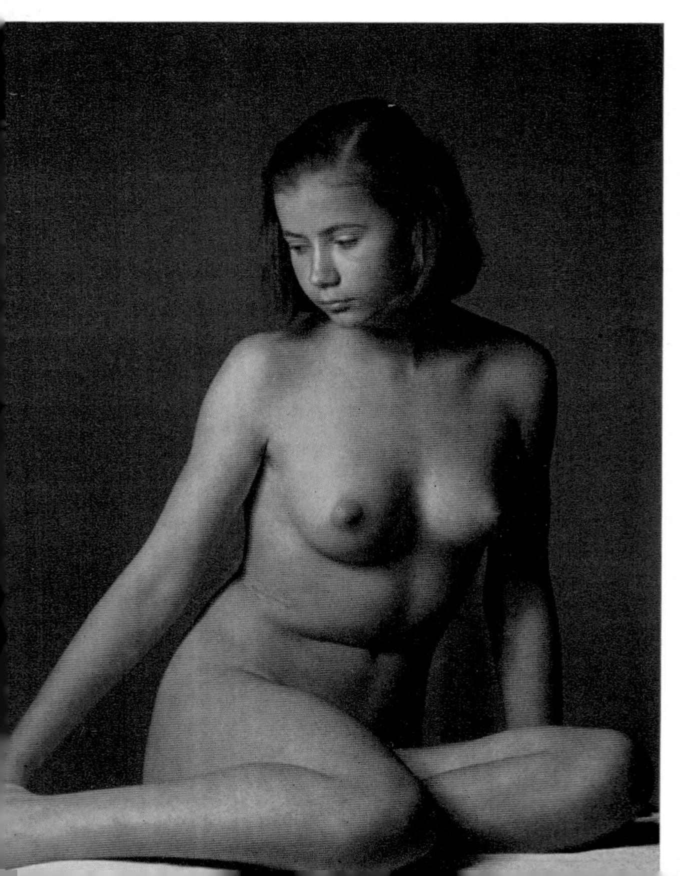

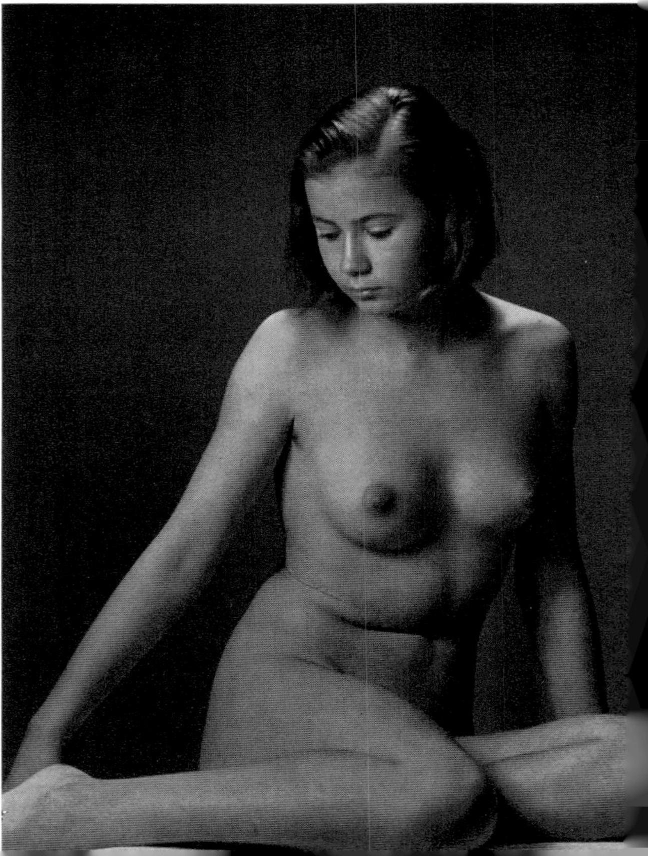

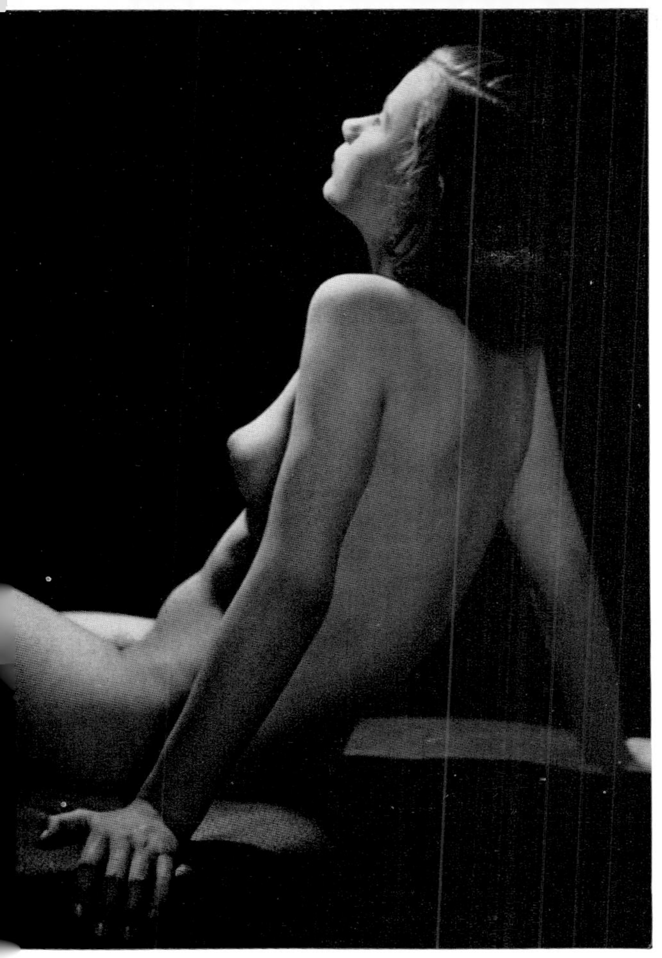

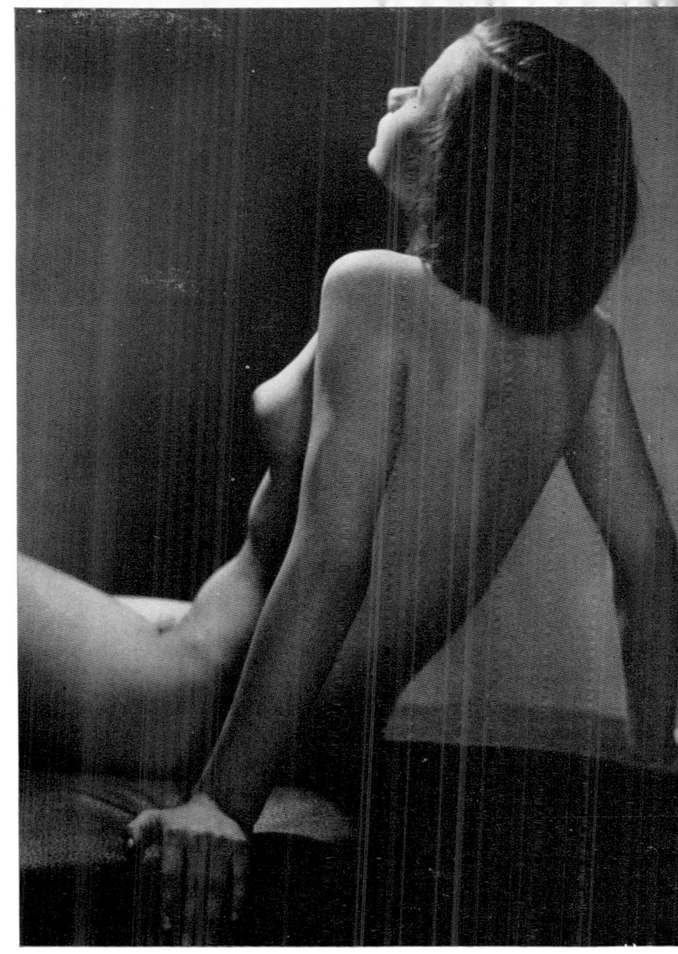

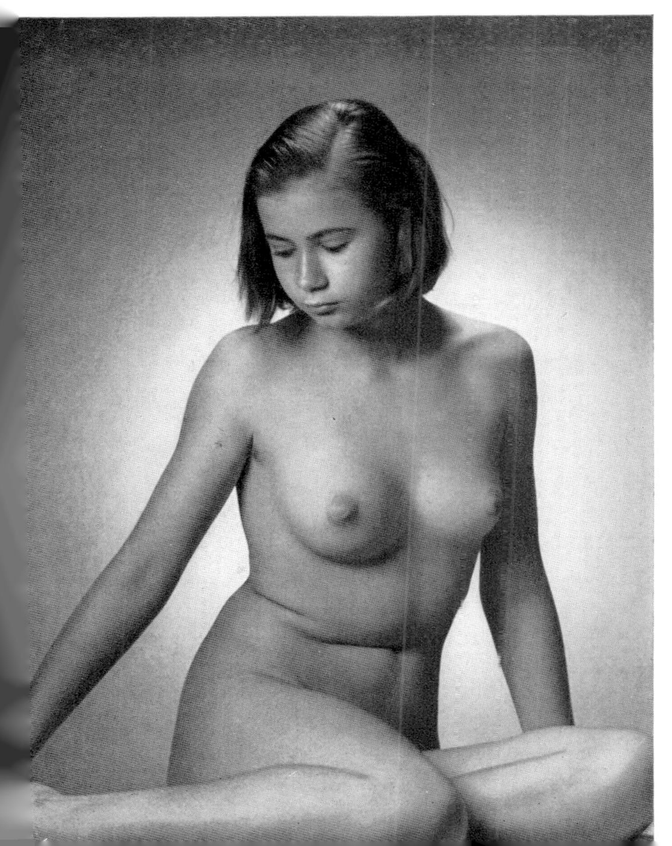

The lamp set-up which produced the photographs on the left also leads to a good lighting effect. First set up the main modelling light without considering the shadows. Next, use a diffuse flood for overall lighting, and finally add top lighting or effect light if required, as in the illustration. Round the picture off by adding a light to give tone to the background.

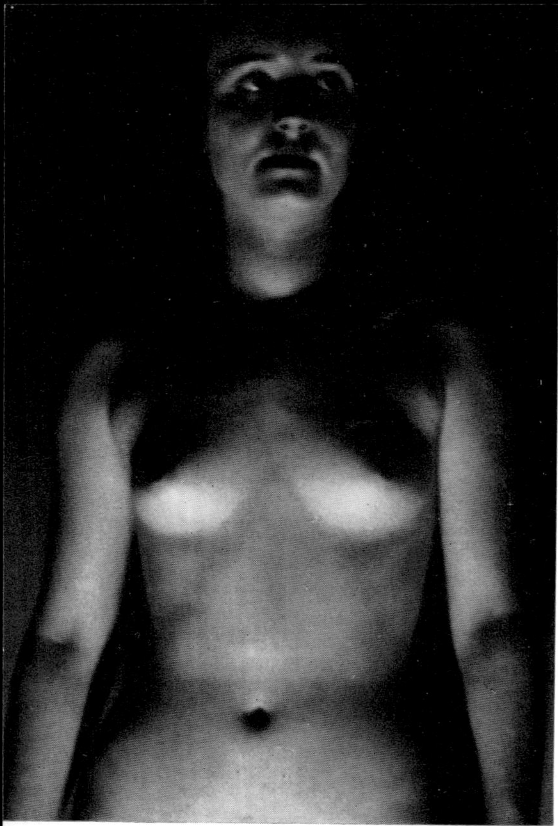

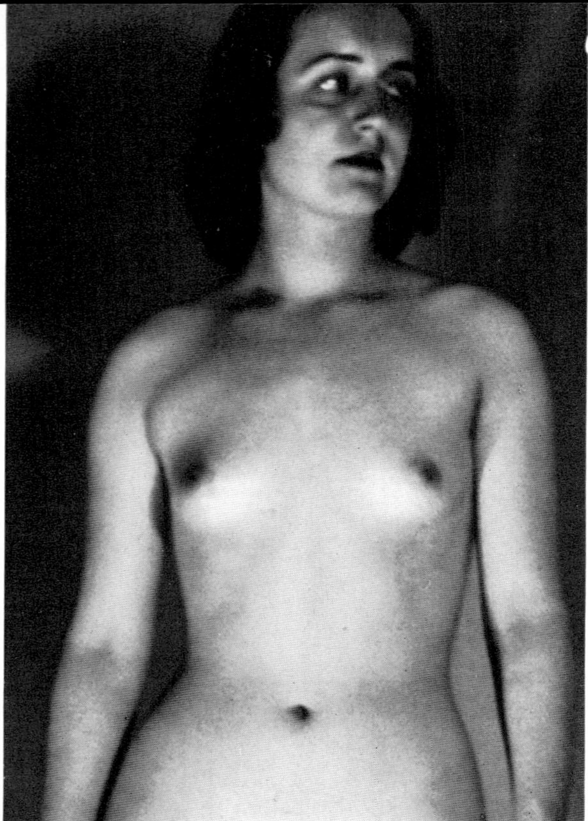

The same model, shown four times but with four very different kinds of treatment. *Above left*—low lighting which improves, *inter alia*, the contour appearance of the breasts. The effect is quickly lost *(above right)* when a second light provides shadow illumination. On the other hand top light *(below left)* works like a slimming diet; the face is left looking like a mask. *Below right*—the body shadows are lightened by an additional lamp.

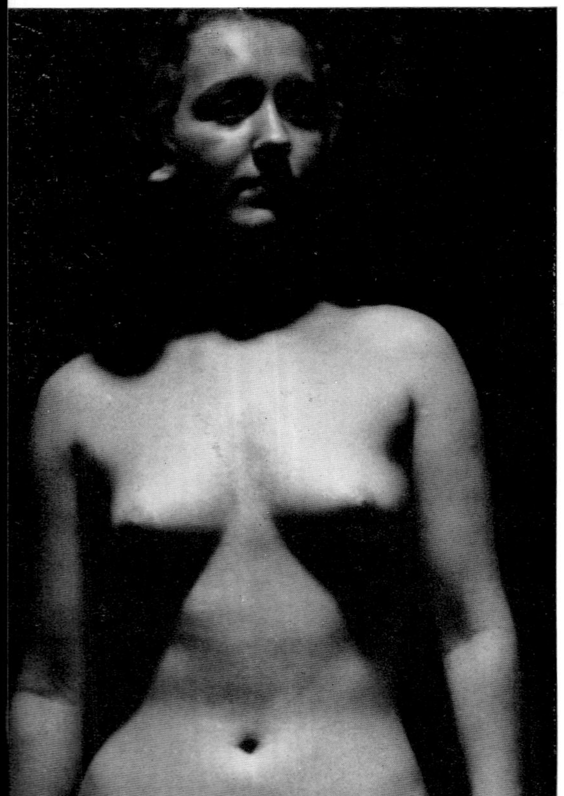

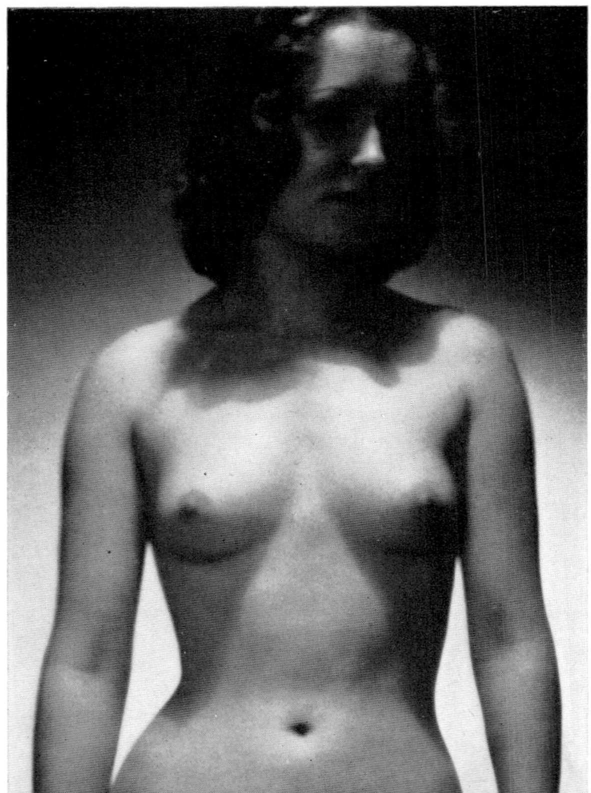

Series below—To create a pose with the model it is possible to start with the basic standing position, although this in itself means nothing. Yet the model has only to raise an arm *(left)* and immediately the simple stance takes on the beginnings of a pose. It becomes even more of a full pose *(centre)* with a turn to the right through about 60 degrees and by bringing the left shoulder towards the camera. *Right*—With the raising of the shoulder and inclination of the head, the pose tends to become over-exaggerated.

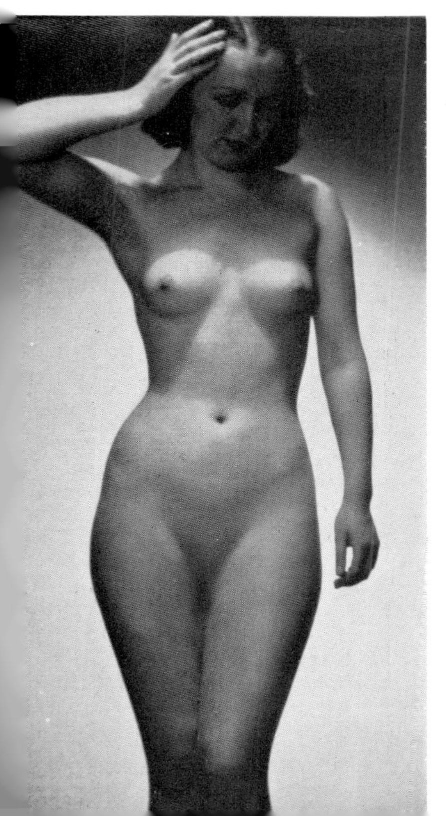

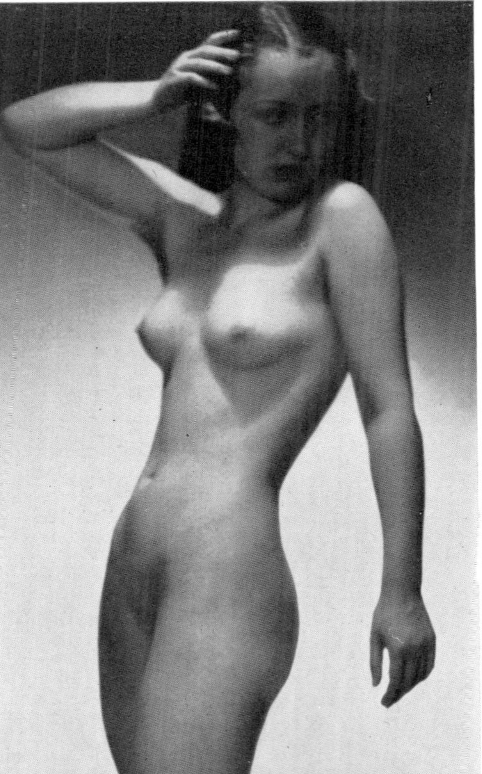

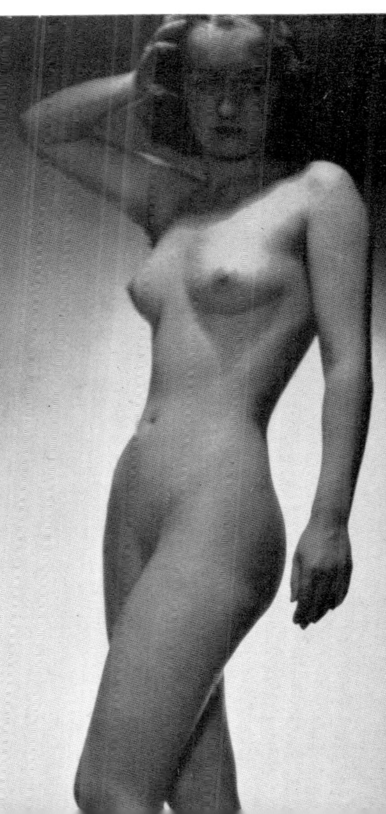

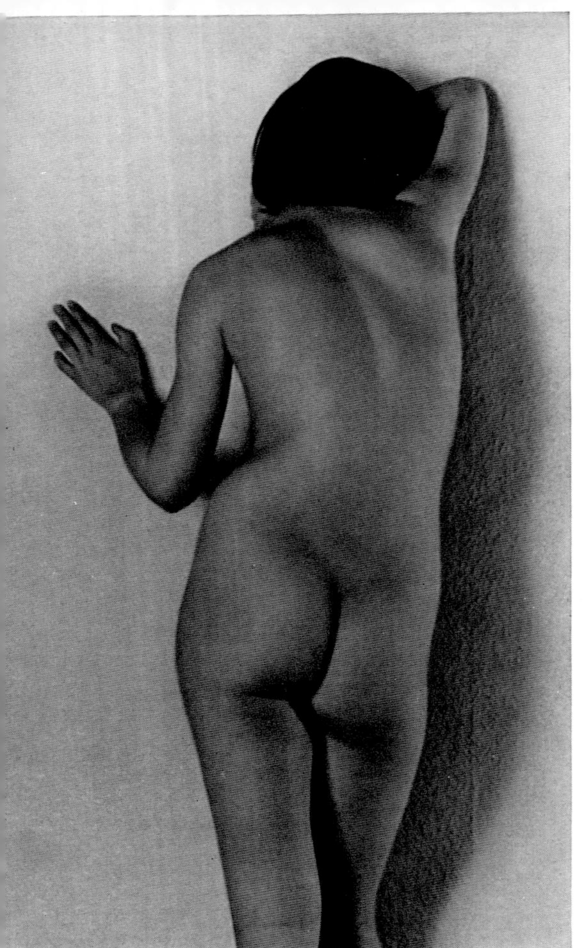
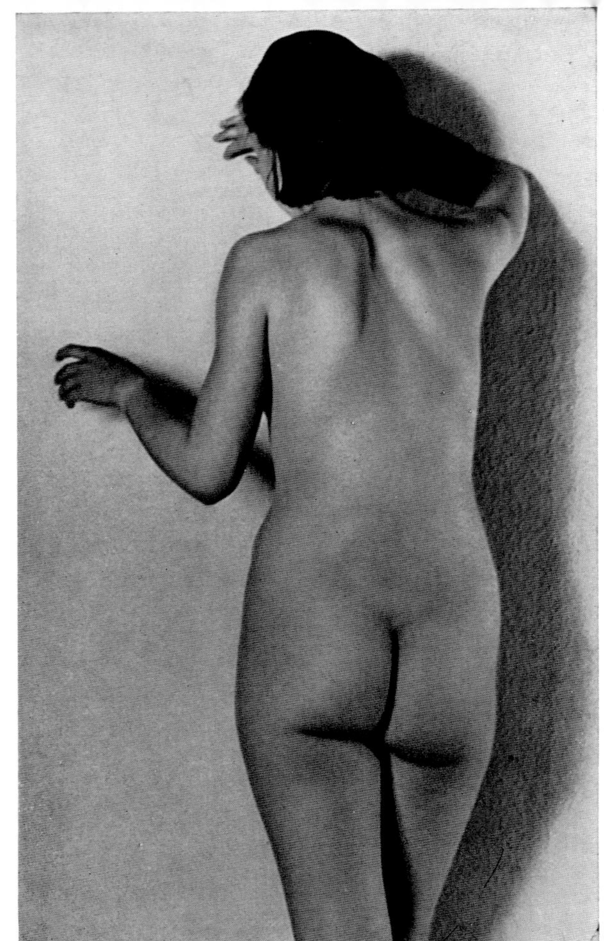

Series above—the line of the back, as the illustrations show in an exaggerated way, is no less susceptible to "anatomic faults" than any other aspect of the human body. Neither pronounced curve nor ramrod straightness of the backbone produces pictures of much value. Other faults shown are unpleasant line formation, cut-off effect of the arm, heavy thigh shadows, angular appearance of the shoulder blade. The right-hand illustration tries to improve on the shortcomings.

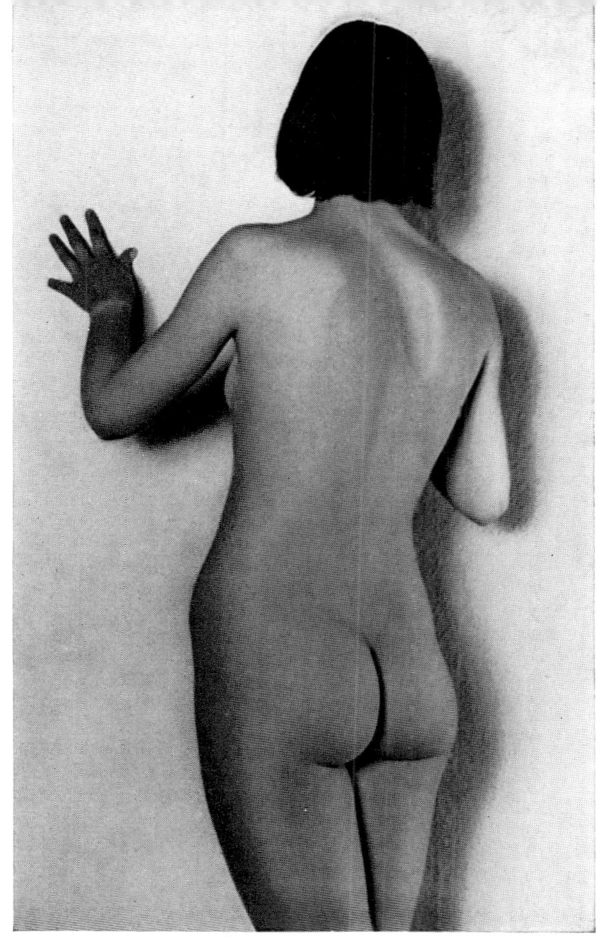

On p. 122—place the model on a turntable—a worthwhile experiment for any ambitious photographer. The props are simplicity itself: a robust packing case on a base fitted with rollers or casters (incidentally, such a turntable is useful in any studio). The two back views are pictorially least satisfactory. The lighting arrangement for the top left illustration consisted of a spot from the right, slightly diffused with tulle; a background light at medium height, and a very weak general light close to the camera.

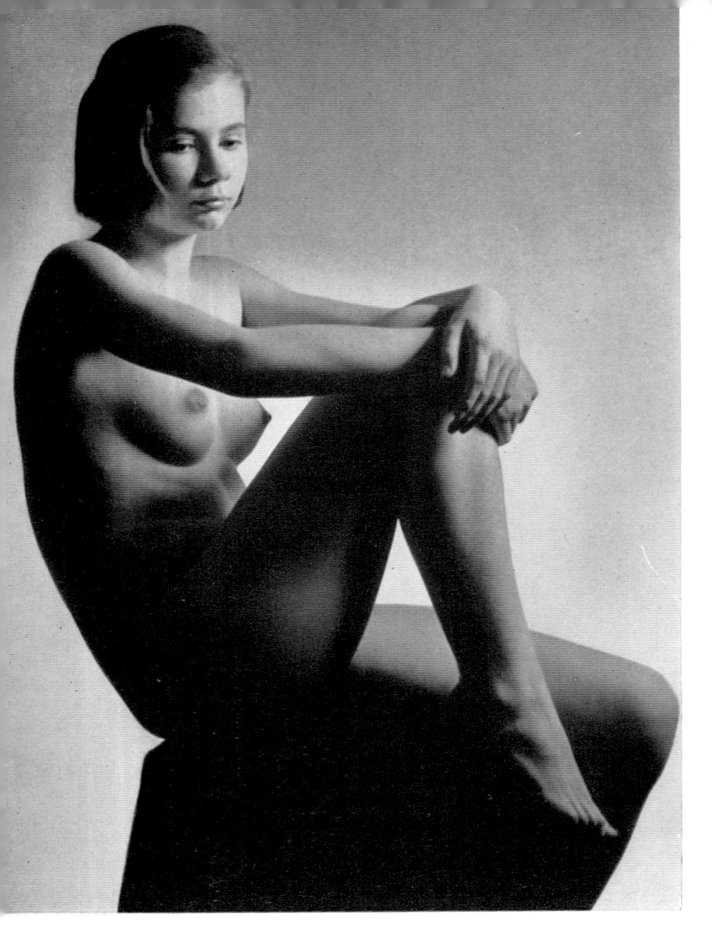
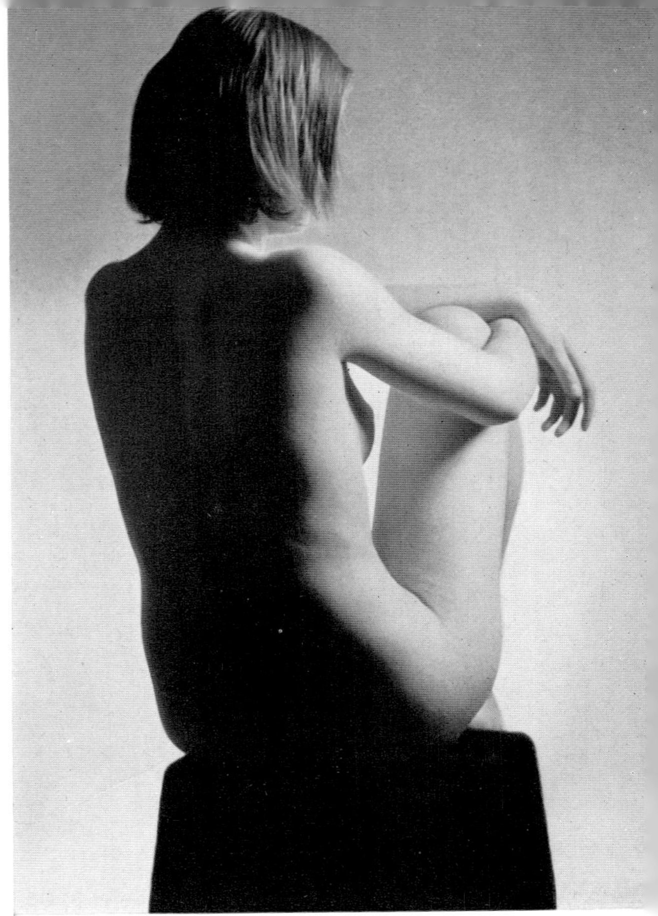
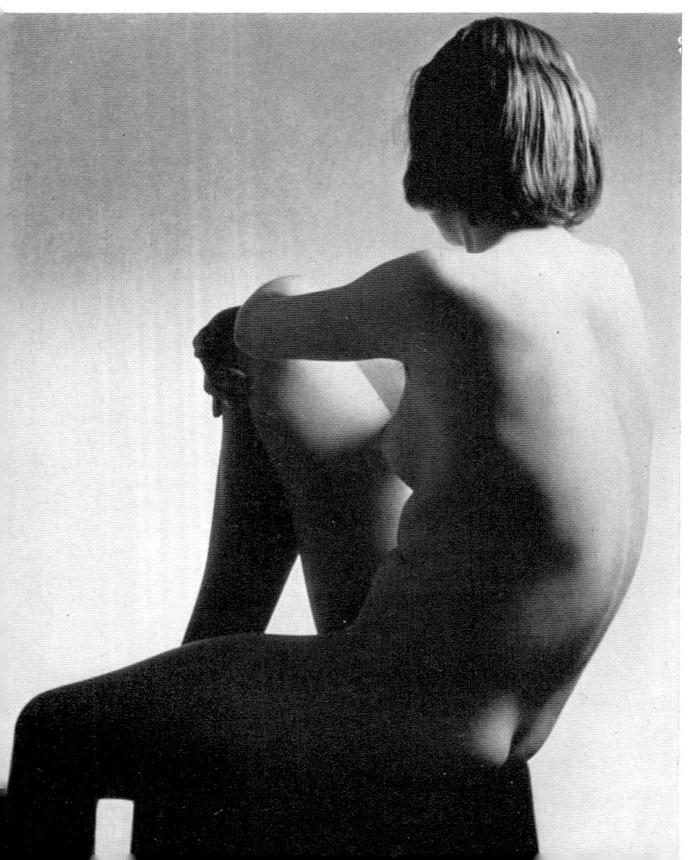
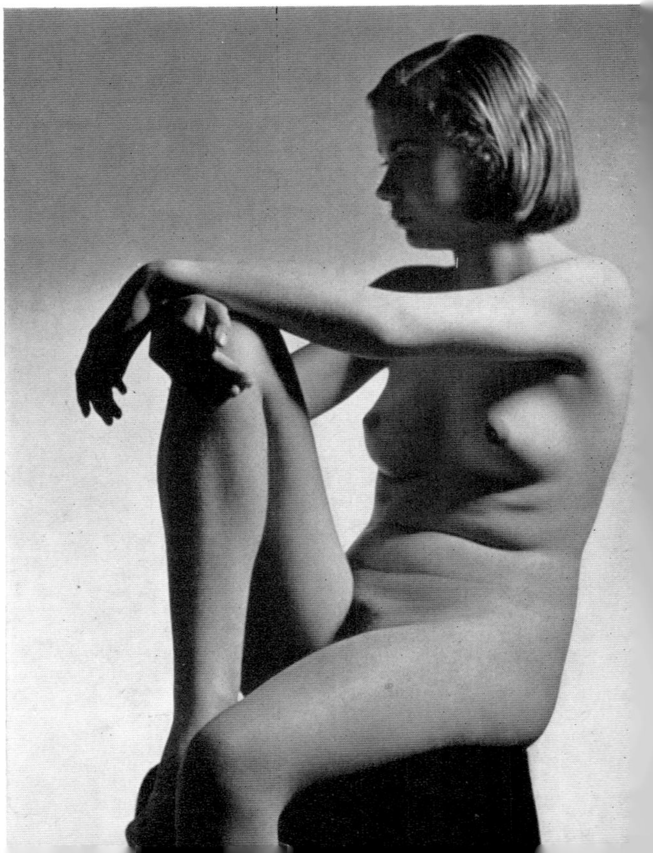

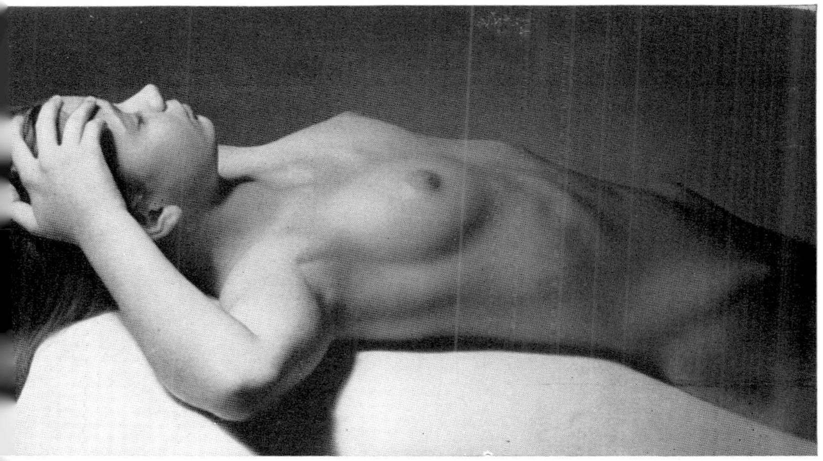

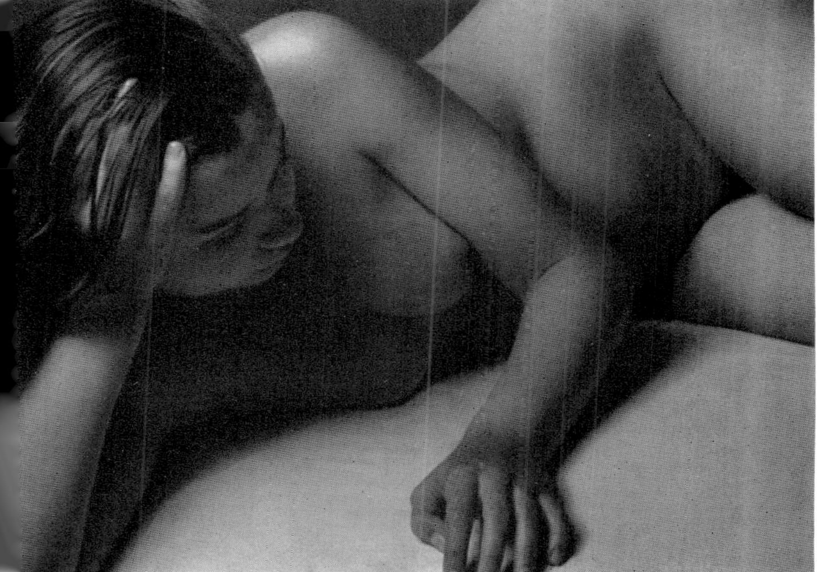

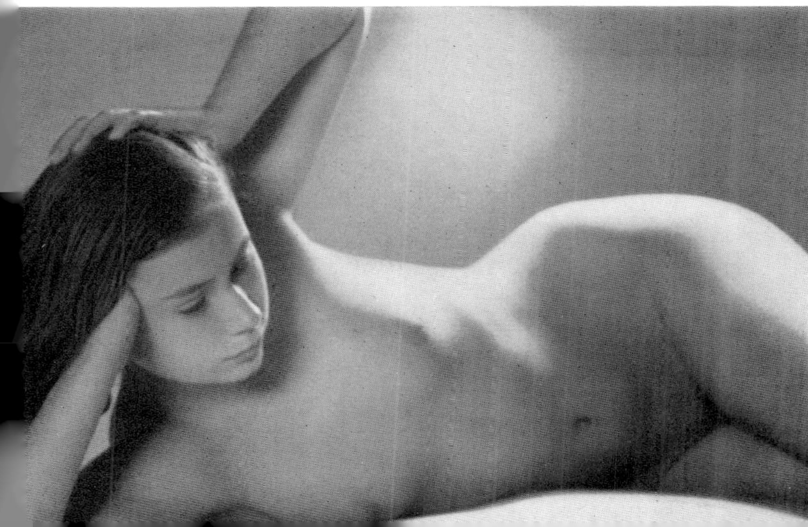

Three pictures – three faults

An unpleasant fall-off in lighting becomes visible when the light-to-subject distance is less than 5 ft. Anyway—only a model with a very beautifully shaped body is suitable for posing on her back.

Intersecting lines frequently provide the excitement in a picture, but they are also often responsible for its rejection. Greater camera distance and more strongly marked lighting might have saved this picture.

The reflected light used for this picture—or perhaps the second light which illuminates the shadows—has destroyed all three-dimensional effect. Furthermore, the hip line protruding at an angle produces another fault. But a pleasing hip line can add much to the effect of a picture.

The final photograph below was lit by a 500-watt lamp with a shallow reflector positioned as side-back light with a diffused flood near the camera. Its effect has been to emphasize the line of the upper torso and at the same time to outline the facial profile with a rim of light. Leica with 12.5 cm. Hektor and reflex attachment.

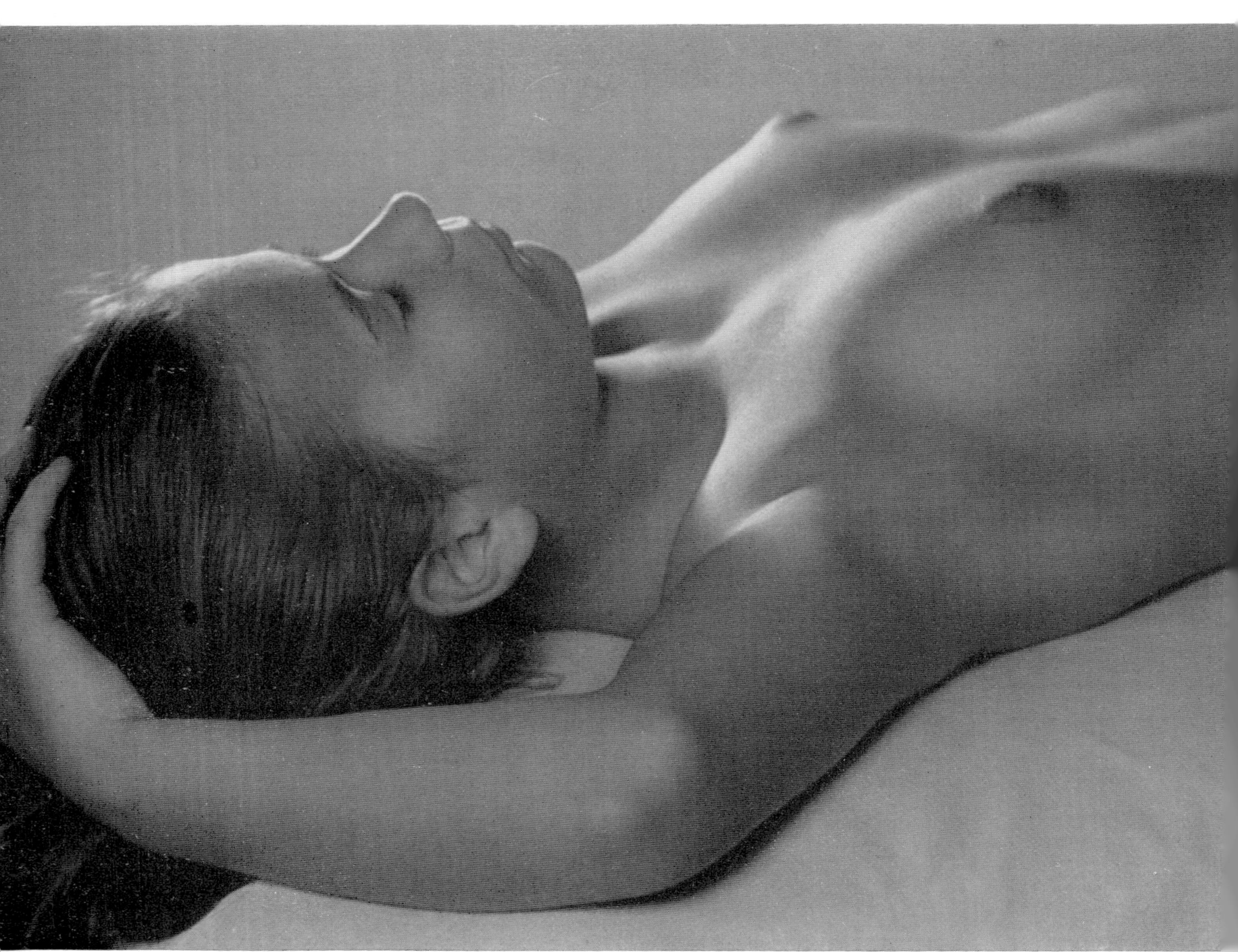

which the decreasing light intensity causes. The concentrated beam of the fully directional spotlight illuminates the subject area much more evenly than the wide angled cone of a flood.

Making up a Studio

The first thing to trouble us in an ordinary room is the horizontal line of the wainscoting which cuts our pictures in two halves. Thus we are straightaway faced with the problem of the background, one of the most important indoors.

Generally speaking the background should not repeat the tones of the nude. If a light-coloured background comes out too dark it can be lightened with a spotlight, slide projector or a photoflood. The beam of the photoflood should not be too wide because it is important for the nude not to receive any light intended for the background. Form and outlines of the figure are well stressed against a lighter background, and the picture becomes fresher.

Neither tricks of lighting nor moving the nude further away from the background will eliminate the troublesome line—with or without wainscoting—between floor and background. The ideal way to neutralize it is by means of a 20 foot length of grey or dark strong paper which should be about 10 feet in width. Each end of the paper is attached to a round piece of strong wood with tacks or broad strips of adhesive cellophane.

One piece of wood is hung from the upper edge of the background framework (if used) or, better still, to the wall immediately below the ceiling. The other piece is then pulled down on the floor towards the camera position so that it forms a sweeping arc, and held down with a couple of weights.

The nude is now placed on this excellent and even surface which forms at the same time floor and background. Its only drawback is that it tears rather easily and shows up grease stains—from an oiled skin, for instance—very plainly.

If space permits the paper can be cut to a trapezoid shape, about 14 feet wide at the top and 9 feet wide at the bottom. If two lengths of paper have to be fitted together to form the required width they should not be made to overlap. When overlapping strips are rolled up they put a visible ridge in the paper. The lengths of paper should be placed side by side on the floor and put together with wide transparent adhesive tape. This will also prevent cockling.

If a second, lighter or darker background can be obtained, it will prove very useful. Equally useful are a few smaller adjustable screens about 7 feet high, which can be arranged to form walls, and some means of raising the nude from the floor. This could be a small pedestal, about 8 inches high of rectangular shape with a surface area of about three to four square feet, a cube, a semi-circular planed beam suspended between two ordinary trestles, or whatever simplified "geometric" makeshift props may be available.

There is no objection to well finished and not too conspicuously grained wood being clearly recognizable as such. If its appearance is unpleasing a light grey, matt, washable paint is to be preferred.

With a little imagination a range of versatile props can be easily made at small cost. Furniture, however well camouflaged with sheets and drapes, is no substitute. The only piece of furniture we can possibly use is an absolutely plain couch with smooth covers and without any projecting woodwork. But can anybody make something even approaching a new picture with a couch?

Everything I have said about props stems from the endeavour, praiseworthy for a beginning, to take the indoor nude out of tormenting reality. That is why I want no furniture, not to mention paintings, objects d'art and such in the picture; nothing, at first, that reminds us of the everyday setting of our own four walls.

The body must be sufficient unto itself, we should only assist it to unfold its grace. It is only from this point of view that I have recommended props at all.

It is quite a different matter when a nude picture, motivated by a shower, bath, washbasin, dressing table or edge of the bed, is intended to illustrate and form part of our daily life.

It is not easy to discover something new in this field, something that has not been flogged to death. Irving Penn once saw a nasty, grey-black fly on a mosquito net, behind it, ghost-like, a cup, some fruit, a fan and a sleeping girl, uncovered from the hips up—in colour.

What a theme—but it was certainly a far better picture than the popular variations of nudes behind frosted glass, nudes behind veils, and nudes behind all kinds of other turbid media.

The volume of hundreds of nudes taken by the Hungarian Zoltan Glass who is working in London, would seem to contradict my opinions. He places the nude in rarely geometric, often deliberately conventional, mostly scurrilous settings in a lumber room or even in artificial snow. A daring venture, justifiable only when handled in a sovereign manner. A man has to be a master of his métier if this type of work is not to fail hopelessly. Particularly in colour.

Colour with Artificial Light

It is obvious that artificial light pictures of nudes in colour must be lit even more carefully than in black and white, and exposed with absolute accuracy. Reversal film reacts to even slight underexposure not only with darker but sometimes with unexpected colours. Also the studio walls reflect more colour into the shadow areas of the body than we like. If we want to cure this once and for all we must at some time or other take the plunge and paint our walls a light neutral grey or plain white. But first we must test the paint. One or two exposures with a photoflood will soon show whether the film recognizes the paint as light neutral grey. Such tests have been known to produce somewhat surprising results.

The background paintwork requires similarly careful attention. If it is not our habit to work haphazardly we cannot get out of making test photographs of all paintwork. All this adds up to the fact that colour costs more.

The money is well spent. We can learn, for instance, how stubbornly even "snow white" reflecting screens and other surfaces can insist on delivering a colour of their own. Only after experiencing such happenings is it possible to turn the chance effects to good use and exploit them for deliberate expression in colour.

Make-up

The model whose complexion will stand up to artificial light without make-up has not yet been found. Red blotches must be covered with one of the many proprietary cosmetics or suitably toned powder. Shiny skin must also be powdered but dull skin should be given a silky sheen. Lipstick should be applied very lightly. Make-up for colour presents fewer problems than for black and white because we can to a large extent rely on our eyes.

The fairly restricted range of skin and flesh tones, possibly relieved only by the colour of the hair, often cries out for complementary colours in the background. In sunshine and under a blue sky they are naturally present but indoors we have to provide them ourselves by selecting suitable colours for the background and floor.

In fact the human figure, whether tanned a deep bronze or possessed of a schoolgirl complexion, seems to come out most effectively before, above or next to medium or light blue, turquoise and similar tones. It can also be made a colour centre between greens and reds, a dangerous but interesting colour scheme. But I have yet to see a pleasing background in glaring red. Red is dynamite.

Our discussion of colour is not meant to suggest rendering the subject in "natural" colour. What I have in mind is a definite colour *character* which we hope, of course, to find again in the processed colour picture. It is a hope that is easily jeopardized, for instance when after a long period of use photoflood lamps present us with a colour temperature which has made a definite move towards reddish tones. This phenomenon has to be allowed for.

Artificial light photography in colour offers wide scope for "documentary" figure studies as well as experimental work which is still too infrequently attempted. Intriguing partial solarization, bas-relief prints and masking effects have already been seen (masks are positive contact copies on black and white or colour film which alter the colour of either the whole negative or a separation print made with a filter).

Negative prints, solarized or not, with or without modification of the colour pattern, also offer themselves as means of creative expression. Soft focus, on the other hand, may now be assumed to have had its day.

Other media that have not yet been overexploited are coloured light effects, obtained by placing not too glaringly coloured cellophane filters before floodlights or spots or indirectly with reflected light from coloured surfaces. With a reasonably sure colour sense in charge of production such effects are another and additional way of freeing colour photography from the fetters of "natural colour rendering". Finally, we must not forget that in colour photography, too, a daring chiaro-scuro is not infrequently a way to heighten expression.

Flash

The purpose of flash is either to make it at all possible to take a photograph of a subject or event, or to use the bulb or electronic tube as a means of expression. The rigid attachment of the flash to the camera, not necessarily a disadvantage when the flash is used to fill in shadows out of doors, gives way to the long extension cable in the studio in order to let one or more flashheads develop their full scope.

Even with one flash arranged to provide side-rear lighting, we can obtain at least one worth-while picture, for instance of a nude pouring a bucket of water over herself. The setting or background must of course match the action. The rush of water, stopped by the 1/700 or 1/1,000 second of the flash, is rendered incredibly beautifully in the semi-backlighting. With a second flash we can even improve the picture. In the amateur studio a single flash proves useful on many occasions. It may happen, for instance, that main and background lighting are satisfactory but the light output of the supplementary photofloods is insufficient, the scene needs more overall light. One flash, bounced from the ceiling or a reflector screen (from a previously tried out distance) solves the dilemma without difficulty. The flash supplies the power missing in the mains. It only has to be apportioned correctly. This can be done in several ways.

(1) Changing the flash-to-subject distance with direct flash;

(2) Changing the angle of the reflector—your outfit may have provision for normal or wide-angle throw.

(3) Using the flash without reflector. This reduces the light output to a quarter and less, depending on the reflecting properties of the room;

(4) Switching to half power, if available, or

(5) Firing an extension flash (but keeping it covered), thus reducing the flash in use to half power;

(6) Bounce flash—pointing the flash at the ceiling or other reflecting surface;

(7) Placing one or more diffusing screens before the flash. The amount of light each screen absorbs can be determined by placing them first before a photoflood and taking comparative readings from the exposure meter.

(8) Normal, i.e. not prolonged development of the negative. Normally, negatives exposed with short duration flash need extra development; if this is not given the share of the flash can be twice that indicated by the guide number table.

All in all, we have in flash, whether electronic or bulbs, a most adaptable form of lighting capable of giving us good service as main or supplementary light source.

Mixed lighting, that is photofloods plus electronic flash, presents no difficulties in black and white but can become an insoluble problem in colour. Daylight material would at best permit the use of photofloods as effect lights, with the flash taking over the general illumination.

Artificial light material, however, will react to electronic flash whose colour temperature approximates that of daylight, with a pronounced colour cast even when it is supplying the supplementary lighting only. Still, experiments are always worth while, even if they have a habit of going wrong at first.

Action with Artificial Light

In the studio action photography, i.e. taking people in movement, can only be done when the models are trained dancers. Along with a sufficiently large room and complete mastery of technique the photographer needs an additional and quite indispensable qualification. He must be a tireless watcher and knowledgeable lover of ballet, artistically minded, and obsessed by materialized musical expression.

As recently as the thirties the majority of pictures of famous ballet dancers, unless taken out of doors, portrayed the protagonists during a slow movement or even in a static pose. Until one fine day a few specialists, headed by the Berlin photographer S. Enkelmann, produced photographs of a different stamp. Enkelmann soon mastered the photography of ballet dancers in full movement in a manner which remains practically unrivalled to this day.

Enkelmann works mostly with a 9 by 12 cm. reflex camera and always exposes his pictures at 1/500 second. A few years ago a photographic magazine had this to say about his work:

"With only the aid of light, mainly two polished faceted reflectors (2,000W each) placed to give side lighting, he achieves startling pictorial effects which correspond in the highest degree to the artistic achievements of the dancers. The ballet is danced in his studio against a snow-white background which he can tone down or render very dark by adjusting his lighting."

The photographer who can call on a total light output of 15,000W, works in a way that is similar to the work of a stage lighting manager, though more difficult. His lighting is intended to stress characteristic movement and to allow grace and tenderness to dissolve like an ethereal phenomenon. The atmosphere of the lighting produces the particular charm that permeates every artistic dancing movement.

Our scope is ever widened but the way to achieving atmosphere has not become easier by one iota for all that. Constant technological progress, only too often a burden or an end in itself, yet presents us with ever new stimuli and possibilities. But in the hands of the master it must never be more than a means to an end, and subject to the message.

Thoughts on Picture Making

There are two ways leading to creative photography, both equally valuable.

Either the photographer sees the complete and finished picture in his mind's eye. In this case it is useful to make a preliminary sketch indicating the pose of the nude and the arrangement of lights and background so that only minor adjustments remain to be made before the exposure.

Or, the second way, he experiments with his lights and props on his patient model until the first vague idea—has taken quite a different shape from what he had envisaged.

With such wide and varied possibilities at his disposal, the photographer should be warned against overdoing his lighting effects. For thirty years we have been looking at them, and we have had enough. And when with all those lights the shadows begin to cross or diverge, the picture is nothing if not primitive.

Similarly, the very popular highlight effects should be used with caution. Of course, we can just as easily play with suntan oil, glycerine and vaseline in artificial light as out of doors. It is even easier ... shimmering splendour, undraped glamour. ... No, it would be better to go all the way and take magazine pictures. To be sure, it will not be many more years before we are no longer able to face that stuff. If we want to create something of lasting value we must bear in mind that precisely in nude photography the simplest expression has the greatest chance of becoming genuine expression.

Simple, or better, strong expression is not dependent on any technical aids. It can be achieved—and this is no contradiction of my recommendations—just as well with one lamp and one reflector screen as in a chromium-plated streamlined studio with 20,000 watts. Here the keyboard is hardly richer, it is only easier to play. Or perhaps more difficult.

From the Camera to the Picture

Every advanced photographer, that is every so-called serious worker, could take a nude photograph with a box camera "in favourable conditions". Nevertheless it has to be said: a box camera will not do.

Above and beyond this fact the choice of a camera, though not a matter of unimportance, is one of personal preference and habit. It really is only a secondary factor as far as the results are concerned.

The advantages of the miniature camera should not be overlooked. But I would say that particularly in nude photography which demands such great care, only the worker who is used to a disciplined taking technique will be able to produce results above the average. The precision instruments among miniature cameras are *liberated* cameras, not cheap snapshot boxes!

Anybody familiar with the working methods of the masters of the miniature knows very well that hardly any of their outstanding pictures were taken as snap shots in the primitive sense of the word. Many were even taken with the tripod. The fact that the best of the miniature cameras remain magnificent instruments even when fixed to a tripod cannot be stressed often enough. In any case the tripod is indispensable with long focus lenses over four inches.

I think I have handled most leading cameras at least once and taken photographs with most of them more than once. I deliberately avoid saying "worked" with them. For to this day photography is for me more a genuine hobby, a labour of love, than work, or worse, a means of making money although it is part and parcel of my job. This should make it quite clear that I am subject to the usual vagaries that always come with a passionate pursuit.

One of these vagaries is my dislike of the square format. Why? Well, every artistic expression rests on a foundation of interesting design. And design is still most expressively arranged in a rectangular picture space—and with the classic formula of the golden section. The square leads much more easily to loose composition than the rectangle.

It can be said of course that the negative is an intermediate product representing

Page 133: *Study in Movement* by Prof. R. Koppitz

An arrangement from the year 1927 by the late Viennese master. Though reflecting the mood of a bygone period, the perfect balance of this symbol-heavy composition will still command admiration.

Page 134: *Looking over her Shoulder* by Zoltan Glass

2¼-in. square Rolleiflex, Super-XX film, 1/5 second, *f*5.6.
Taken by daylight coming from the right of the picture. A fill-in light on the left produced the delicate shadows; the props fit in cleverly with the space available.

Page 135: *Fantasy* by Ingeborg de Beausacq

The Baroness de Beausacq, who works in New York, has made her nude and fashion photographs known through her highly original ideas. The picture is reproduced in the vertical format as taken, but when viewed horizontally—as the photographer meant it to be viewed—the figure appears suspended in air.

Page 136: *Before the Night's Rest* by Michael Neumüller

Stegemann 9 × 12 cm. studio camera, 8-in. Rodenstock Imagon, rotating stop plate H 7/9, half closed, Isopan F film.
Neumüller, perhaps the best known Austrian soft focus specialist of recent years, used two 500-watt photofloods for this picture. One light was used from the front with a diffusing screen, the other was the effect light without diffuser. The negative was developed in Rodinal following the three-bath method introduced by Heinrich Kühn. The negative was first desensitized to enable the photographer to watch the development of the delicate luminosity of the soft focus effect.

Page 137: *Exercise* by Stephen Glass

2¼-in. square Rolleiflex, Super-XX film, 1/10 second, *f*5.6.

Page 138: *The Long Stride* by Fernand Rausser

Though taken some years ago the dynamic power and boldness of the framing of this Swiss photograph have never been surpassed.

Page 139: *Negro Dancer* by Ferenc Berko

2¼-in. square Rolleiflex, Super-XX film, 1/100 second, *f*11, extended development in Dektol.
In this picture Berko used a coloured dancer to achieve an abstract effect. To get the movement sharp and produce shadowless lighting, he used a short exposure and extended development.

Page 140: *Pose* by Gerard Oppenheimer

Here, Oppenheimer, who works in New York, contrives a pose that appears effortless. However, a high degree of technical and artistic ability was necessary to master the many intersecting lines.

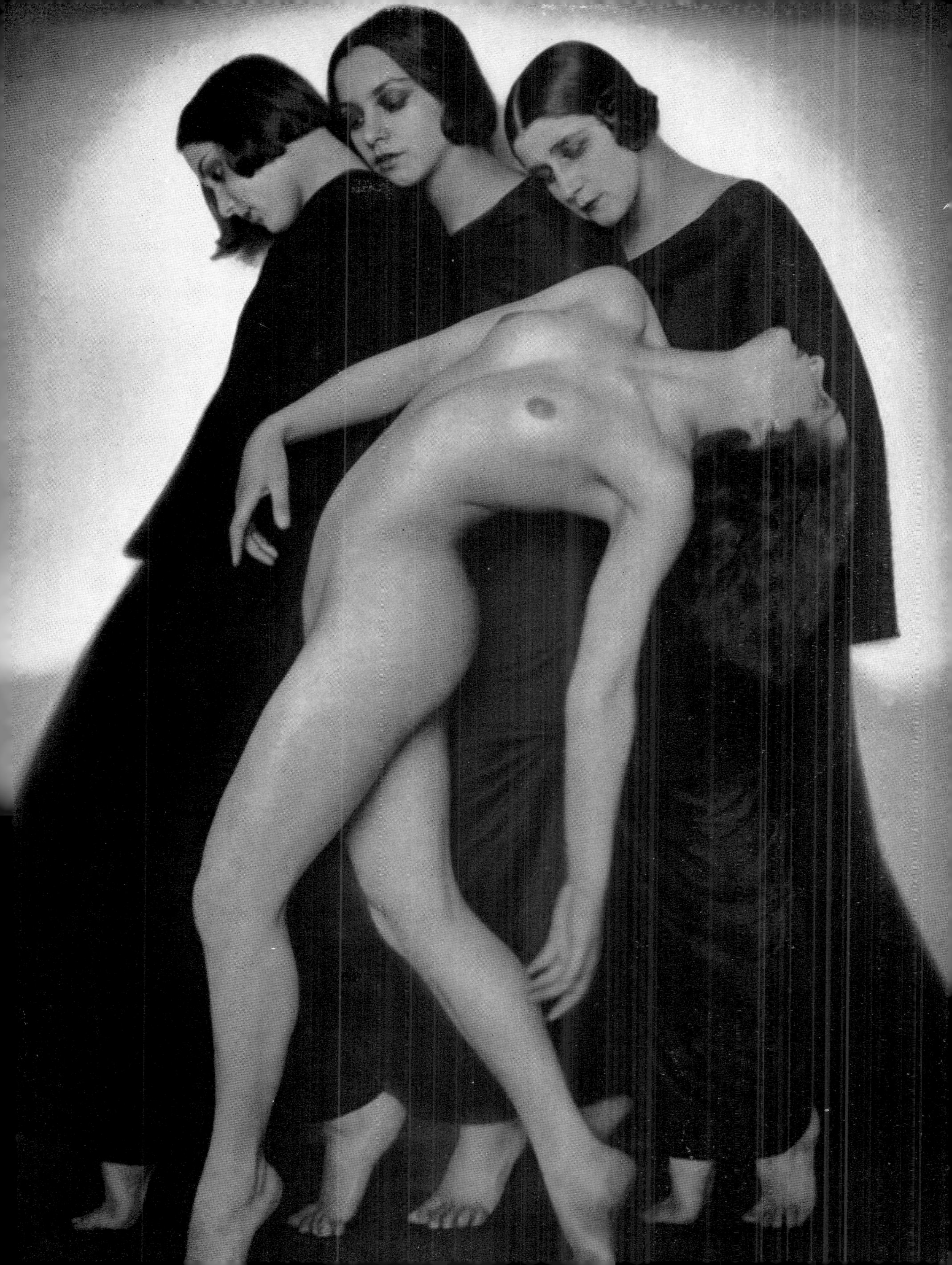

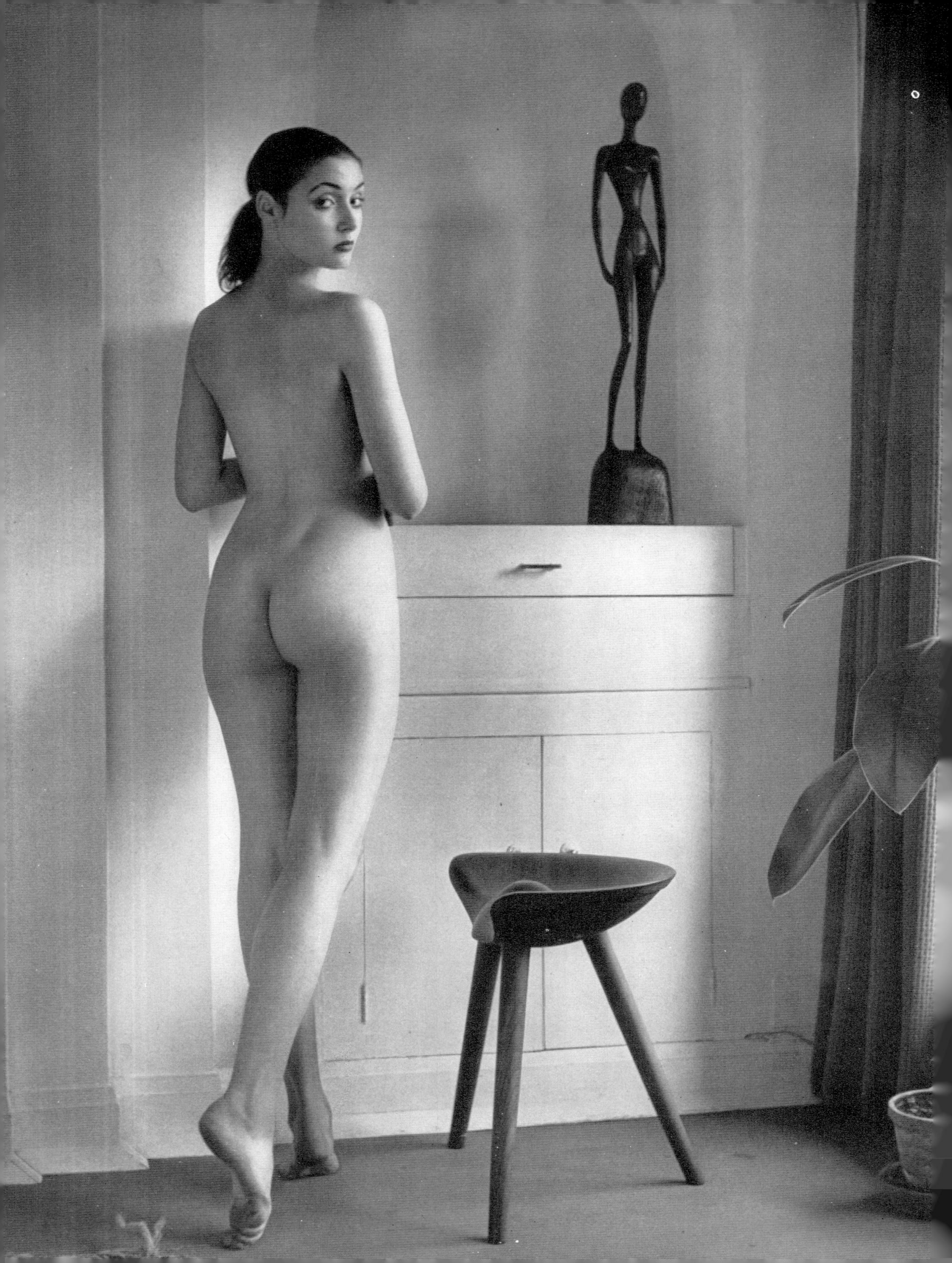

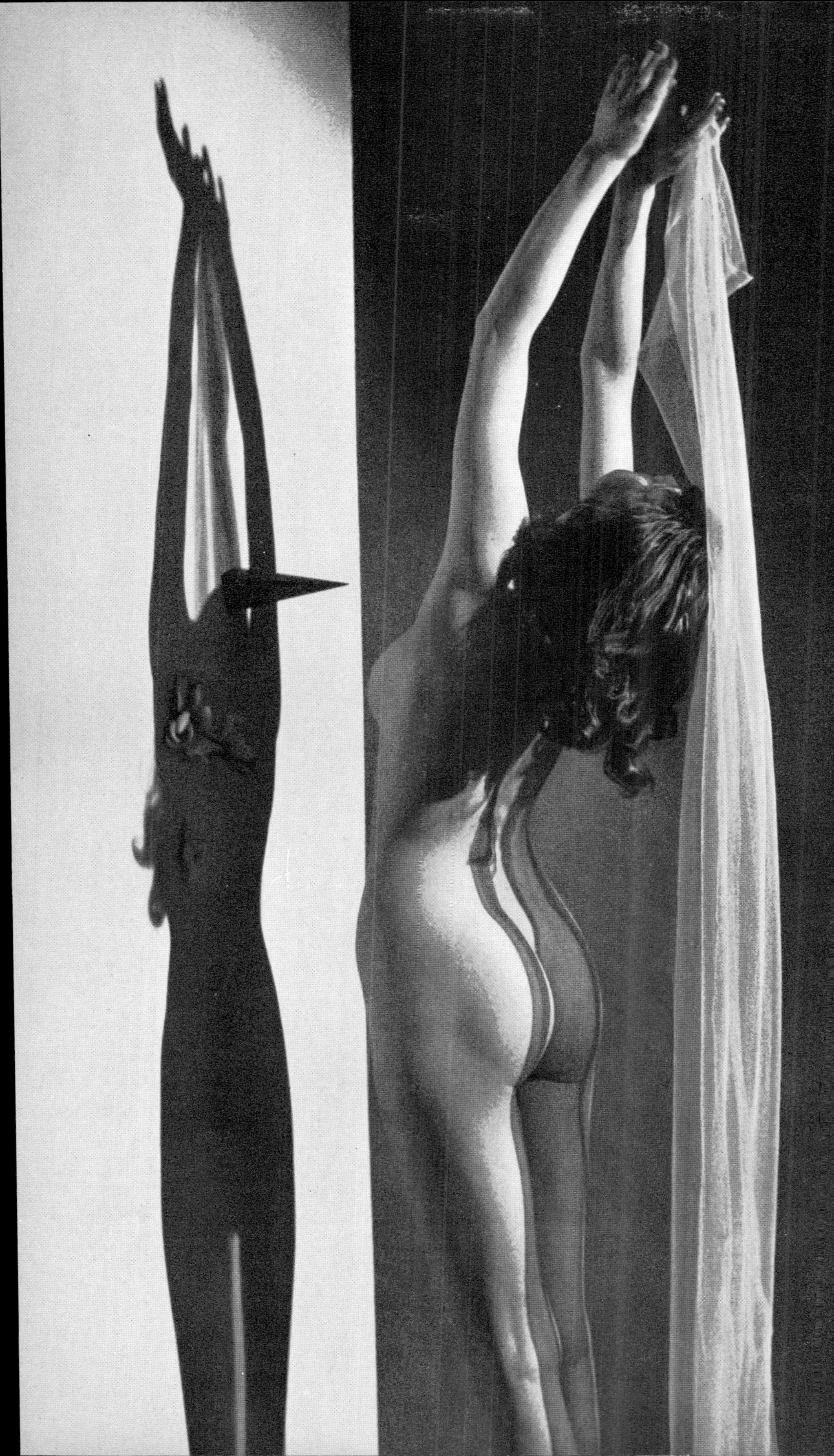

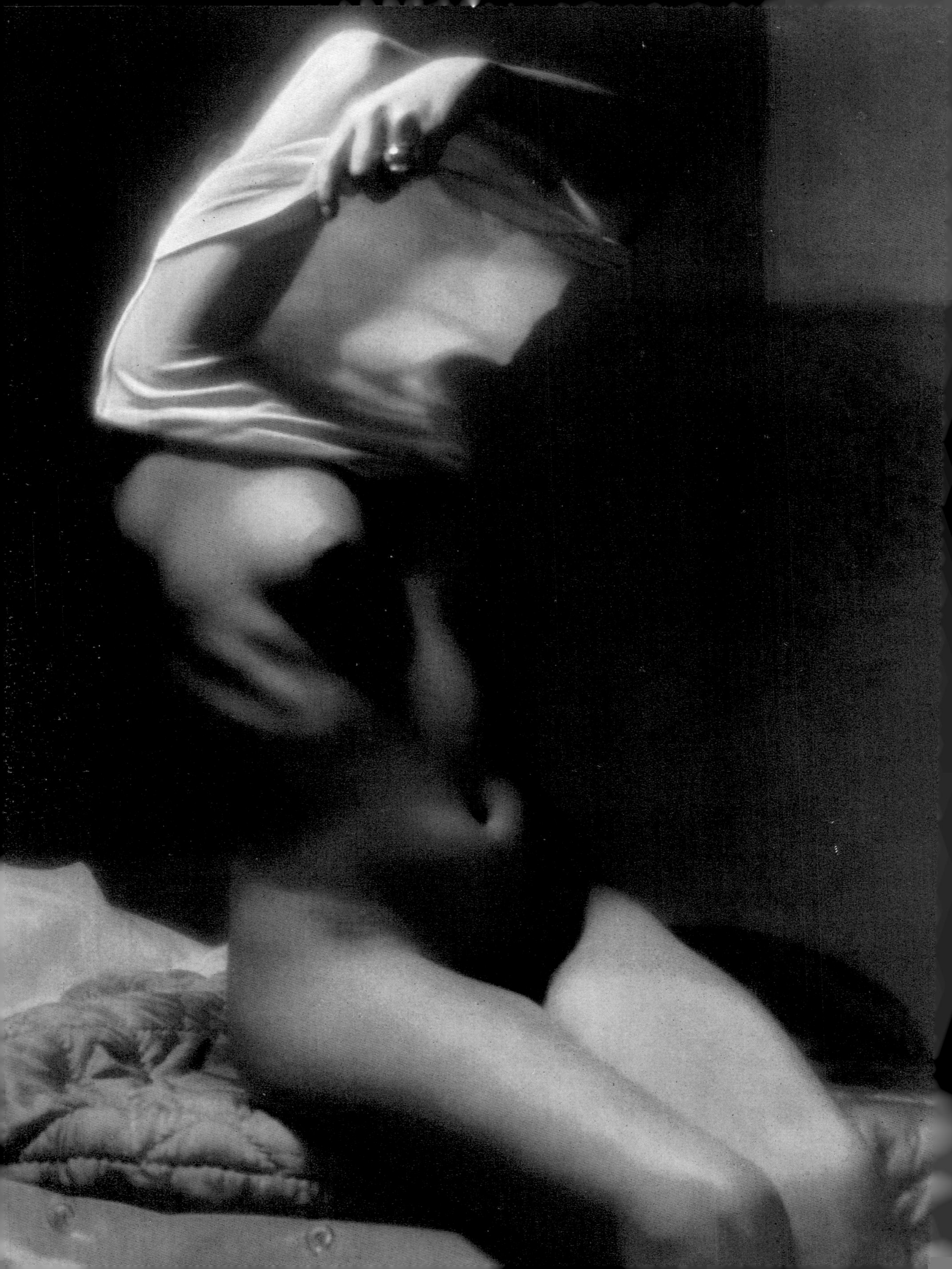

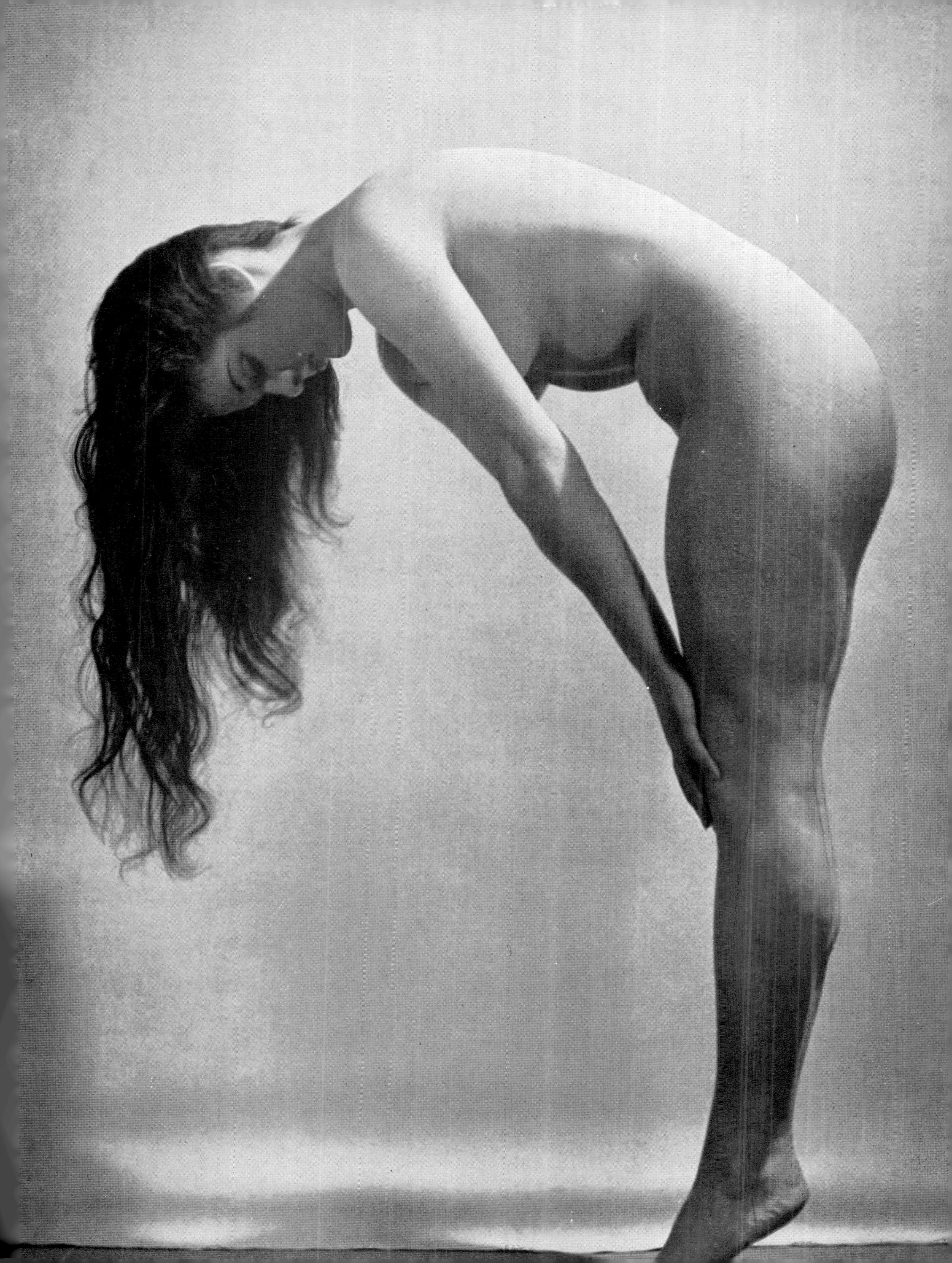

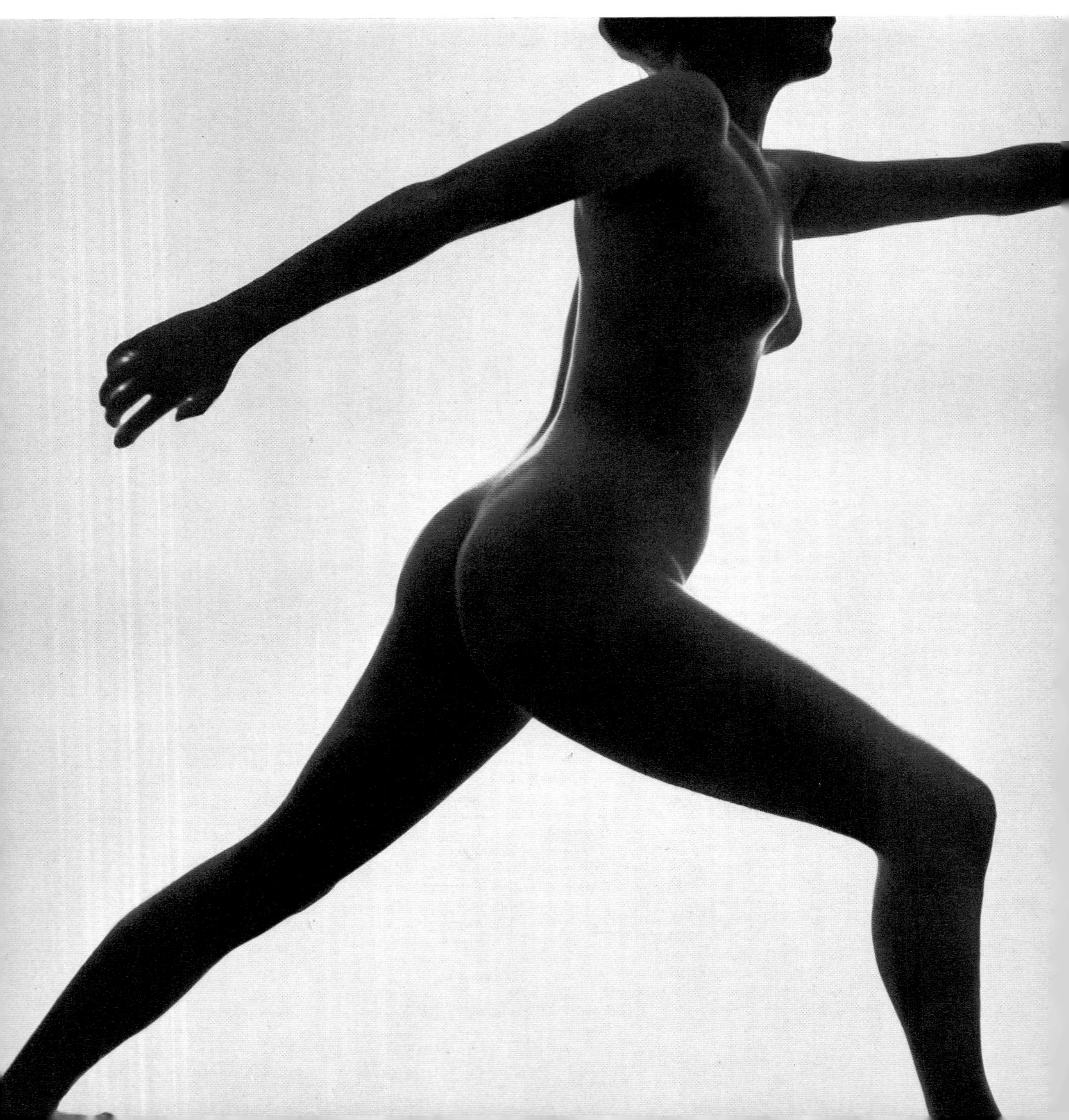

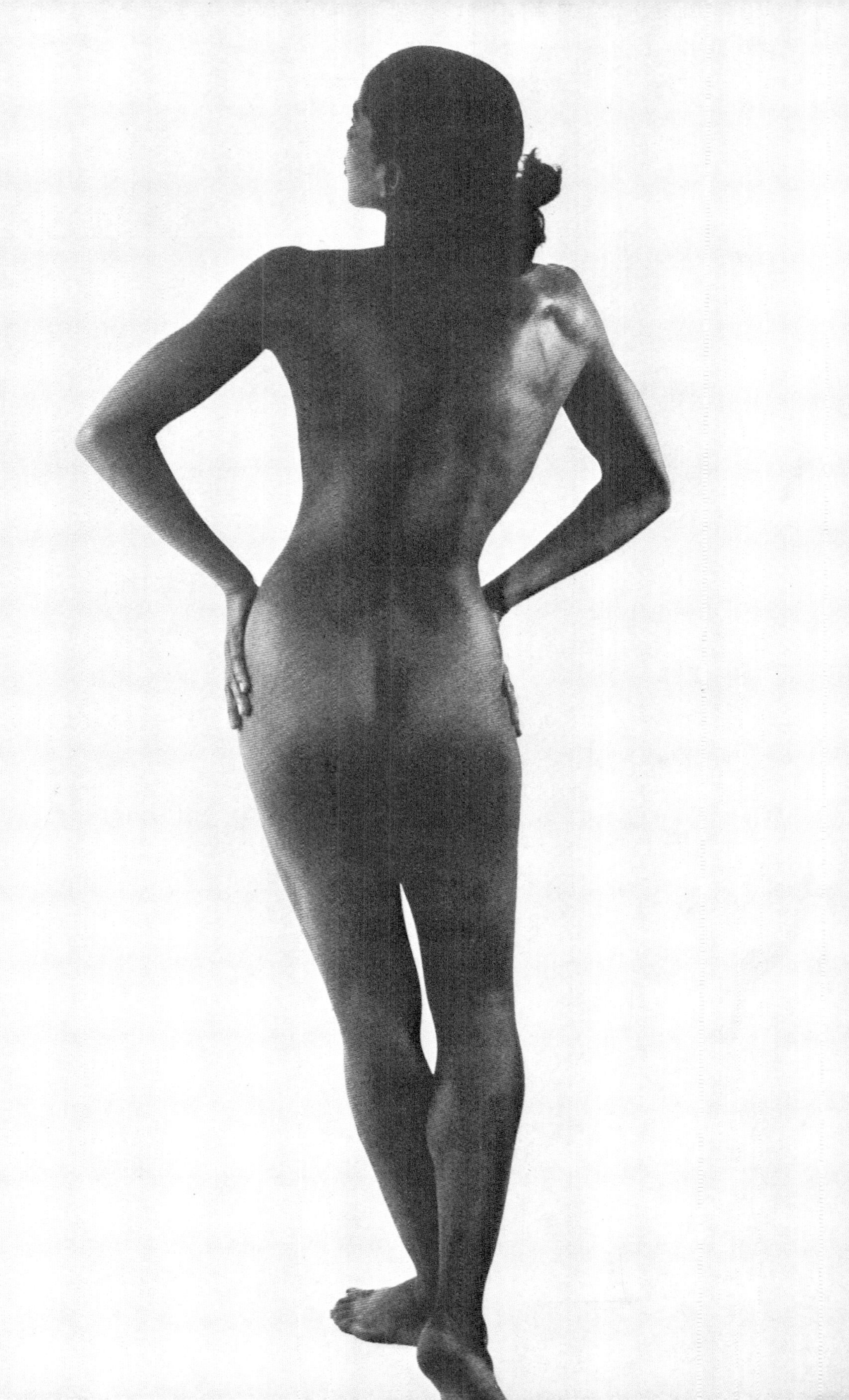

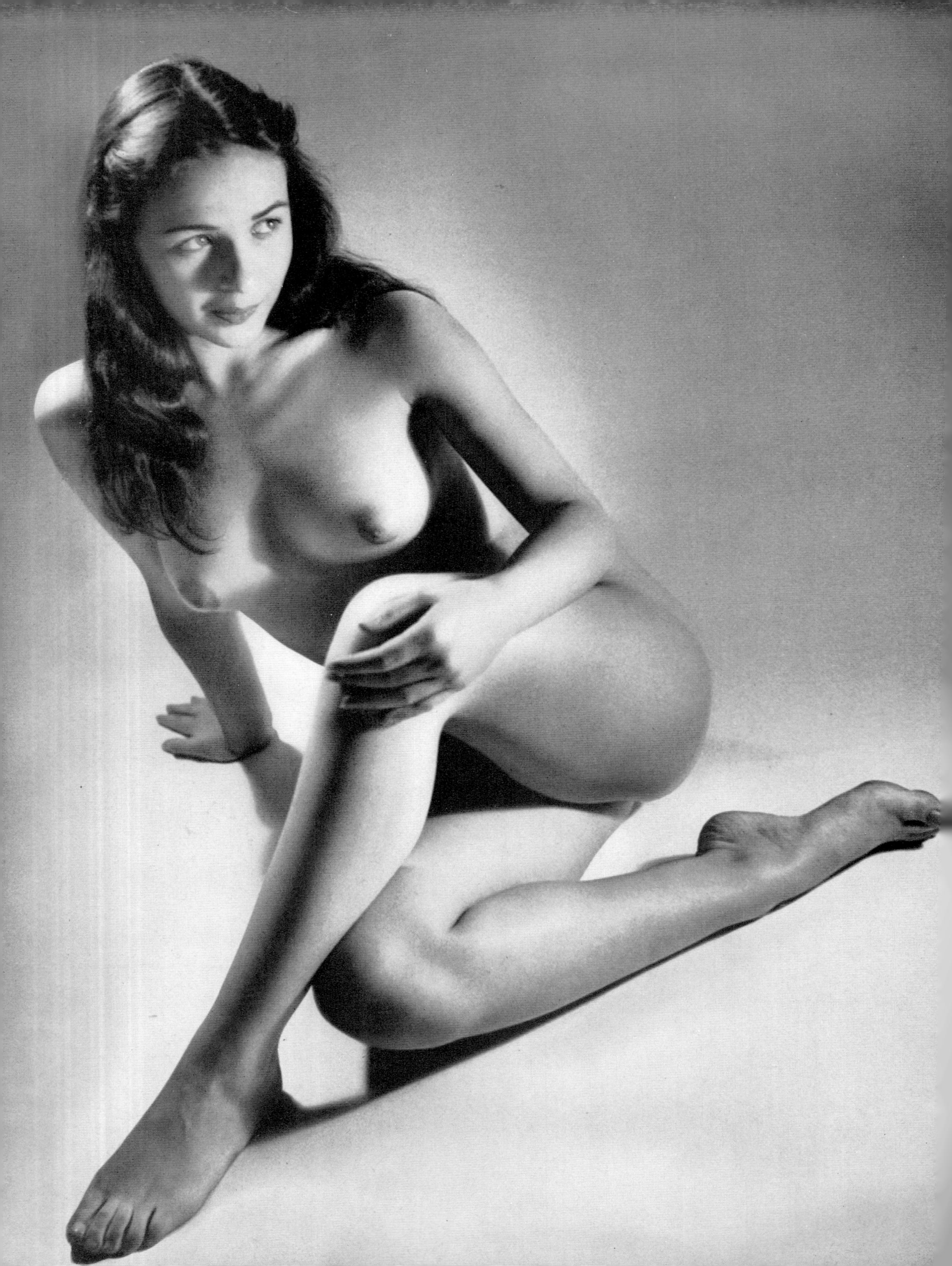

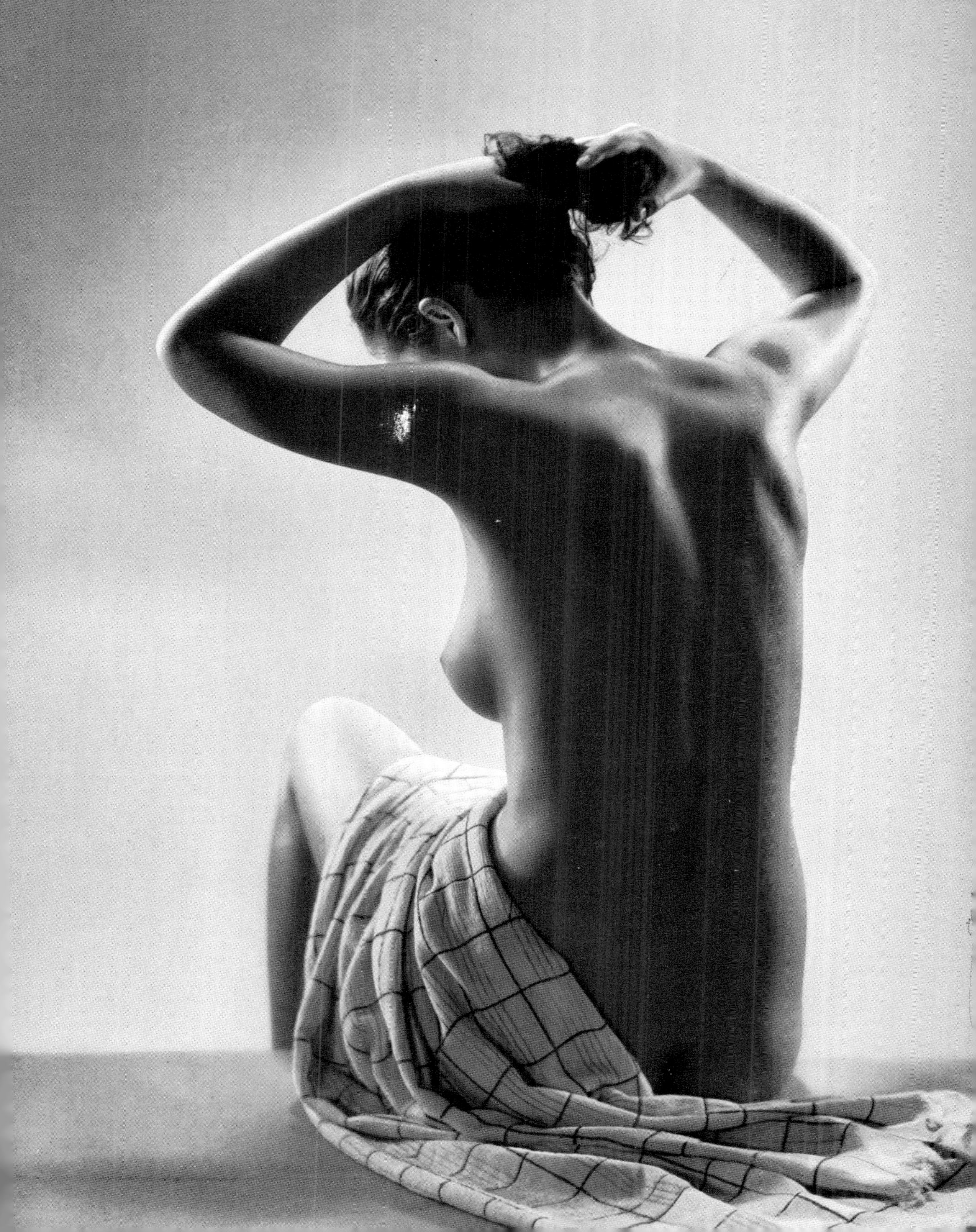

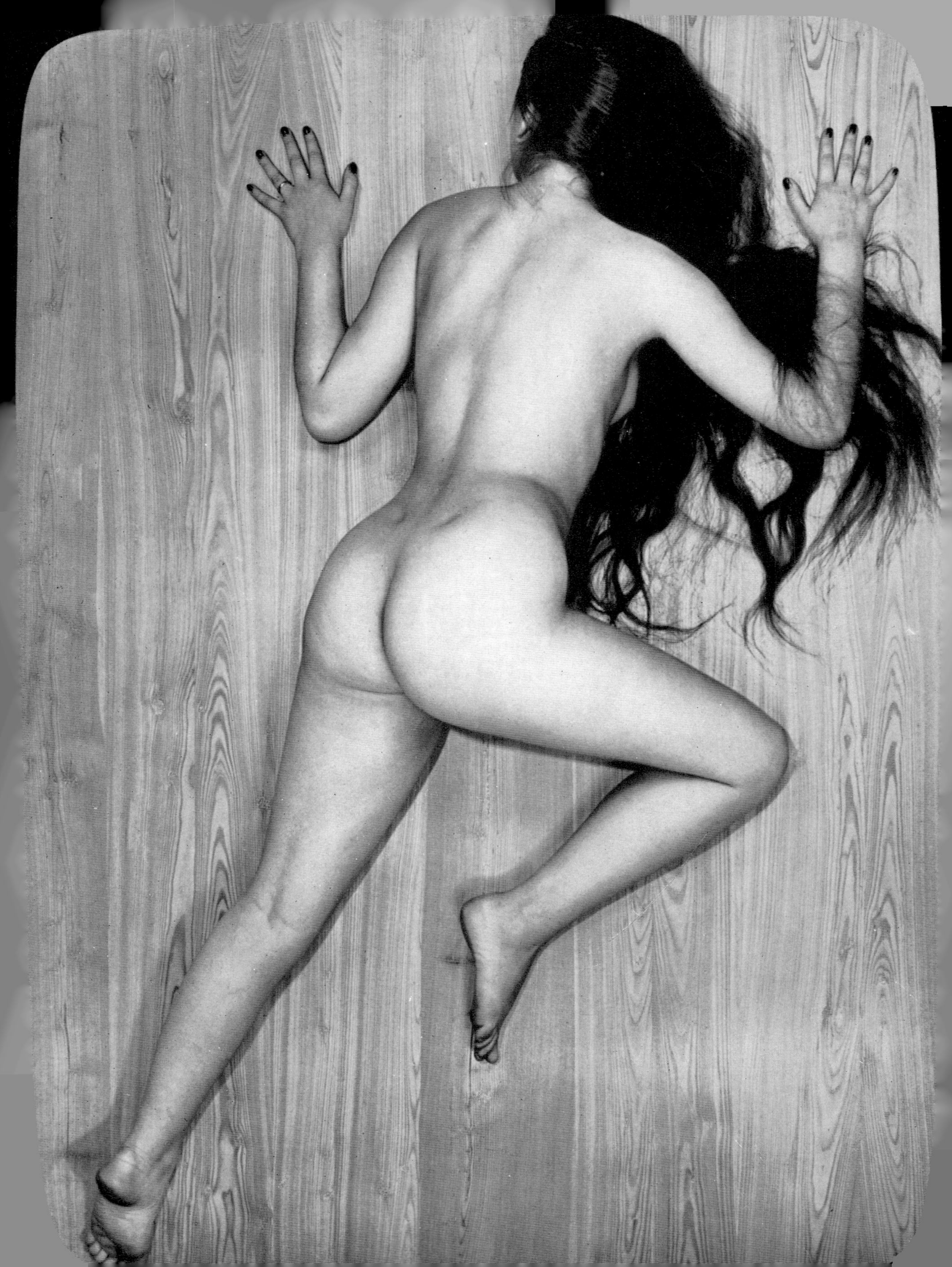

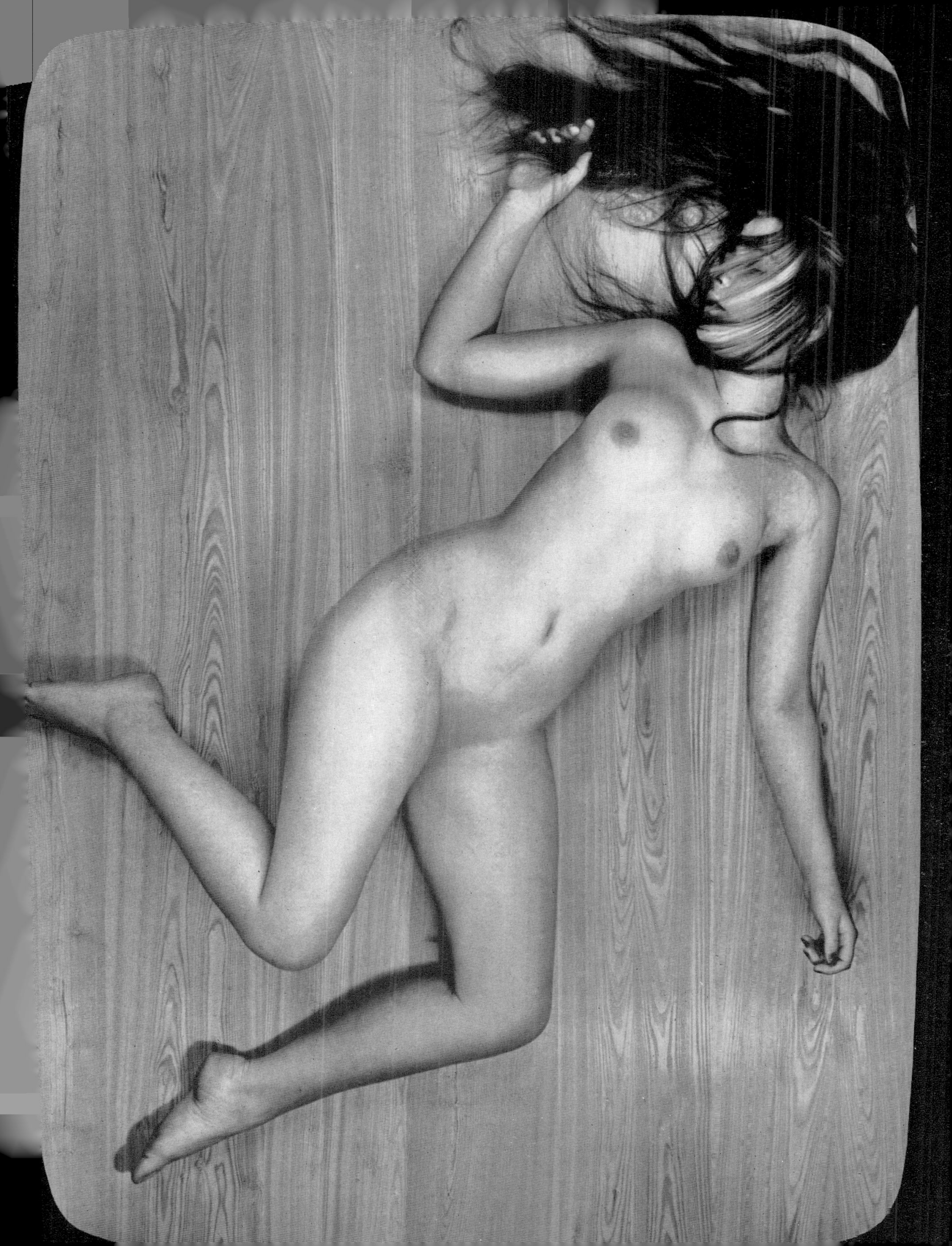

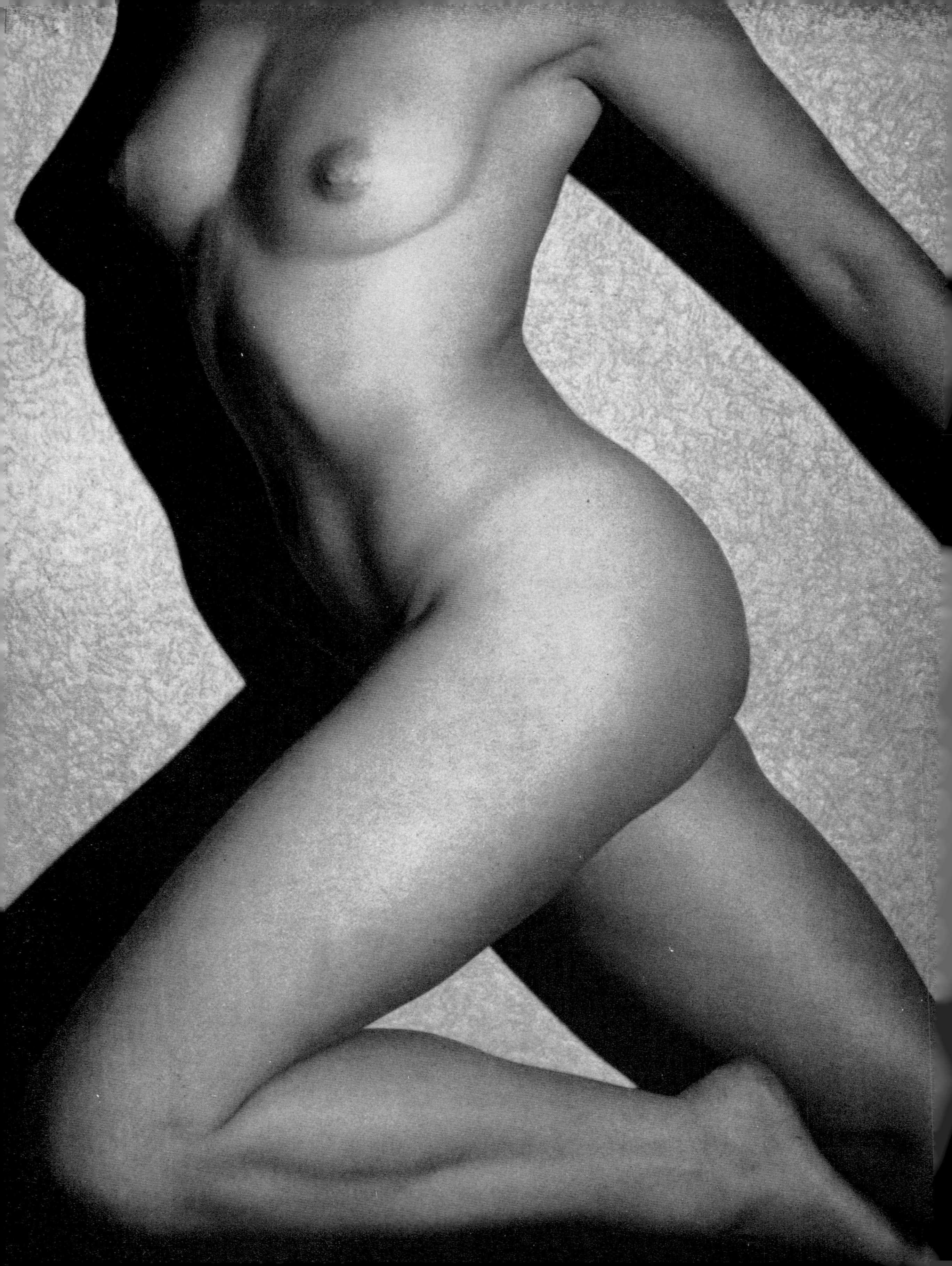

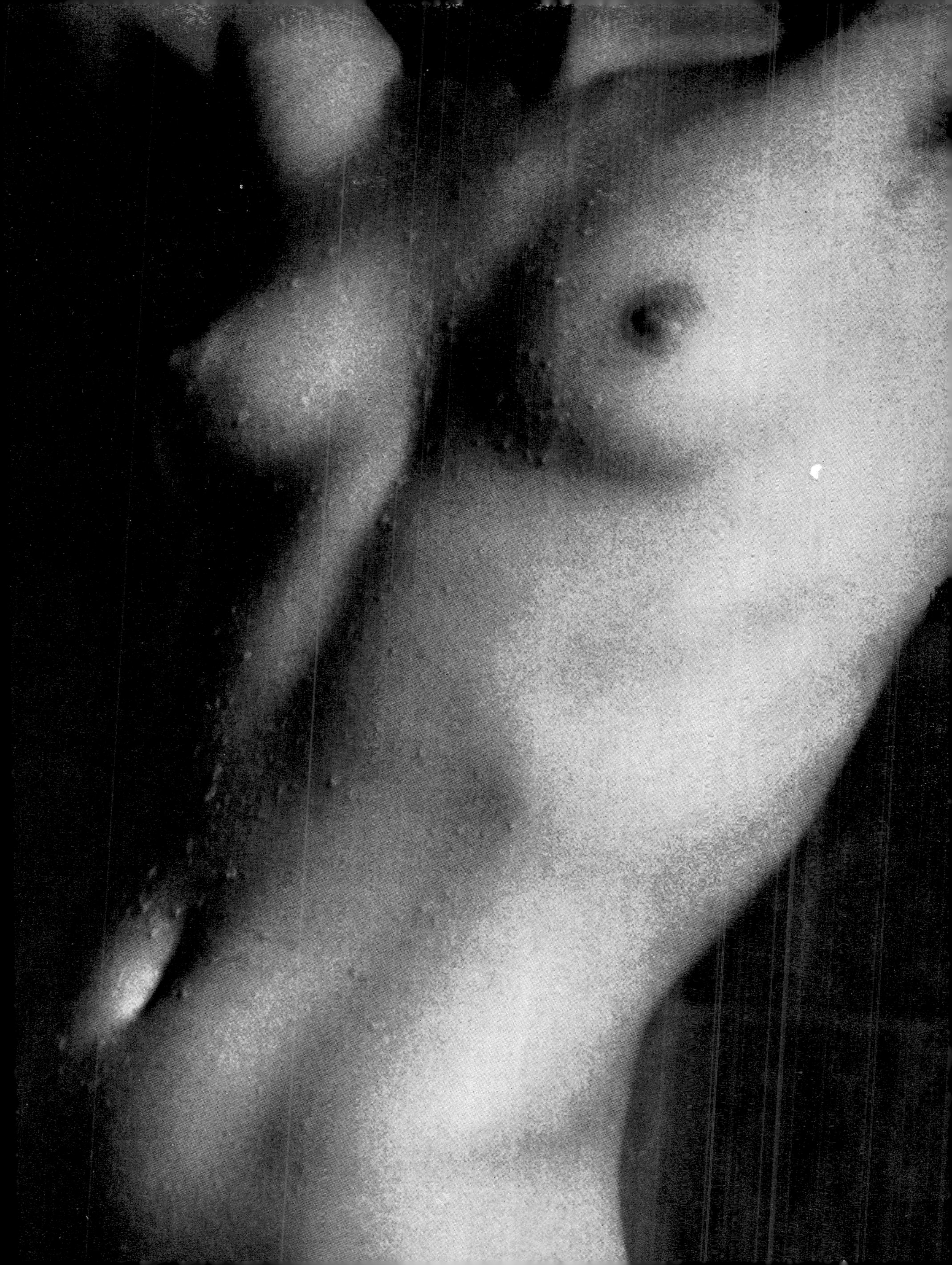

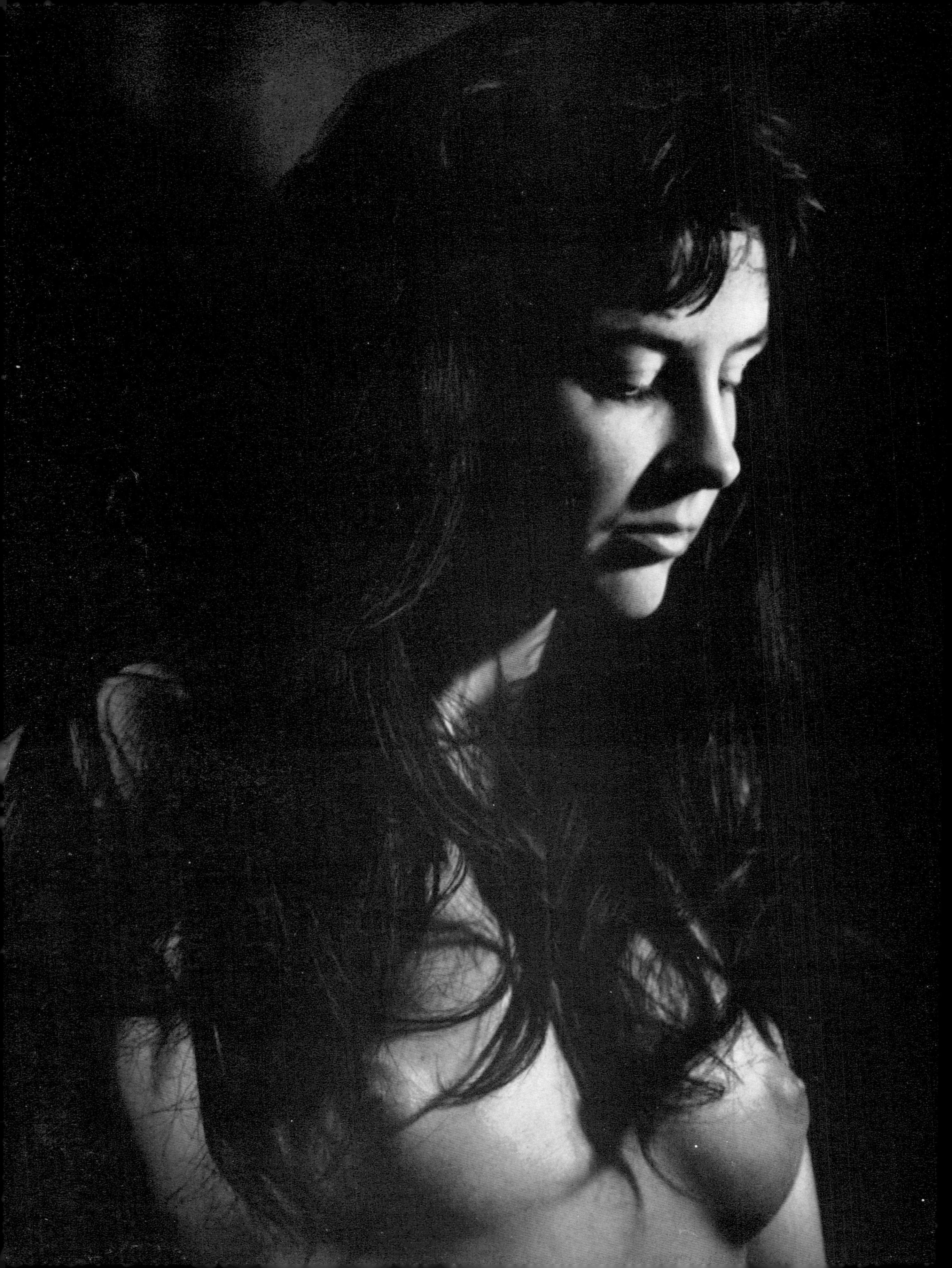

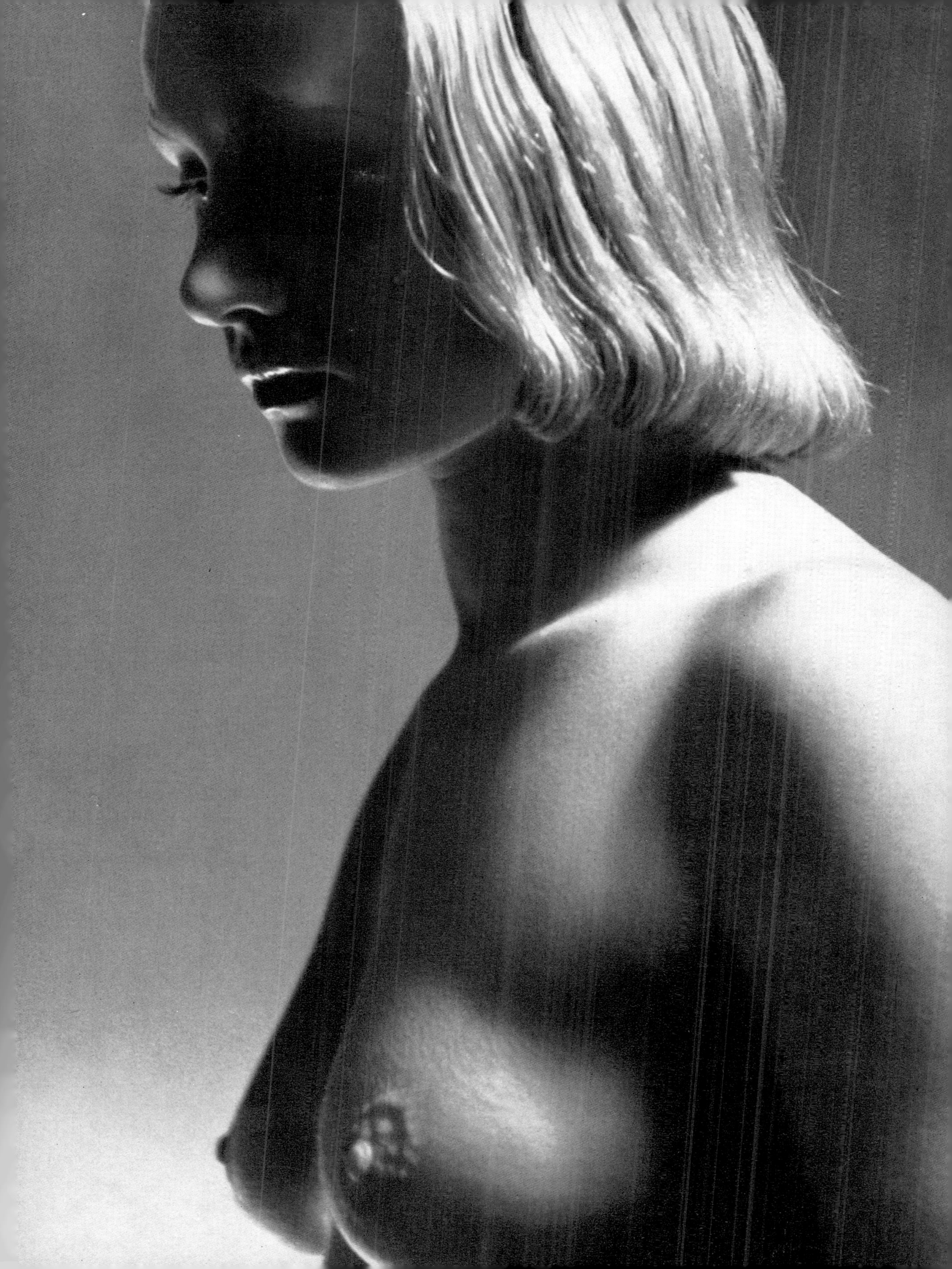

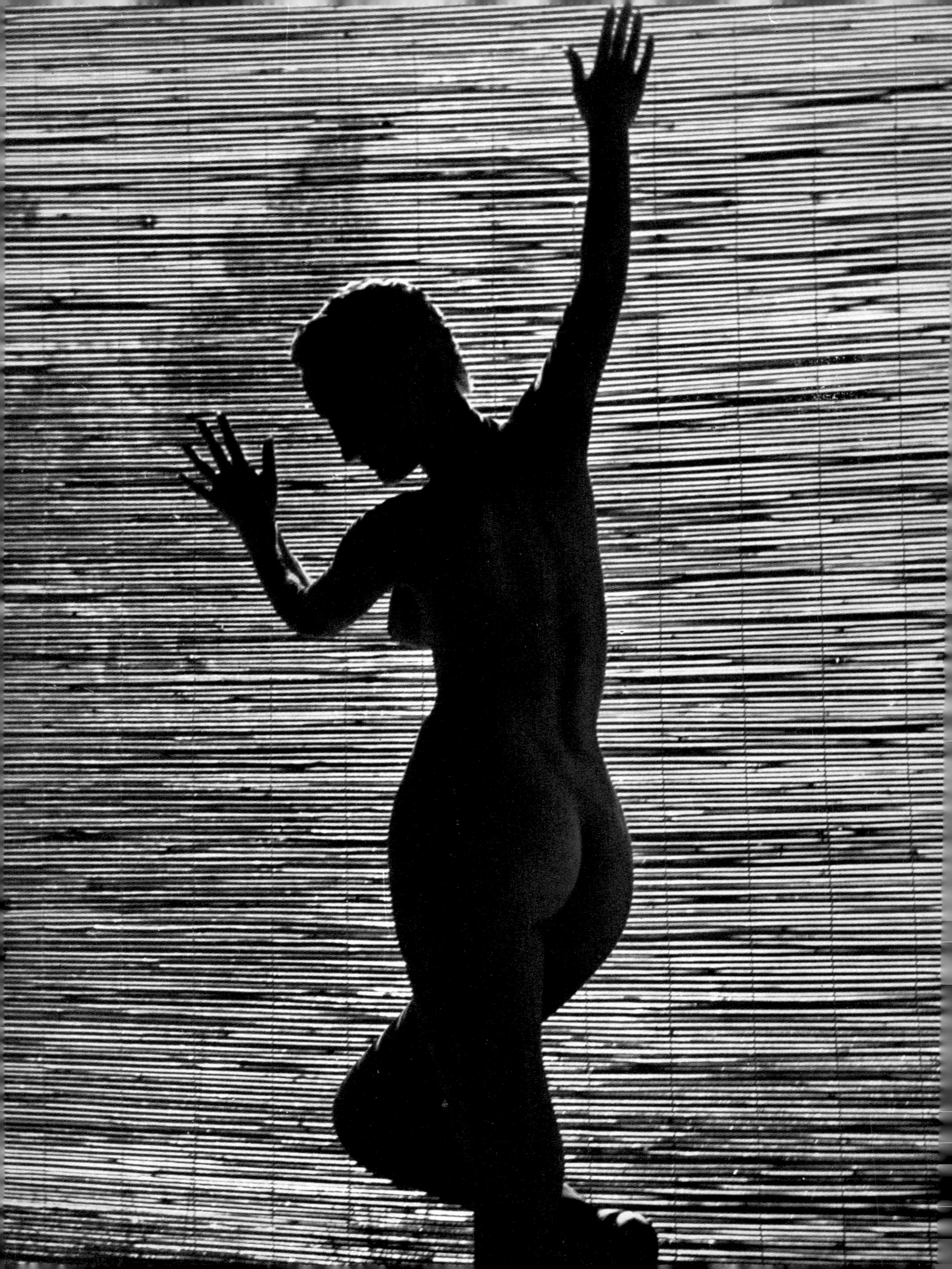

Page 141: *The Bath* by Urs Lang-Kurz

13 × 18 cm. Linhof Technika camera, Kodak Portrait Flat film, 1/25 second, *f*11–16, Pyrogallol developer.
A studio shot taken in artificial light. The photographer used spotlights to get a three-dimensional lighting effect. He applied a small amount of oil to the model's skin.

Pages 142 and 143: *Girl in Repose* by H. Heidersberger

9 × 12 cm. camera, 6-in. Heliar, Perutz Peromnia plate, four 500-watt photofloods almost fully overhead, 3 seconds, *f*22.
The girl is lying on a table with the camera vertically overhead.

Page 144: *Movement Phase* by Reinhold Lessmann

2¼-in. square camera, 40 ASA film, electronic flash, *f*16, part enlargement.
After several experimental exposures this movement study was shot with an electronic flash unit fitted in a spotlight reflector. The flash duration was 1/5000 second and the spot was focused down to the narrowest beam in order to get the right width and height of the shadow which outlines the body itself. The model was placed close to the wall.

Page 145: *Under the Shower* by Reinhold Lessmann

35-mm. camera, 2-in. lens, 40 ASA film, 1/25 second, *f*2, hand held.
A shot which proves that good nude photography does not necessarily need extensive apparatus. The light source was one 500-watt photoflood placed at 8 ft. from the model. The light walls of the small bathroom reflected light back into the shadows. Lessmann took this picture 25 years ago as one of his first experiments in this field, and it has had many successes.

Page 146: *Modelling by Darkness* by Pan Walther

2¼-in. square reflex camera, 16 cm. Tessar, 1/10 second, *f*8.
This shows economic use of lighting. The main light was a 500-watt photoflood with a 100-watt lamp fill-in.

Page 147: *Semi-Nude* by Dr Wolf Strache

Leica, 9 cm. Elmar, two 500-watt lights.
A minimum of light was used for the face and body because Strache holds that complex lighting easily turns this type of semi-nude study into glamour trash. The low angle of the light on the left produces the necessary outline of the profile of the face; the high angle of the light on the right adds brilliance to the skin and hair.

Page 148: *Early Morning* by Andre de Dienes

2¼-in. square Rolleiflex, Super-XX film, 1/100 second, *f*11.
An almost complete silhouette, this picture achieves its impact through contrasting the subtle, curving form of the model against the straight horizontal lines of a bamboo screen. Careful positioning of the head resulted in the highlight outline of the girl's hair.

the best possible reproduction of the subject while it is at the enlarging stage that we finally select a horizontal or vertical format or leave it square. I am sorry but I must differ.

The picture takes shape at the taking stage and not during printing. But are any users of the square negative format able to visualize the final shape of their pictures without straining their imagination as to which parts of the negative are to be trimmed off? It is possible to make the decision easier by drawing the outlines of the horizontal and vertical formats in the viewfinder. But my nightmare as a photographer is that some day the manufacturers will leave me no choice but to take only square pictures. ...

However, since I am only human, I did a few years ago buy a camera with the square negative format I am so little fond of. And not only that but the negative measures only 24 by 24 mm. and is therefore still smaller than the standard miniature size. (This camera is now also available with the standard negative size of 24 by 36 mm.)

Admittedly the smallness of the negative ceased to present any special problems as long ago as the early fifties. It was about that time that the new thin emulsion films and new developing methods brought important progress to miniature photography.

Obviously I do not use this camera because of its square format but in spite of it. My real reasons are its technical and particularly its dynamic advantages, due to the fully automatic operation. The format was merely something I had to accept as part of the bargain. But I have never been able to get used to thinking in terms of the trimmed enlargement. Even with the quickest action shot I must have the finished picture before my eyes in the viewfinder, complete with all its lines and with light and shade or colour patterns.

At first I also played about a great deal with vertical and horizontal trimming on the masking frame. Since then I have discovered that my 24 by 24 mm. pictures are square and remain square and, golden section or no golden section, do not look too bad either.

The opposite numbers of the thoroughbred miniatures are the larger cameras of the Plaubel Makina, Hasselblad and Linhof Technika type, all great names to the advanced worker. With their versatility they approach the sphere of studio photography but that does not make them any less suitable for our purposes. To enter into a detailed discussion of these cameras would be as much out of place here as idle speculation on a non-existing ideal universal camera combining the refinements of the miniature with the advantages of the larger negative.

However, I must say a few words about a third group, the twin lens reflex cameras of the Rollei and Ikoflex type.

Many photographers of high standing, men like Feininger, Henle, Relang and others are determined twin lens reflex specialists. Most fashion photographers work with them. This did not come about without good reason.

The twin lens reflex cameras are basically simple rollfilm cameras with all their advantages, and also with the disadvantage of the fixed lens. Their technical scope is no greater than that of a rollfilm camera fitted with a good lens. But in their built-on coupled, focusing screen cameras which sometimes even incorporate parallax compensation, they possess an outstanding viewing system. It permits close scrutiny of the subject matter and assessment of the effect of the complete picture in all its detail.

Since the fields of fashion and nude photography are closely related the suitability of the twin lens reflex camera for our purpose is obvious. For the rest, Feininger believes the square format to be the *ne plus ultra* of photographic functionalism because it is the logical product of the circular shape of the lens.

Maybe. I am still convinced that its present-day predomination is in some cases the logical product of the design of the camera.

My own basic equipment is as follows.

(1) A $2\frac{1}{4}$ by $3\frac{1}{4}$ roll film camera for "the picture that must have the lot", texture, detail, close-up. For life-size conception, and for negative colour film.

(2) A miniature camera for all dynamic subjects, picture series, movement, action —and when the other camera is not at hand. Also for reversal colour film.

Since I travel a great deal I try to manage whenever possible with these two cameras, if only for the sake of mobility. They complement each other perfectly, and with a few interchangeable lenses (wide angle and moderately long focus) plus filters I should have enough. But this is not always so.

I have one more bee in my bonnet, my $4\frac{1}{2}$ by 6 cm. Super Ikonta. Why, oh why has this beautiful format been so completely abandoned? I may have voiced a few objections to the square format but surely $2\frac{1}{4}$ by $3\frac{1}{4}$ and still more 24 by 36 mm. are terribly elongated "stripes". When we enlarge them on the usual 8 by 10 inch paper size we lose a shocking amount of picture space from the top and bottom of the negative. Or we have to leave an exaggerated margin on either side, for the 24 by 36 mm. has nothing like the classic proportions of 9 by 12 cm. or even the 6.5 by 9 cm. plate.

My $4\frac{1}{2}$ by 6 cm. negatives are always the most fully utilized. Besides, this format has the eminent advantage of supplying a negative that is quite large by modern standards. For all practical purposes it is the same as 6 by 6 cm. ($2\frac{1}{4}$ square) for when it comes to professional work for the press, publicity, advertising or fashion the enlargement must nearly always be made vertical or horizontal.

The Super Ikonta has still more advantages. Getting 16 frames instead of 12 from a film is considerably more economic, the *f*3.5 lens is good and fast, the Albada viewfinder large and clear, and the Compur Rapid shutter yields 1/500 second. Yet the camera is so small and flat that it really does fit in my coat pocket, protected by a chamois bag. Small wonder that I guard it like the apple of my eye.

Here end my personal views on the camera problem. On occasion I take only one of my cameras with me. For big jobs and when I have to travel they go together into one of the usual shoulder bags. No ever-ready case, but each camera has its own carrying strap or chain. The case is not exactly streamlined but it bears the marks of age with dignity. I had it adapted from a shooting bag years ago by a saddler to my own ideas. It is fairly sandproof (important when you work on beaches or, as I do, travel through deserts). Four big compartments with subdivisions take, in addition to the cameras, a couple of additional lenses, all filters, cassettes, a few films and small accessories, and my notebook without becoming too unwieldy.

Films

In my 2¼ by 3¼ inch camera I frequently use ultra-fast films of the ISS, Peromnia or Ilford HP types, indoors and out. And why not, when the solid size of the negatives is unlikely to present me with any grain trouble. These films have the advantage that their increased sensitivity to red brings out rich tones not only in artificial light but also, for instance, on sandy beaches, always the domain of the most striking outdoor nude pictures.

Another characteristic of these films, their soft gradation and long range of intermediate tones, is usually also an advantage. Only occasionally is there a risk of the skin coming out too smooth and idealized. This is a matter for being sparing in the use of filters, which is all to the good. Despite the wide exposure latitude of this type of film care should be taken not to overexpose or overdevelop.

A good all-round film for summer use is still the medium speed film of 16–17° DIN and normal red sensitivity. It has a steeper gradation and finer grain and will yield practically unlimited enlargements and part enlargements from 2¼ by 3¼ and 2½ inch square negatives.

When the finest possible rendering of materials or skin texture is required and for abstract photography I use 14–15° films.

As far as 35 mm. films are concerned, I enjoy working with the modern 17° DIN films. No half-measures for me; I swear by the extremely fine grain of the Adox KB 14, Agfa FF or Ilford Pan F type of film. I expose them as for 17° (18° for Ilford Pan F) and develop them in a once-only developer of the Neofin or Isonal type.

These developers bring the last ounce of speed out of the film and are specially meant for the slower fine grain emulsions. Once the correct balance of exposure and length of development has been found, there is no need to fear either the empty shadows of a too steep gradation or grain. The image will come out with maximum definition and "kick".

Some well-tried "once only" developers that have made a remarkable comeback in recent years are the quite different developers of the Rodinal or Perinal type. They have been known for decades and are not subject to any ephemeral fashion. I call them "once only" because they are so cheap that it does not hurt anybody's pocket to pour them away after use. Consistently safe results are the reward. They are *not* fine grain developers but they do produce lively negatives with maximum definition. Nor do they require extra exposure as they retain the film speed fully and have excellent compensating properties. Their working can be easily controlled by adjusting length of development and dilution.

As long ago as A.D. 1949, still in the age of para-phenylene diamine and the Sease formulae, Heinrich Stöckler pointed out the drawbacks of the so-called "genuine" super fine-grain developers. They have the undesirable secondary effect of attacking the sharp lines between light and shadow areas. Even at that time Stöckler recommended the Rodinal type of developer. As the emulsions have been considerably improved and the grain problem minimized since then, there is no longer any reason to renounce the use of this simple and cheap developer.

A few data for Rodinal:

13–15° films; Dilution 1:100; development time 15–18 minutes at 65° F. (at 70° 1–3 minutes less).

With subjects of normal contrast expose as for 15°; with low contrast subjects (under soft lighting) expose as for 17° and dilute to 1:75.

17° films; Dilution 1:75; development time as above. With subjects of normal contrast expose as for 19° DIN.

Shake the developing tank lightly and agitate the film once every minute. Keep exactly to the correct time and temperature, and take the intermediate washing into account. Test and standardize your development.

For faster 35 mm. films a developer of the type of Atomal-neu is recommended because of the grain.

Solvent fine-grain developers must not be used with some of the latest films (DK 20).

The Problem of Grain

For two decades photographers used ultra fine-grain developers in order to obtain evenly balanced but extraordinarily delicate, as it were under-nourished negatives which did in fact yield almost grain-free enlargements. But to-day it is generally admitted that it is not possible to obtain negatives with maximum sharpness and the previously mentioned "kick" with genuine fine-grain developers of the old kind.

The new edition of genuine fine-grain developers are a little more soft working. They get more speed out of the negative, corresponding at least to the values given by the makers. But even they have not been able to dispense altogether with solvents which prevent the clumping together of the silver grains. Nevertheless, they do not, unlike their predecessors, dissolve the sharp lines between light and shadow areas together with the silver.

Side by side with the new types the old ultra fine-grain and compensating developers are still in existence. They require ample exposure, that is roughly twice the exposure indicated by the meter for the film in use. If the gradation still comes out too steep, development must be curtailed or the developer diluted a little more than recommended in the directions. These are problems which can only be solved by personal experiment and for this reason test film is always a good investment. Time and temperature must of course be standardized, the time taken by the intermediate washing counted in the development time, and the time increased to compensate for exhaustion of the developer.

These simple directions for standard development yield negatives of brilliant harmonious tones with good shadow detail. The silver grains will not clump together but maintain their original structure in the lower layers of the emulsion. The negative can easily be enlarged on soft paper which also tends to suppress grain, and only in exceptional circumstances is a normal or even hard paper required.

Workers who are used to this method may as well keep to it. But if they are grateful for being able to use 1/30 second instead of 1/8 while still obtaining sharp, fine grained and soft to normal negatives with good shadow detail, they will profit from a change. The once-only developers mentioned earlier will do all this but since they contain no potassium bromide they tend to produce slight fog. But they are not quite so suitable for high speed 35 mm. emulsions which need rather long development—30 minutes and more.

But why use high speed films? After all, we now use for a 17° film only half the shutter speed previously given to a 21° film—less, if the lighting is soft. Yet we get finer grain and at least equally good gradation.

Since the lighting makes a difference to the exposure we have to learn something new. We must learn to see the gradation of the negative in relation to the brightness range of the subject. This is possible only as long as the contrast range of the subjects taken on one film does not vary too much.

The softer the lighting the shorter can be our exposure and the longer our development. What is important is to accommodate all tones on the straight part of the characteristic curve, that is the straight line whose slope indicates the gamma. This seems to require some mental acrobatics, but only of those who are unwilling to ponder a little on these matters.

Special Effects

The beginnings of modern photography in the twenties encountered a boom in bromoil and other pigment processes. The forthright craft and genuine worth of the black and white picture, our most excellent optical abstraction whose pitiless brilliancy on a smooth white surface enforces the greatest devotion to craftsmanship, remained in undisputed possession of the battlefield.

Notwithstanding the problematic former position of the old pigment processes which borrowed so much from painting, one man may be mentioned whose work I admire without reservation; Leonard Misonne.

Unaffected by new and old practicality this Belgian photographer worked for fifty years creating his pictures. Unique of their kind, they were mostly landscapes in oil, gum bichromate and bromoil. In spite of their arty romanticism the atmosphere, mood and light of Misonne's work are so characteristic and so unthinkable in other media, that it always managed somehow to remain specifically photographic.

To-day we have other special techniques, every one making exclusive use of photographic means.

Multiple Exposures

Two or more negatives whose subject matter must have been matched specially for this purpose, and which have to be kept thin, are sandwiched in the negative carrier and enlarged together. Similar effects can be obtained with deliberate double or multiple exposure of one negative. Such pictures cannot be composed in the viewfinder and the arrangement has to be exactly outlined on the focusing screen.

In a different process a positive transparency is made on positive film from a negative. Negative and positive are enlarged together in perfect register. The result is a tone separation print of a particular quality. In theory negative and positive should cancel each other out leaving no detail whatever, but in practice this does not happen because their gradation and tones are rarely identical. The enlargement looks like a drawing compressed into few highly contrasting tones. A montage of two or more matched negatives and positives can be made on reversal film. If this is then enlarged on bromide paper poster-like pictures are obtained.

A technically simpler variant of the above process is called bas-relief. Negative and positive are again enlarged together but are kept very slightly out of register. The degree of displacement determines the character and width of the partly light and partly dark outlines of the print resembling bas-relief. Negative and positive are held together with cellulose tape. This is a most suitable process for subjects whose appeal is derived from form and simple lines, such as a negative filling picture of a nude.

Page 157: *Study* by H. Hajek-Halke

2¼-in. square Rolleiflex, *f* 8, daylight and 500-watt photoflood, printed through mottled glass on top of the printing paper.
For many years Hajek-Halke has been devoting his talents to experimental photography, but nevertheless returns to nude photography time and again. He always seeks to eliminate the personal and accidental aspect from his work and to achieve pictures of form on a grand scale.

Page 158 (top): *Changing Shadows* by Fritz Henle

2¼-in. square Rolleiflex, Ansco Supreme film, 3 × 1/25 second, *f* 11.
For this studio photograph Henle used six flash bulbs in addition to daylight. He bounced the flash from the ceiling and exposed the figure three times in succession.

Page 158 (bottom): *Shadow Play* by H. Heidersberger

9 × 12 cm. camera, 6-in. Heliar, Agfa Isopan Portrait film, 1/5 second, *f* 11.
The shadow patterns were projected with a home-made 1-KW projector; the plain white background was illuminated by two spotlights of 500-watts each.

Page 159: *Shadow Pattern* by Willy Zielke

9 × 12 cm. Kühn Studio camera, Kodak flat film, Nitraphot lamp, developed in Glycin and Rodinal.
The picture was taken thirty years ago; its shadow pattern effect has been repeated many times since.

Page 160 (top): *Nude Duet* by Annemarie Heinrich GDL

9 × 12 cm. Linhof camera, Meyer Satzplasmat, Perutz film, 1/25 second, *f* 11.
In this photograph the model appears twice on one negative. The photographer drew the outline of the girl on the focusing screen of her camera with a chinagraph pencil. Illumination was from two spots from the right and one from the left. After the first exposure, the photographer moved the camera slightly to the left while the model maintained her pose for the second exposure.

Page 160 (bottom right): *Mirror Play* by Reinhold Lessmann

9 × 12 cm. camera, wide-angle lens, 125 ASA plate, three photofloods, 1/25 second, *f* 9.
This is what can happen when a large looking-glass breaks so luckily in two that both parts can be used to make a picture.

Page 160 (bottom left): *Experiment with Glass Wool* by Reinhold Lessmann

9 × 12 cm. camera, 10-in. lens, 1/10 second, *f* 8.
This study in lighting owes its special effect to a length of glass wool foil suspended between the camera and subject. It is eminently suitable for experimental work because it can be made to produce a wide variety of different effects.

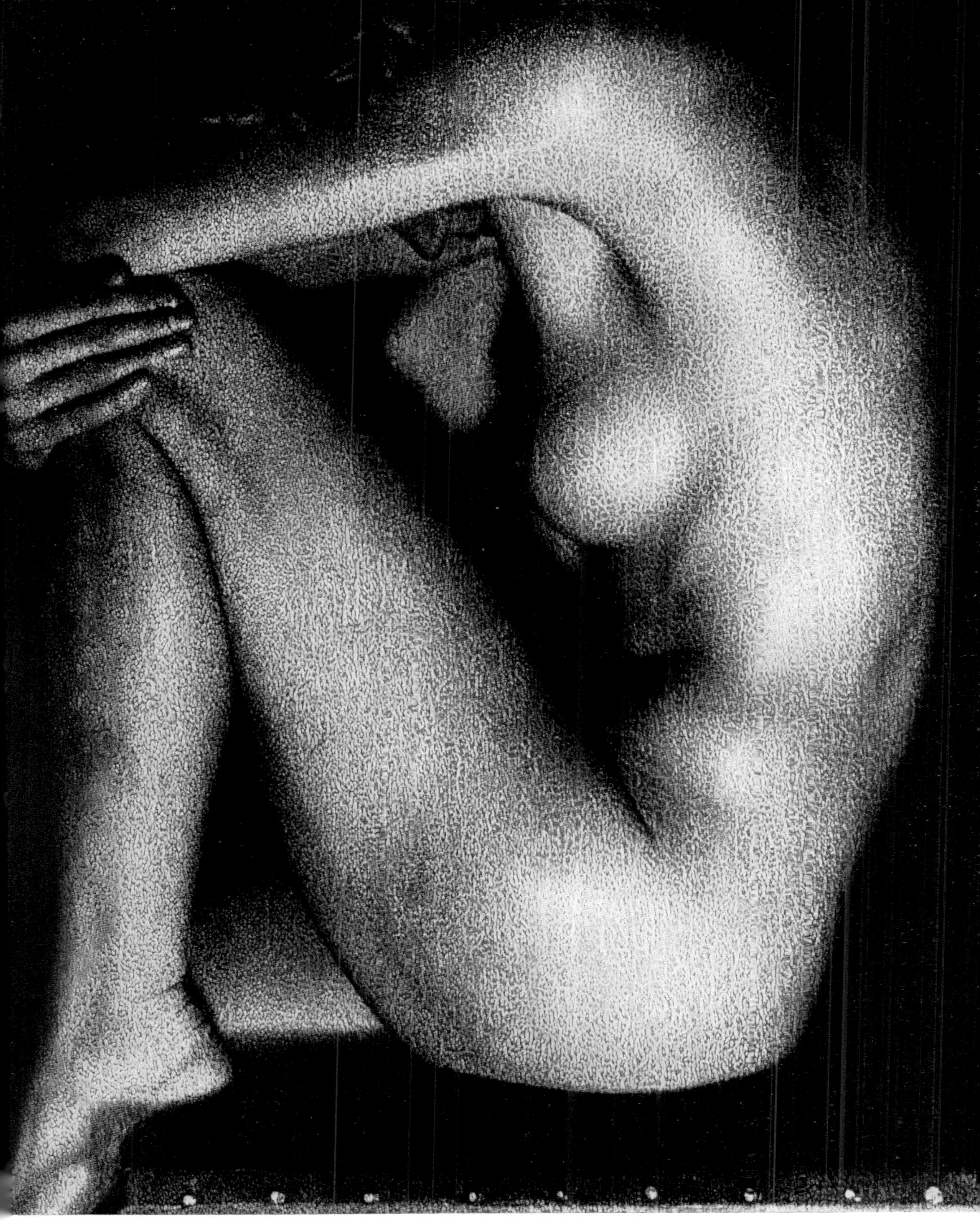

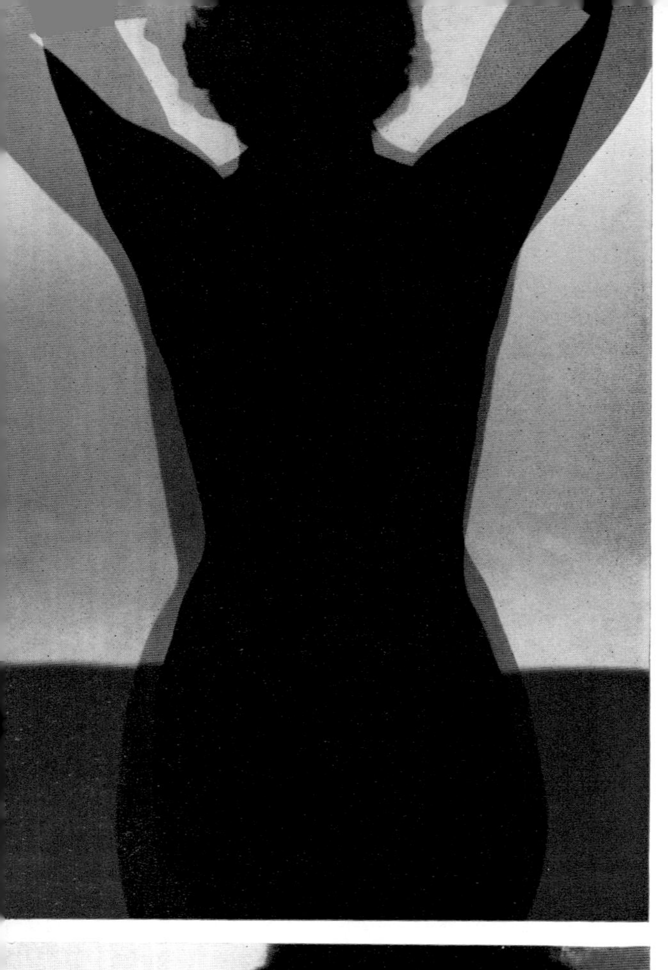

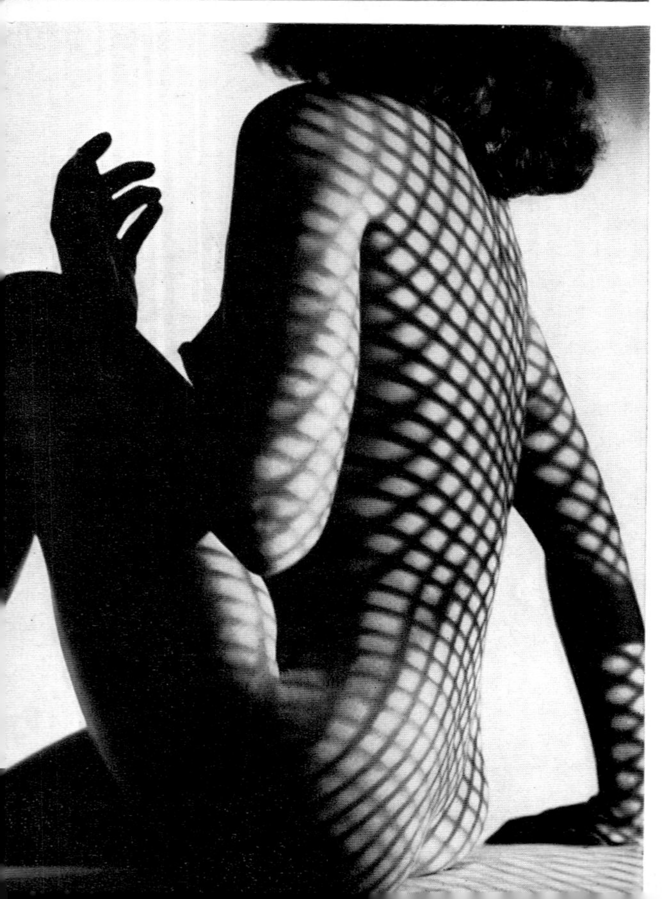

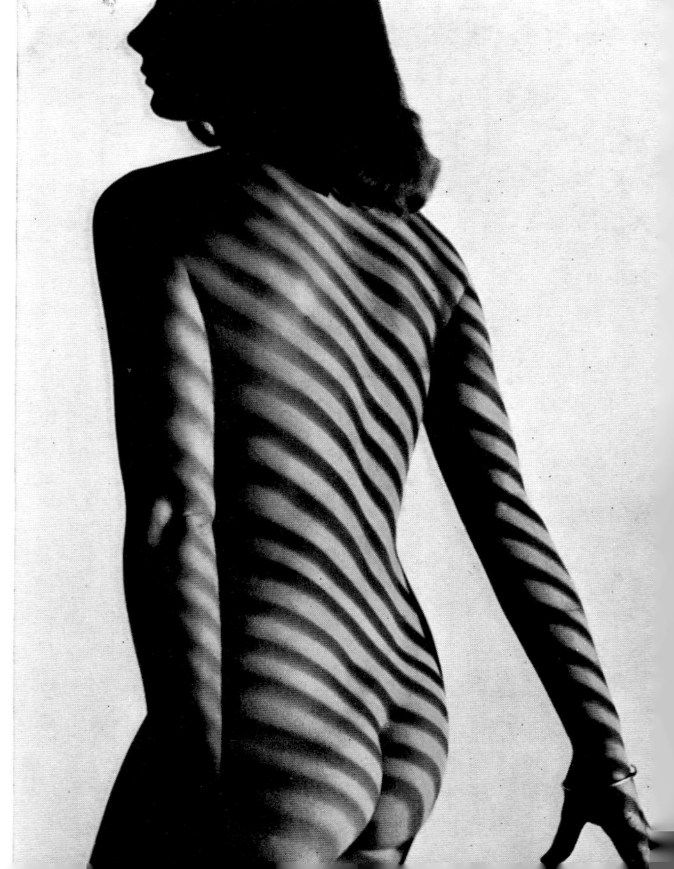

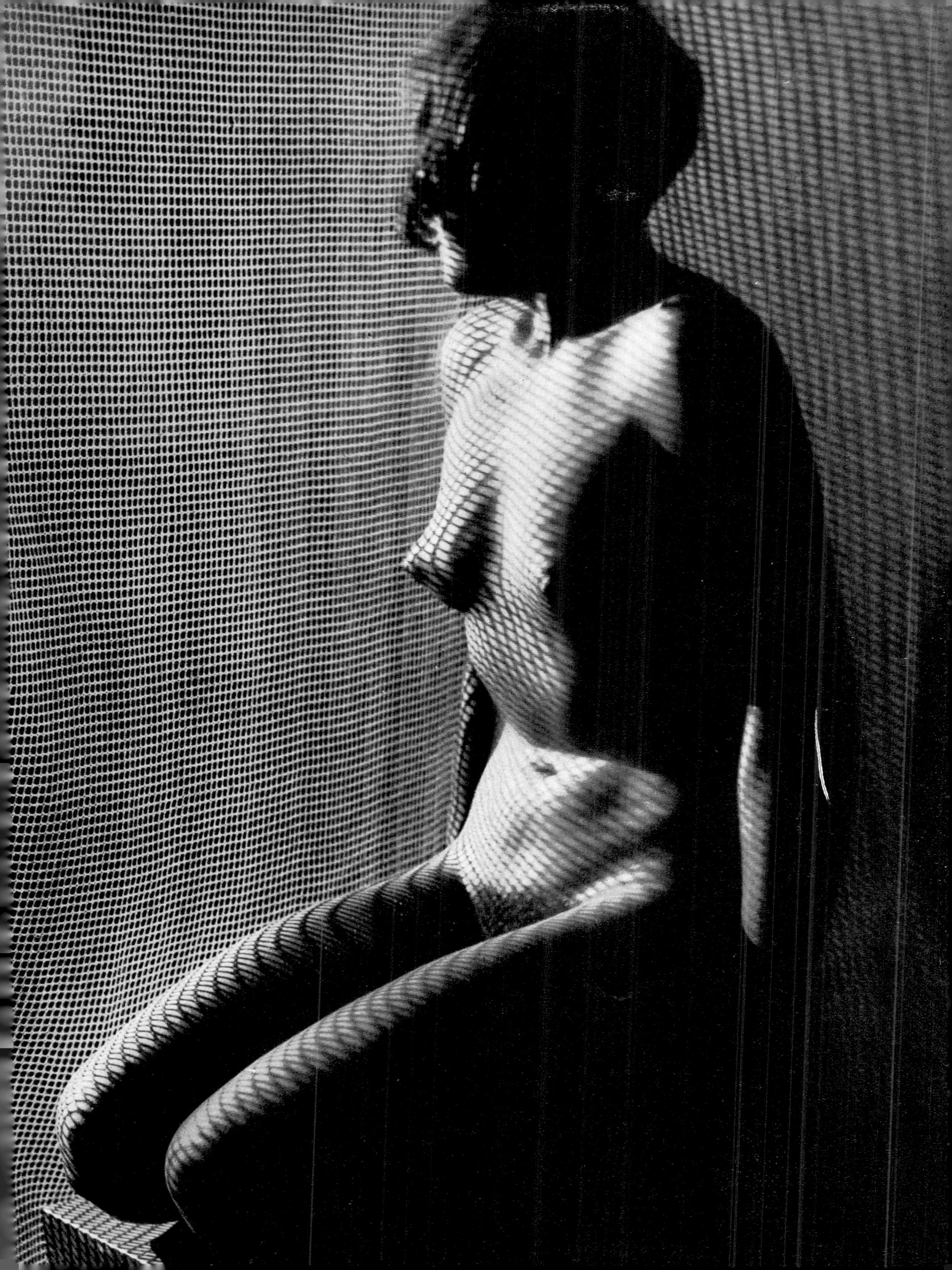

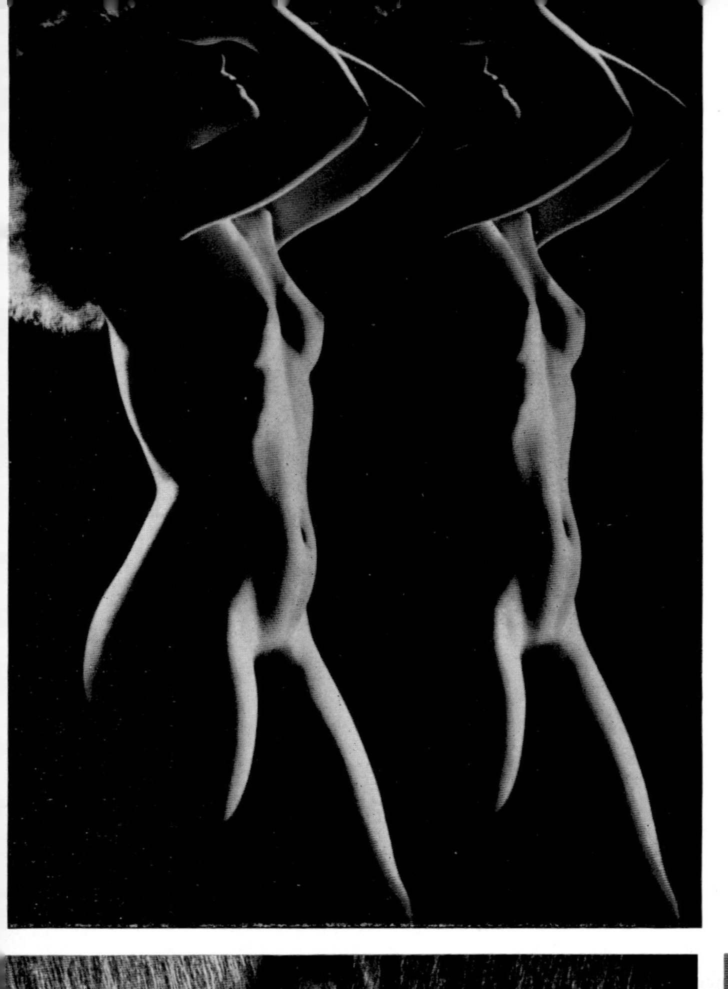

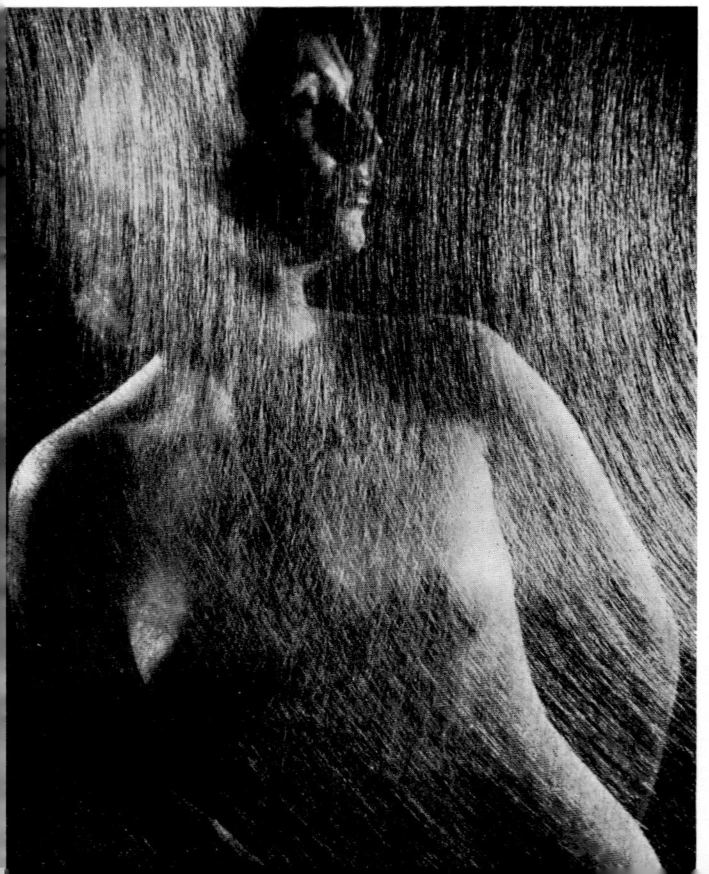

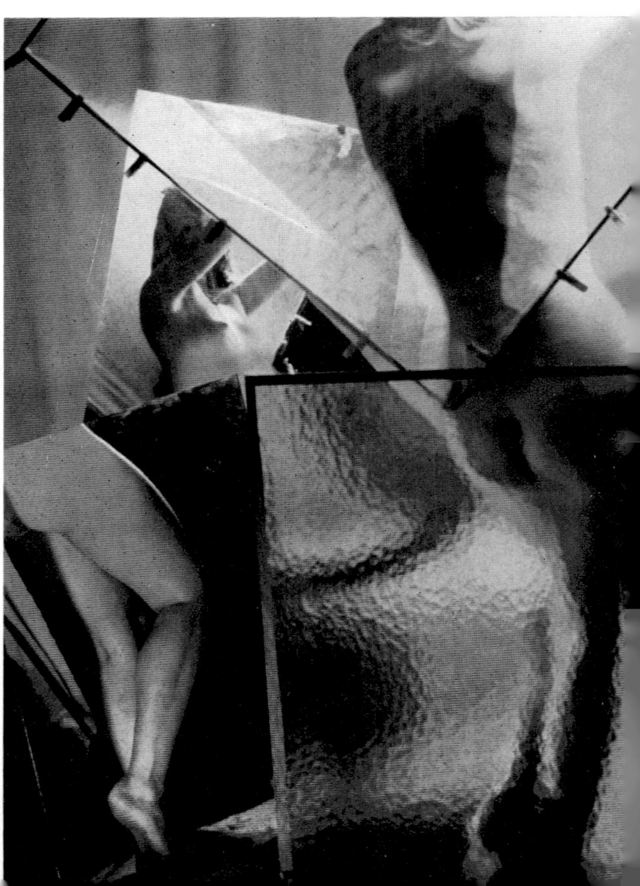

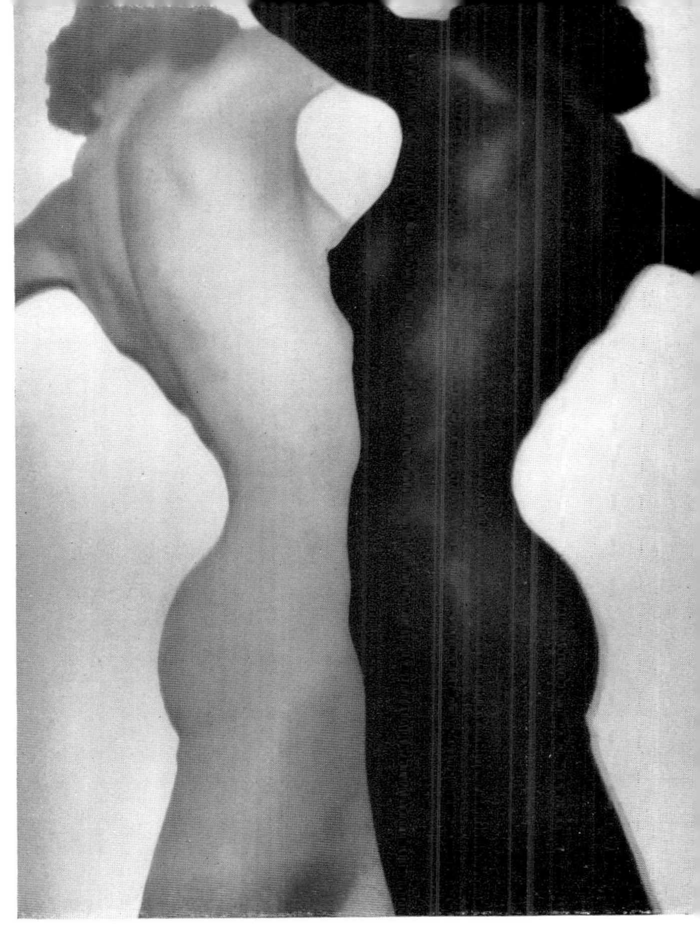

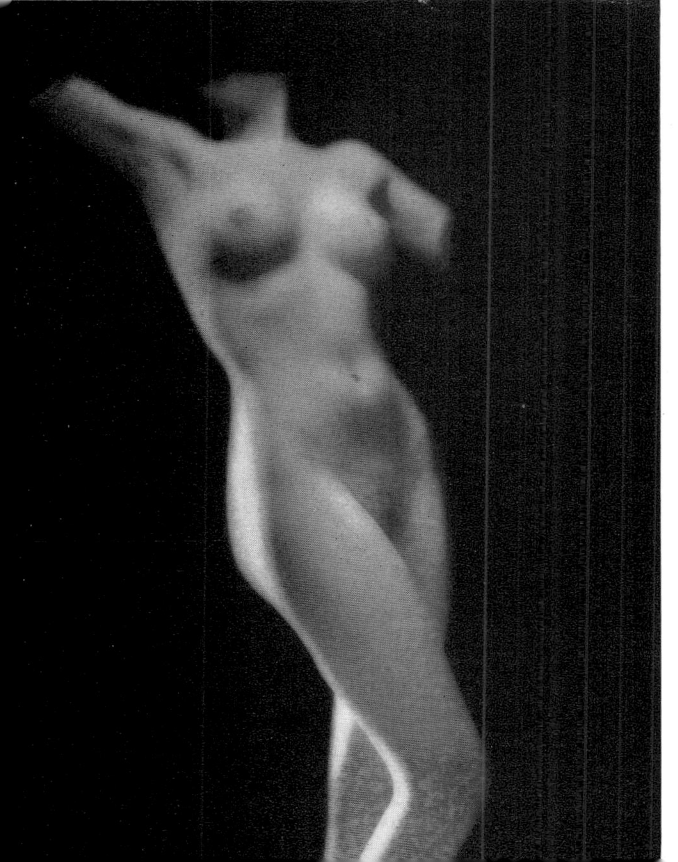

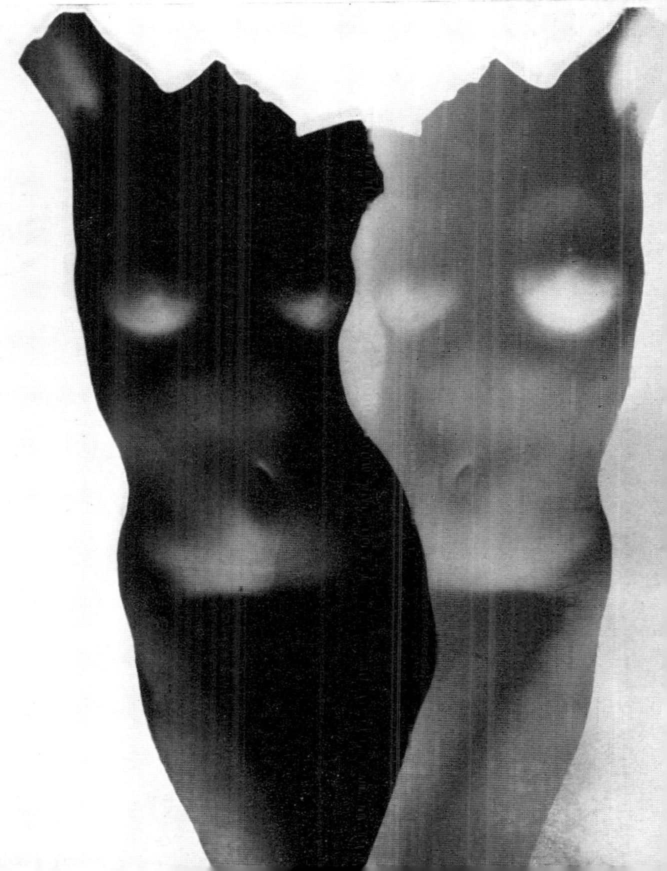

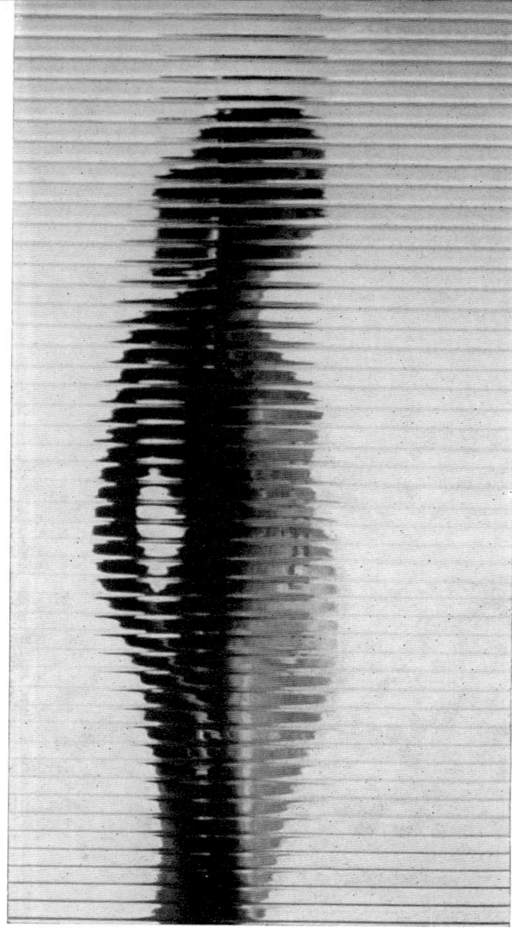

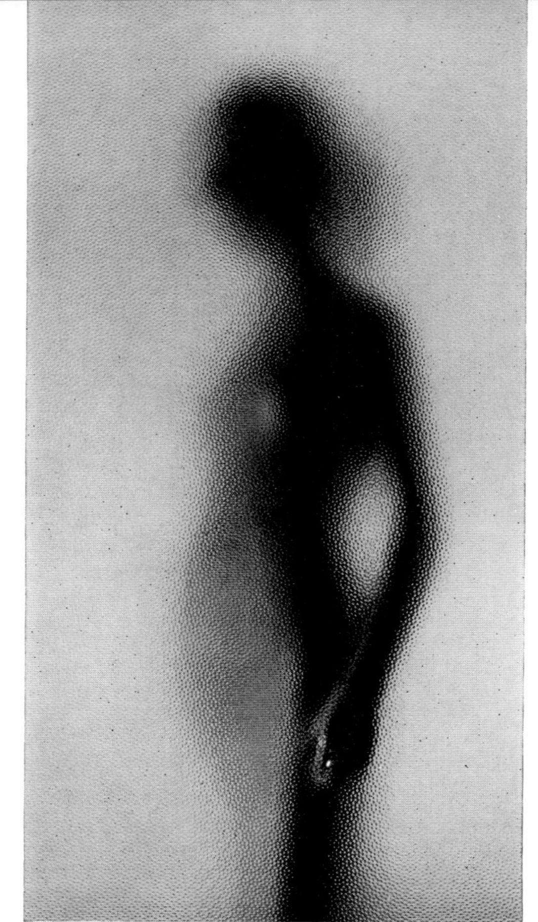

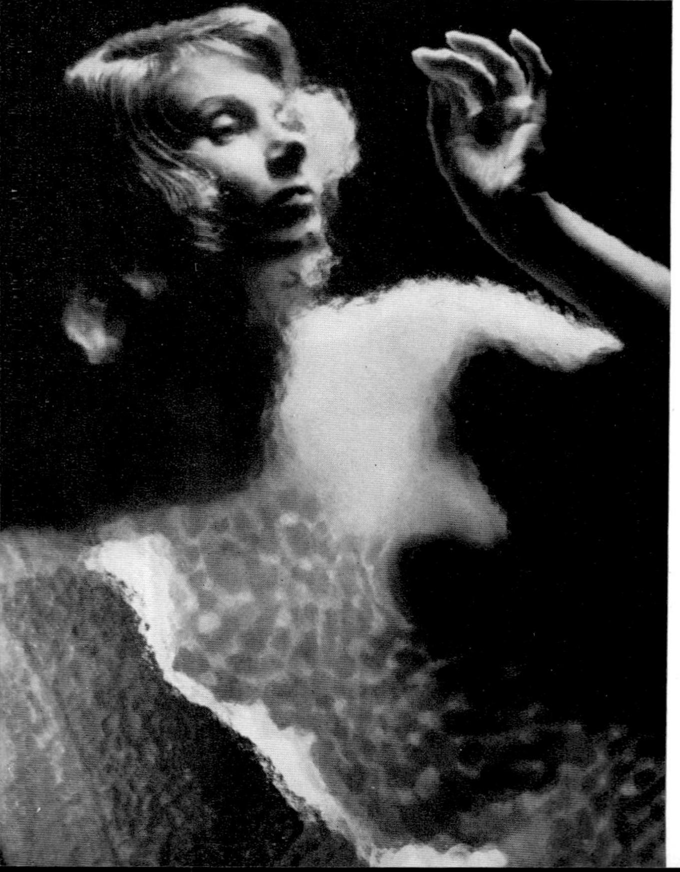

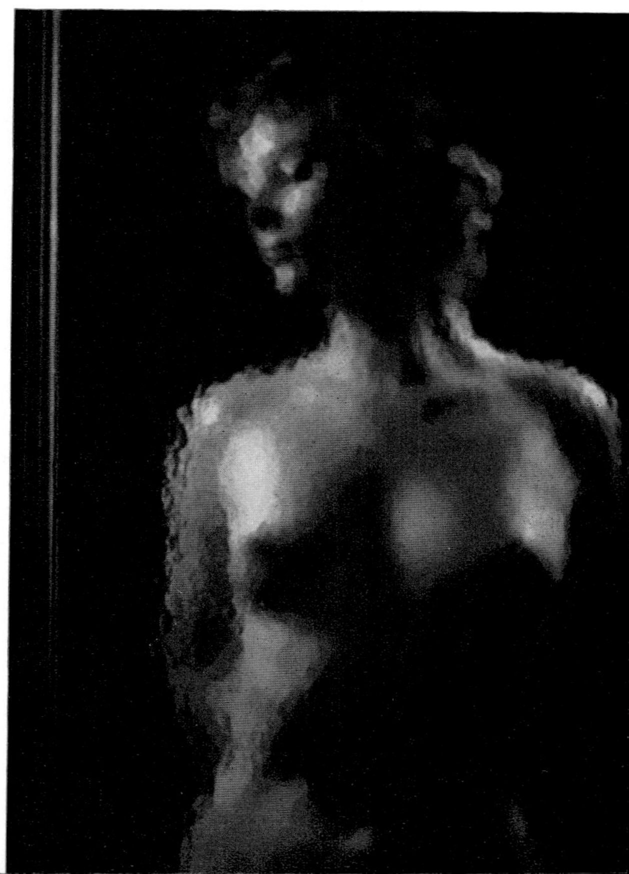

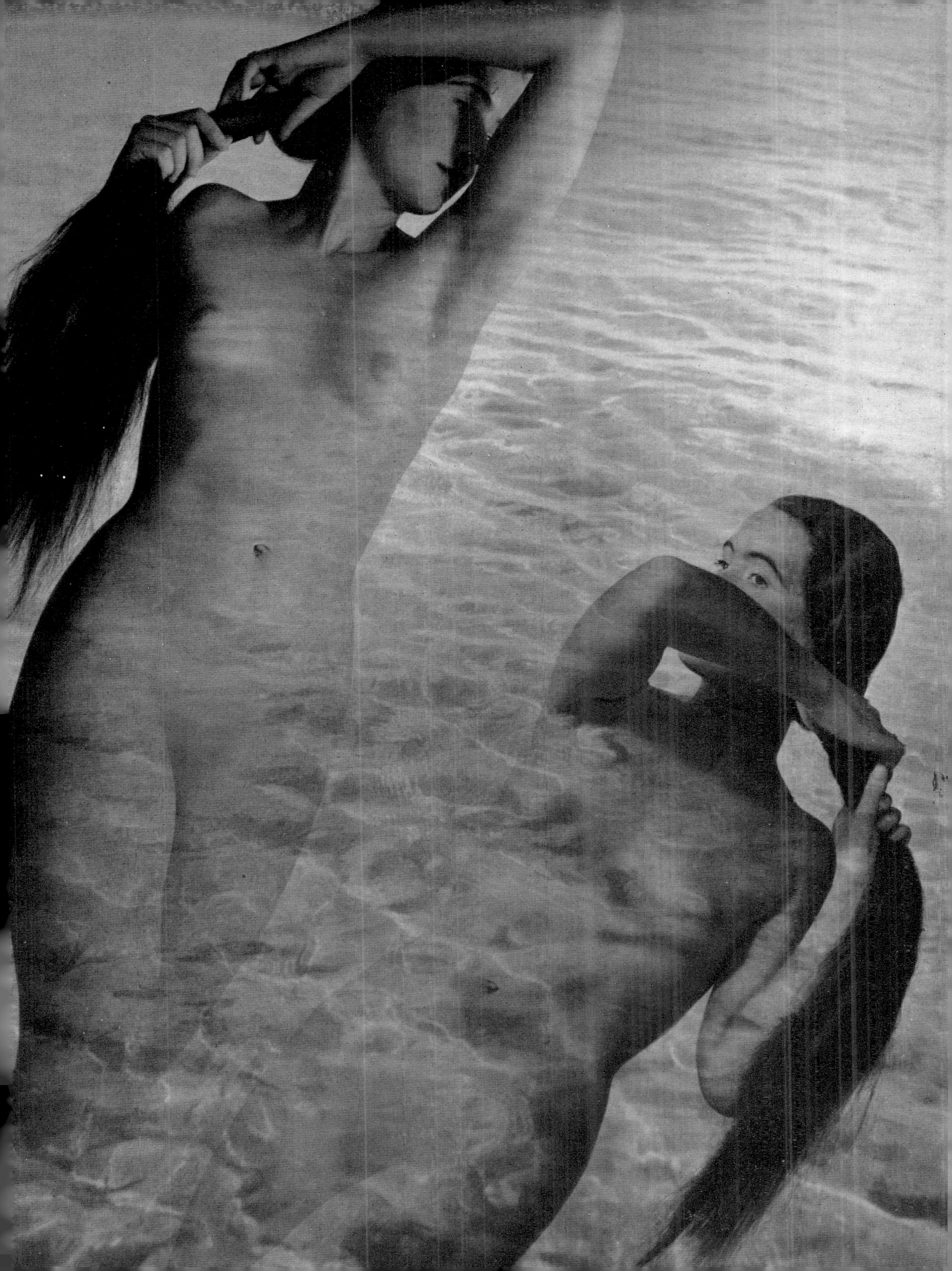

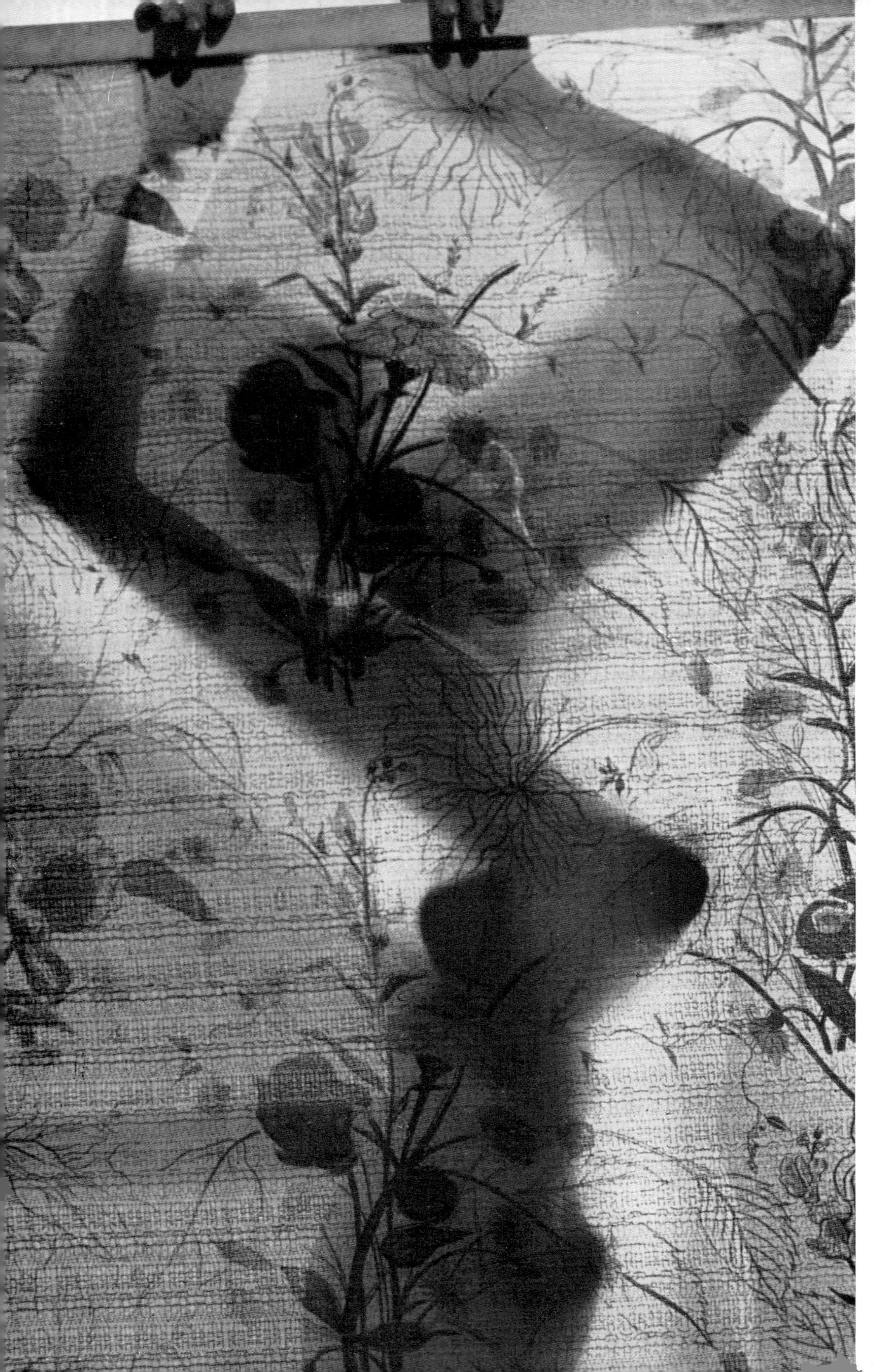

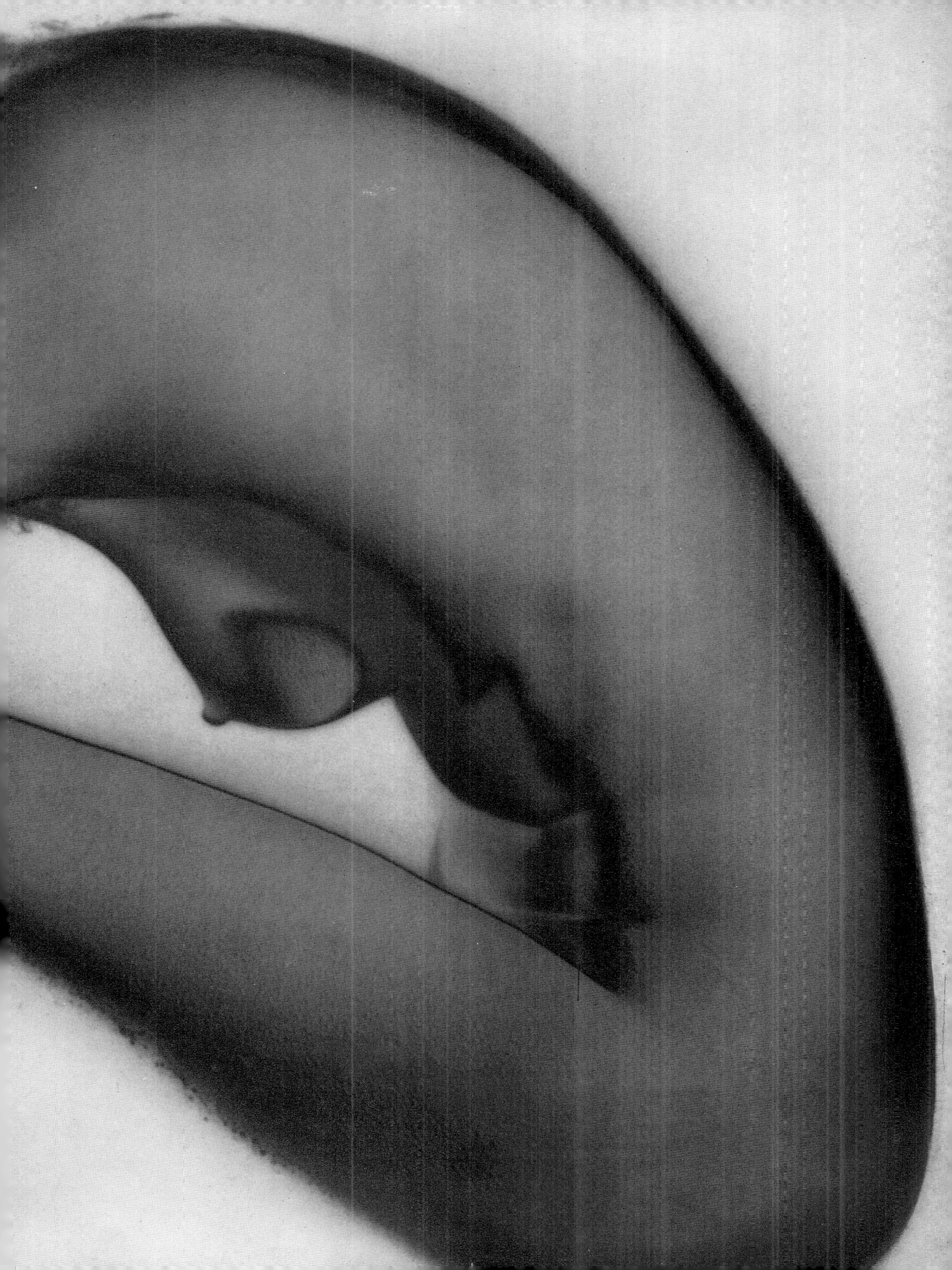

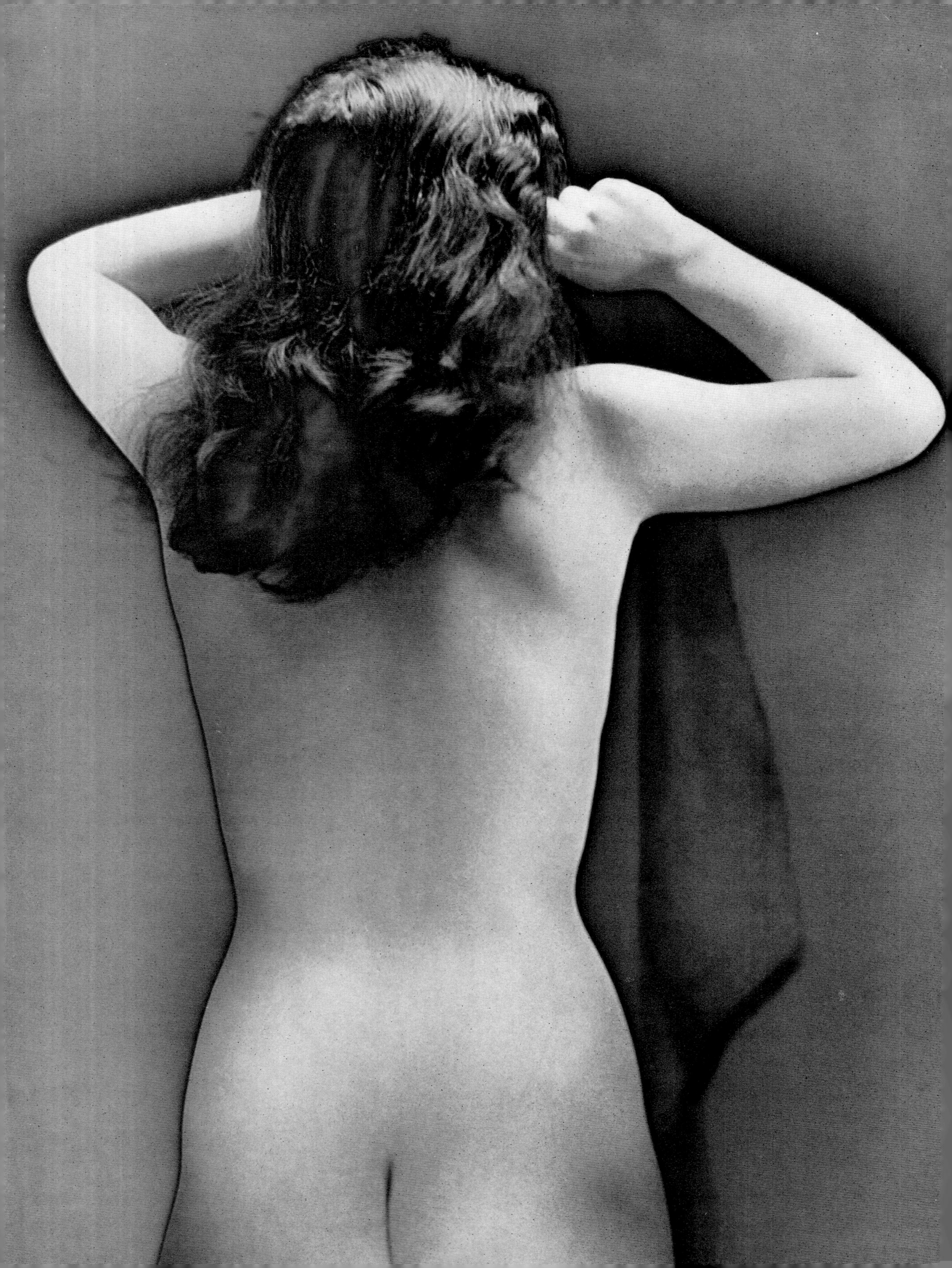

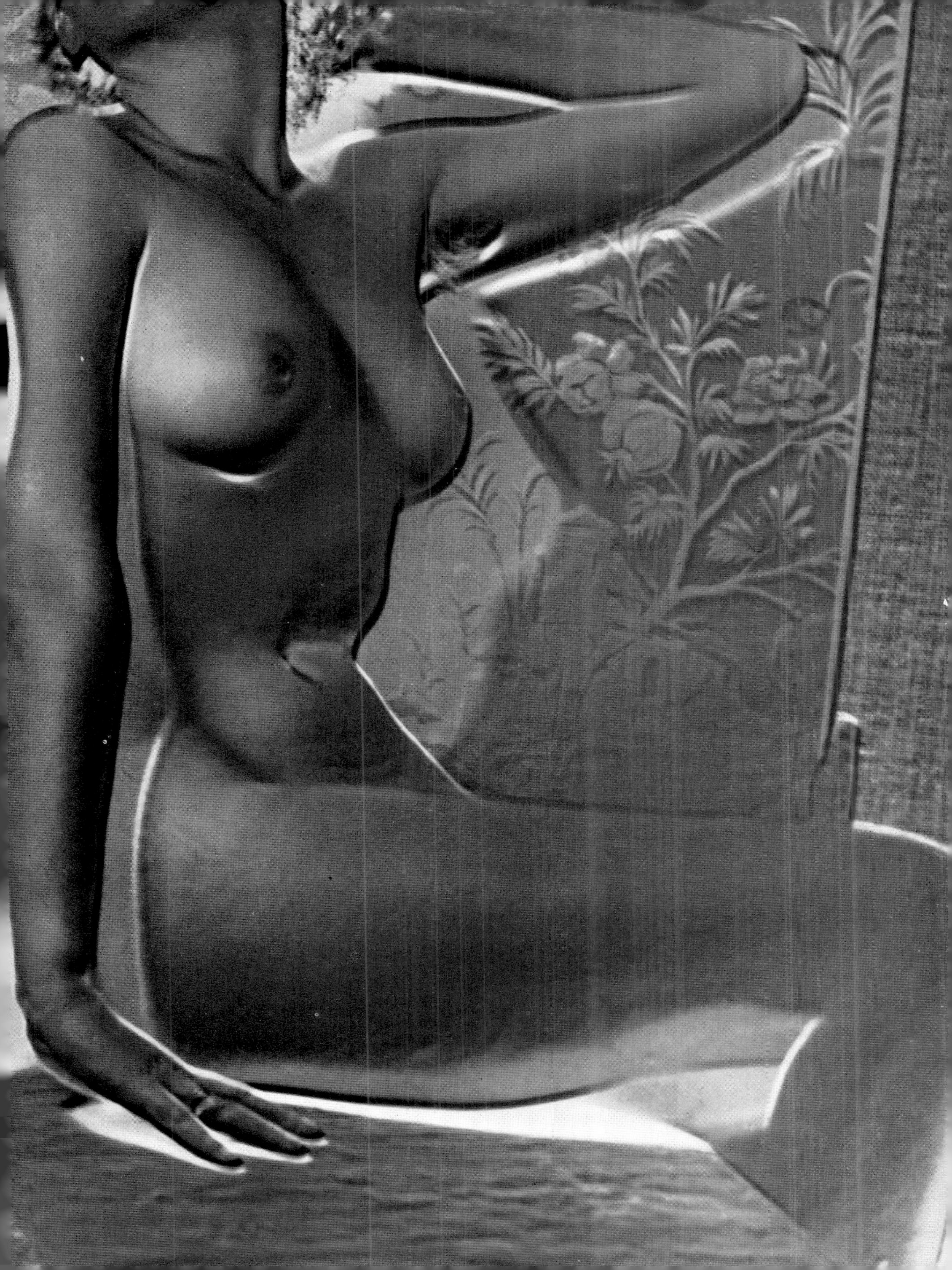

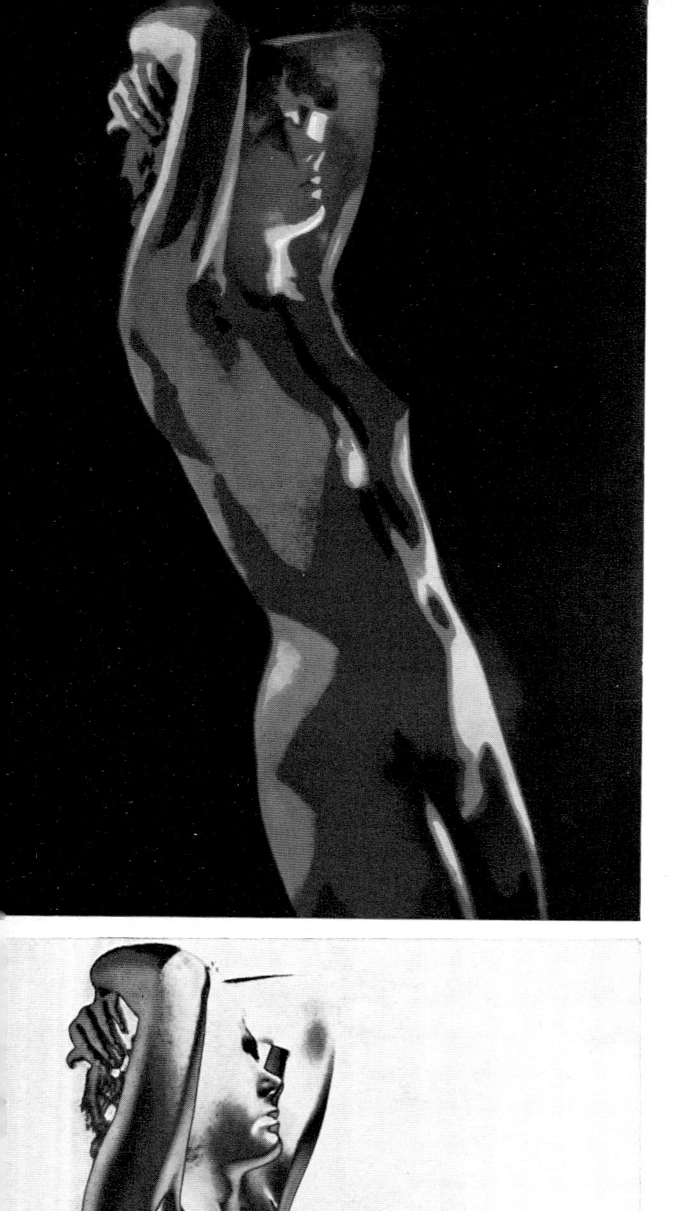

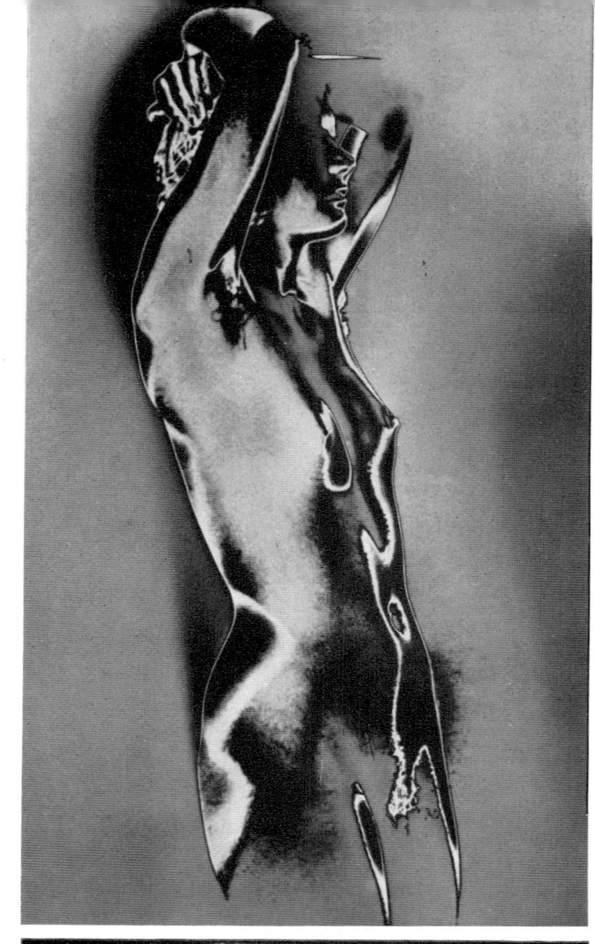

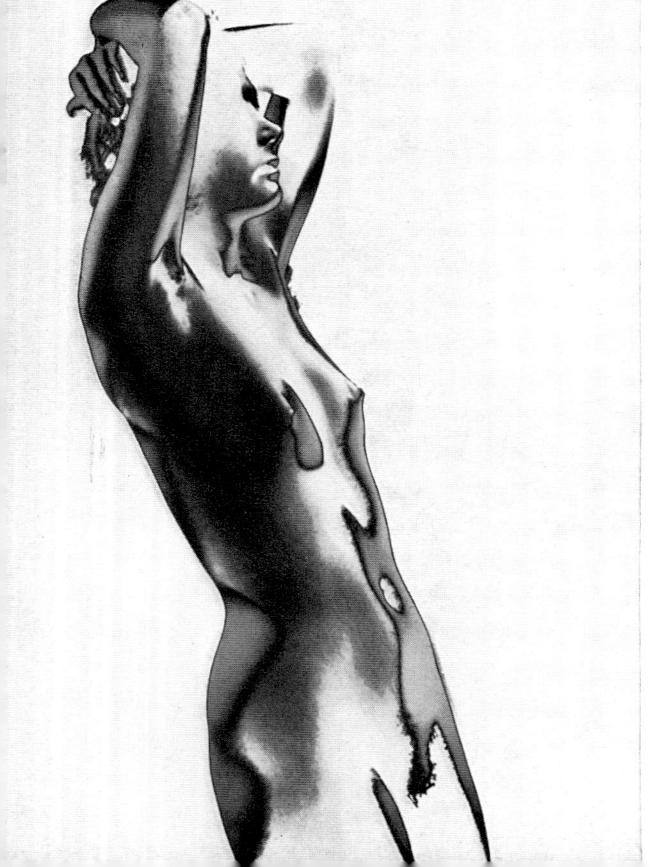

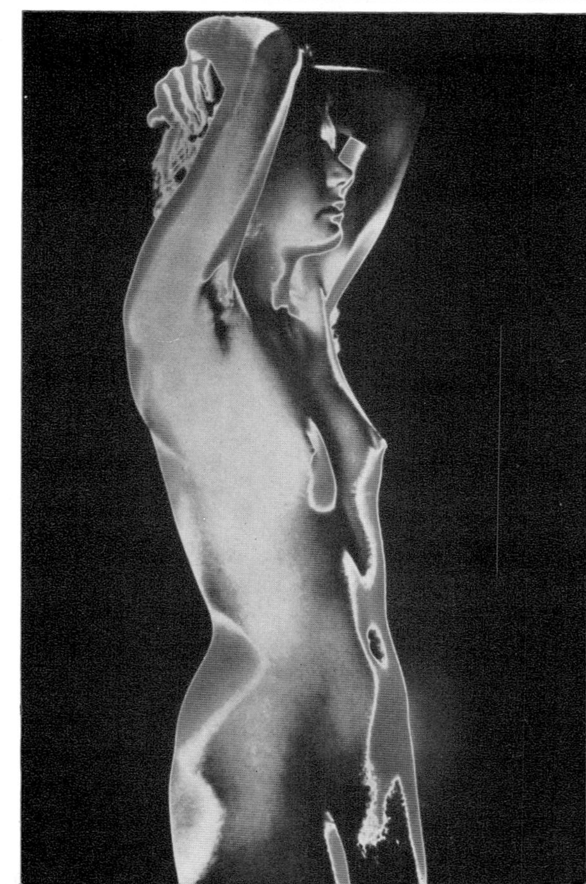

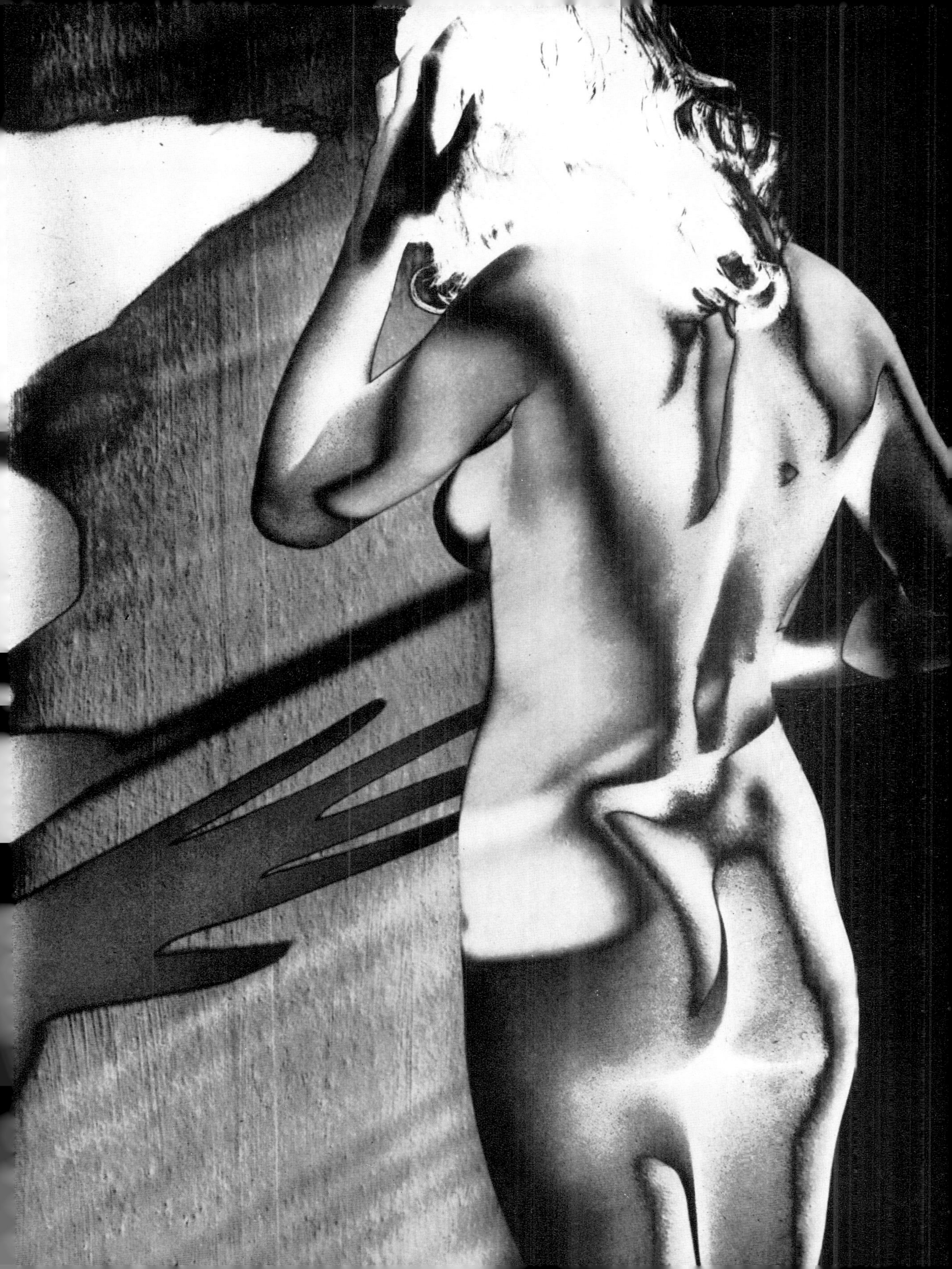

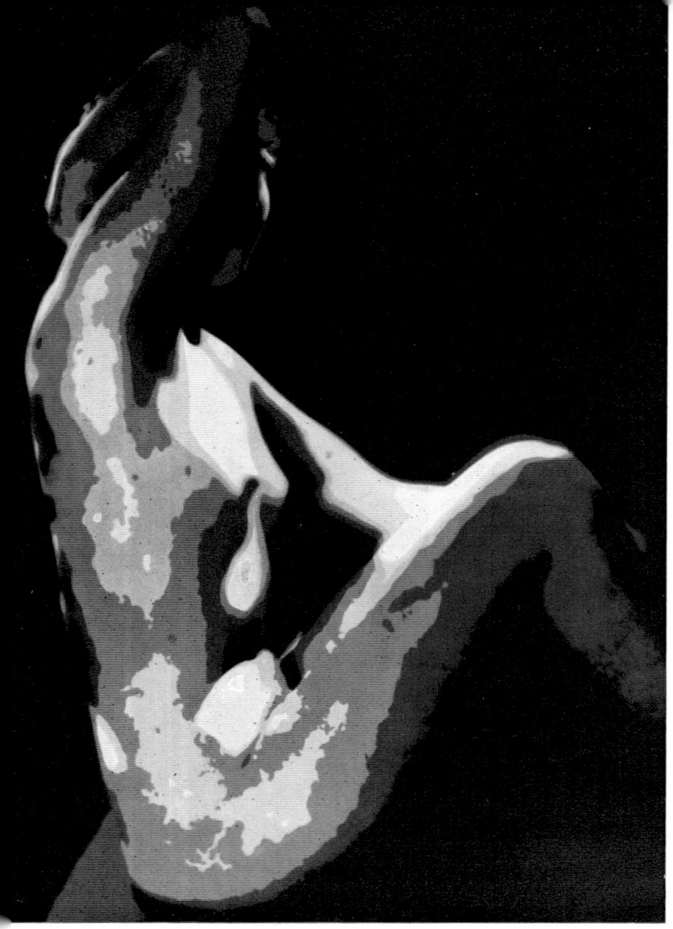

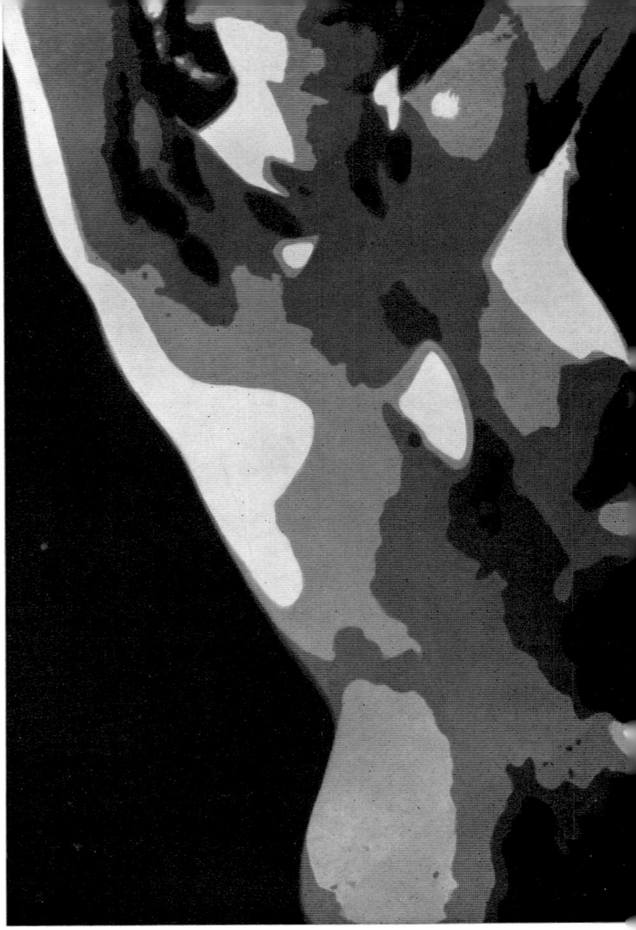

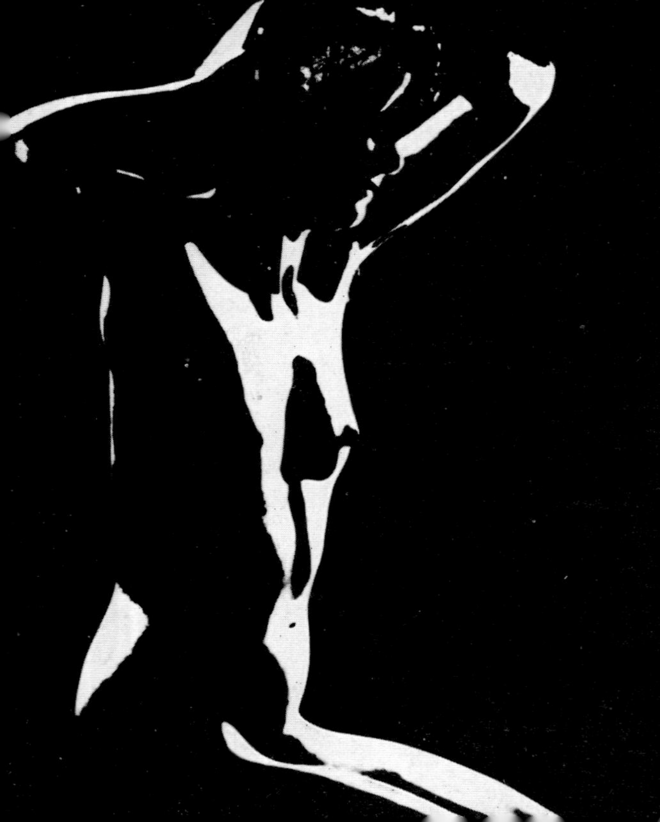
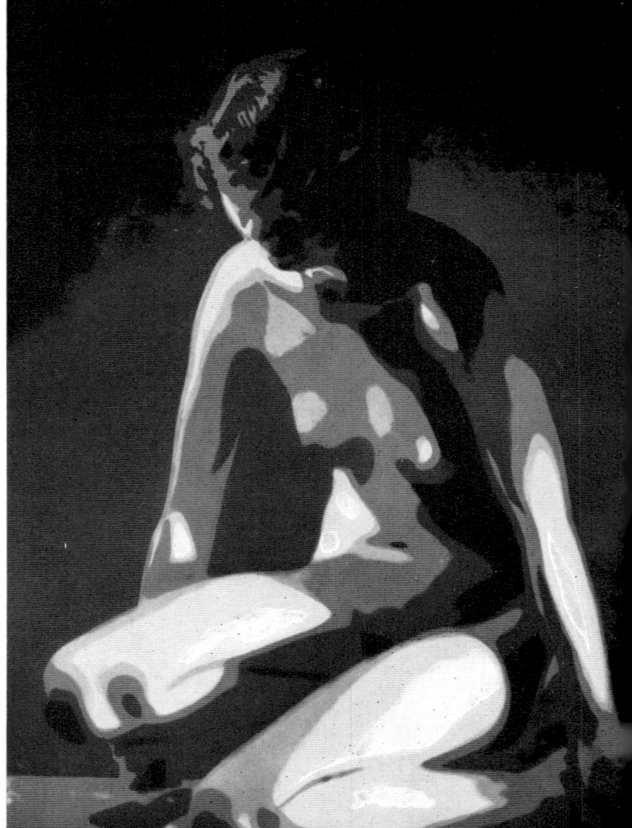

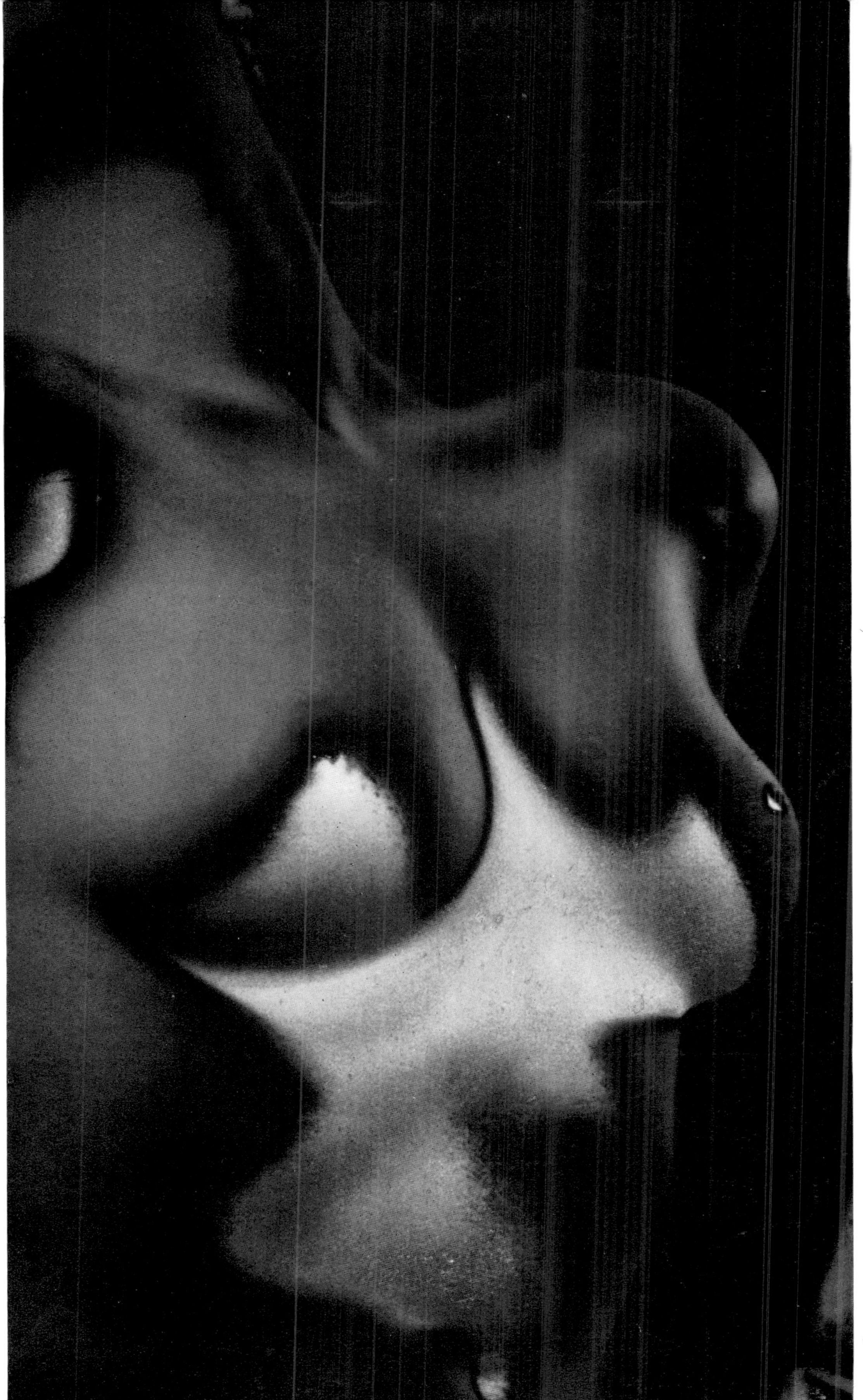

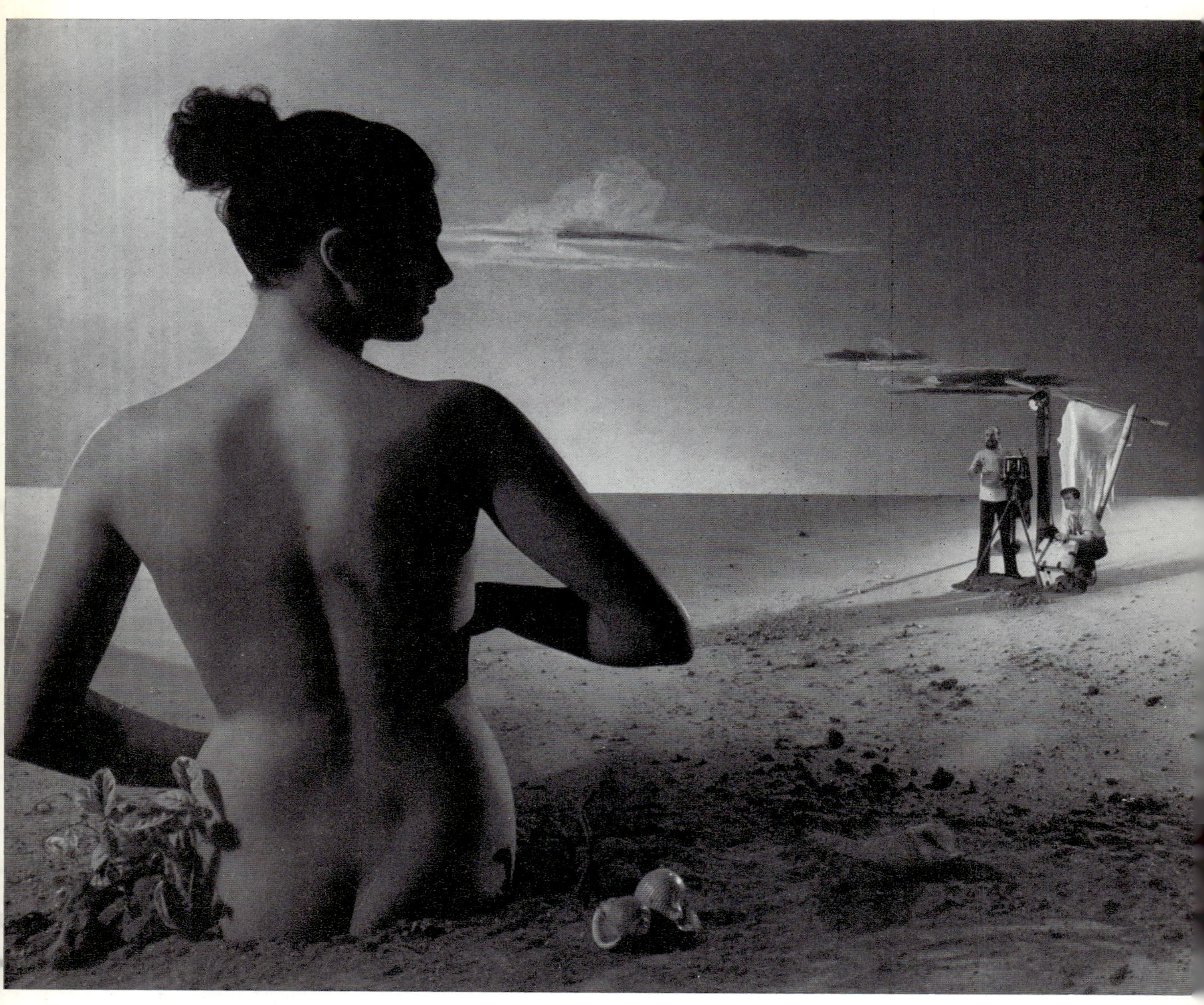

Page 161 (top and bottom right): *Variations* by H. Hajek-Halke GDL

These against-the-light pictures were taken in 1932 on glass plates. The glass sides of the plates were blackened with candle smoke. The soot was then removed with a dry water colour brush as much as was necessary to obtain the desired effect. The negatives were enlarged with a prism placed before the enlarger lens to get two images with one exposure.

Page 161 (bottom left): *Torso* by J. von Santho

Here the soft focus effect is overdone. The photograph was taken some time about 1930

Page 162 (top): *Through the Glass* by Dr. A. Gutschow

Bermpohl camera 9 × 12 cm.
The two figures seen through the panes of patterned glass are, in fact, a sculpture by Gerhard Marcks.

Page 162 (bottom): *Through the Glass* by Reinhold Lessmann

9 × 12 cm. camera, 10-in lens, three 500-watt photofloods, 1/25 second, *f* 5.6.
In both photographs the girls were standing behind panes of mottled glass with the camera focused on the glass. The success of this type of picture depends entirely on correct lighting and focusing.

Page 163: *Water-Nymphs* by Urs Lang-Kurz

Figure photographs: 13 × 18 cm. Linhof camera, *f* 4.5 Tessar, Kodak Portrait film, 1/50 second, *f* 16, developed in a Kodak Pyro solution.
Water photograph: 2¼-in. square Rolleiflex, Isopan F film, light yellow filter, 1/100 second, *f* 8-11, Atomal New developer.
A combination print made from a negative of the two figures and a negative of water. The photographer made a number of water photographs, selecting the most suitable one. She made the print by exposing the paper successively under two enlargers, each with one of the negatives.

Page 164: *Shadow Caricature* by Rudolf Müller-Schönhausen GDL

Stegemann 9 × 12 cm. camera, 24-cm. Heliar, Perutz Peromnia plate, 1/5 second, *f* 6.
The model was placed behind a curtain of flowered material. The photographer moved the light to one side and back until the shadow of the figure fell on the curtain, then the parts of the figure nearest the curtain appeared sharper and with deeper shadows. Then the curtain was moved until the shape of the flower pattern matched the shadow pattern of the figure.

Page 165: *Profile* by Dr. Mario Finazzi

6 × 9 cm. Plaubel Makina.
Dr. Finazzi, an Italian amateur photographer, has been working for many years with pseudo-solarization or the Sabattier effect "for fun". His pictures prove his mastery of this field.

Page 166: *Outlines* by Dr. Mario Finazzi

6 × 9 cm. reflex camera.
This print was also made by pseudo-solarization, but only the outlines have been darkened.

Page 167: *Bas-Relief* by Rudolf Müller-Schönhausen

Stegemann 12 × 9 cm. camera, 24-cm. Heliar, Peromnia plate, 1 second, *f* 11.
Produced by printing a negative-positive combination.

Page 168: *Four Variations* by Lothar Grün

2¼-in. square Primarflex, 10.5 cm. Tessar, two spots as side-back lighting and one diffuse light from the front.
From the original negative a transparency was made on Agfa Printon K film and exposed to light during development. The result was a solarized positive transparency. The picture on the bottom left on page 168 is a print from the transparency (i.e. a negative print). Next, a negative was made on Agfa process film by contact printing the solarized transparency; the bottom right picture is a print from it. Then Grün made a duplicate negative of the solarized transparency on Printon K film, exposing it to light during development. This produced the print at top right, a negative-positive solarization. Finally, the top left picture is a posterization with four tones made from the original negative.

Page 169: *Sunlight* by H. Heidersberger

9 × 12 cm. camera, 6-in. Heliar, Agfa Isopan F film, 1/5 second, *f* 11.
The negative had vigorous development and was contact printed on to a contrasty process film. The resulting transparency was partly developed, then given a second exposure to bright light. Finally, it was completely developed.

Page 170: *Examples of Posterization* by Lothar Grün

The four illustrations on this page continue the examples on page 168. All demonstrate posterization; top left, with four tones; top right and bottom right have five tones; and finally the picture at the bottom left has two tones only.

Page 171: *Abstract Nude* by Rudolf Müller-Schönhausen

Stegemann 9 × 12 cm. camera, 24-cm. Heliar, Perutz Peromnia plate, 1 second, *f* 11.
From the negative, a contrasty transparency was made but with good detail in the shadows. A second negative was then made on a lantern plate; this was given a flat gradation by means of full exposure and curtailed development. The negative was quickly passed through a greatly diluted fixing bath and given another exposure to direct white light. Finally, it was developed in a developing solution containing a large quantity of potassium bromide.

Page 172: *Surrealistic Landscape* by Angus McBean

9 × 12 cm. camera, Kodak P 1200 plate, 1/10 second, *f* 16.
This picture is not a montage. The scene was set up before the camera and photographed with a single exposure. Even the group in the middle distance is real—except for the photographers; they were represented by cut-out photographs.

Solarization

Pseudo-solarization or Sabattier effect are more correct names for what is usually called solarization. Readers will know that extreme overexposure causes a reversal of the image. Black in nature becomes again black on the negative, white becomes white. The positive print looks as the negative should look.

This effect can be utilized by exposing the partly developed negative for a short time to a diffuse lightsource (e.g. pan film for 3 seconds to a bright safelight) and continuing development as usual followed by fixing and washing. Thus the shadow parts of the negative receive a second exposure while the already strongly blackened highlights are scarcely altered. The outcome is a fairly dense negative from which prints or enlargements with very light shadows and a fine black outline round the subject are obtained.

Again the effect can be widely varied by adjustment of the lighting and exposure of the subject, the second exposure, and finally the length of development. This process requires much experience, discrimination and instinct.

A variation is positive solarization where the paper print is very briefly exposed (2–3 seconds as a rule) under a 100W lamp to diffuse but normally bright light. Martha Hoepffner, who has done many successful experiments with positive solarization, says:

"A very hard and contrasty negative is enlarged on ultra hard paper so that there are hardly any middle tones. Develop fully and then expose the print for 2–3 seconds to a bright light. Put the print back into the developer for a short time only until the light areas begin to turn grey and show a fine white line. Rinse quickly and fix.

"The smallest change in exposure and development causes a different effect. Where very bright tones adjoin very dark ones the intermediate exposure produces a fine white line which lends the nude an abstract effect supported also by the reversal of light body tones into dark grey tones."

Other special effects can be obtained during enlarging, for instance by interposing various materials between lens and bromide paper. Anybody who likes to experiment and has the necessary skill can add new interest to nude photography. Above and beyond that he may achieve new expressions from which the fields of advertising, poster, and all graphic art may ultimately profit.

The Enlargement

I should like to stress once again that what we want is a clear incorruptible enlargement on bromide paper that ruthlessly shows up any technical shortcomings. Formulating our requirements in the categorical imperative, we must have *deep, clear blacks—rich greys—brilliant whites.*

I wonder why so many otherwise capable amateurs and even professionals produce enlargements with muddy greys and chalky studies of grain?

Enlarging is also an art of finding the only correct exposure and developing correctly. The correctly exposed print that has not been overexposed must not lose its brightness in the developer. Nor must development be prolonged in order to make up for underexposure. A print has been correctly exposed when its brilliancy remains almost stable at the end of the recommended development time for the paper.

Highlights that are too dense may have to be "printed in", i.e. they have to receive additional exposure without causing undesirable stains or obvious edges. Masks and other aid to print control may have to be used. Sometimes a very brief rinse in weak Farmer's reducer clears the highlights.

Once I have found the "only correct" shape of the picture I trace it with a pointed pen and ruler on the transparent negative envelope, but not before I have given it very serious consideration. Since I was 15 years old I have regretted my decision only $3\frac{1}{2}$ times. I do this also with negative colour film.

I acquired this habit because for years I have had to let other people print my negatives during my travels in East Asia, Turkey, Australia, Peru, and on the islands of the Sulu Archipelago. A willing and helpful photographer could always be found and I have not had too many disappointments.

Part enlarging can only too easily become a bad habit. I have already voiced my opinion which is that we must see our picture finished and complete in the viewfinder. Of course I have also made the occasional part enlargement. And sometimes the expression of the picture may require an unusually high or wide enlargement. But in normal circumstances I am sorry for every part of the negative I lose.

A small white margin looks out of place on whole-plate and bigger prints. So from half-plate upwards leave either a good white margin or none at all. A deckled edge torn by hand off a sheet of hand made paper looks lovely. The deckled edge made with the specially shaped guillotine is only a sham.

Printing paper with semi-matt, matt, velvet, satin and similar surfaces are suitable for special purposes, for instance as presents or for hanging on the wall.

High gloss on a tinted surface is an abomination. The only suitable surfaces for cream and ivory paper are semi-matt to velvet.

There is no point in glazing a glossy print when a dirty glazing sheet leaves intricate matt patterns all over the paper. Glazed glossy prints can be quite easily spotted with a thin brush and diluted Indian ink. Small areas showing traces of knifing are less unpleasing to the eye than pinholes, telegraph wires, stress marks and similar blemishes. Knifing is best done with half a razor blade, but only the old fashioned three-hole blades are rigid enough for this work.

Any retouching that goes beyond spotting and eliminating scratches and other damage to the emulsion is bad. We must leave the smoothing out of wrinkles and putting highlights into the negatives to the professional photographer. He has to do it to please his sitters. Painting, lightening, and enlarging highlights with crayon or other media is phoney photography.

By the way, we can manage quite easily without glazing. No glazing sheet will give the print a depth and brilliance it never had before. For 12 by 15 inches and bigger exhibition prints the most suitable paper is plain white smooth glossy.

Nude photographs in the shape of $2\frac{1}{4}$ square contact prints (with deckle edges) stuck in the family album are not nude photography. The album is nothing whatever to do with photography, only with souvenirs. I use double weight paper and Leitz files. They give me the easy filing I want.

Large prints can be stored like artists' drawings in appropriate portfolios. The best filing method resembles a card index system. There is no limit to personal preference and inventiveness in finding the most practical and convenient system. It is nice, of course, when a collection is presented with style.

Peeping Toms who do not know the difference between pictures of naked girls and nude photography—they exist—are best kept away. Let me close by giving this apt quotation:

"Associating the naked body always with sex is about as intelligent as thinking of food every time one sees a mouth."

Viewpoint

Everything simple and natural is difficult. In everyday life too empty phrases are more easily come by than truth and natural humanity. And there is no Salvation Army to save good taste. But one can make appropriate and inappropriate claims. The question is whether the claims we are making for our subject are too high.

What we all seek to achieve is a work of great, if possible unique, expression. Masterpieces are rare. But if they are to be created at all they must be born of a high standard of average work; without it they are unthinkable.

Finally, what of the nature of our photographic medium, the medium that is still accused by laymen and people who cannot free themselves from ancient notions of being too lowly and too circumscribed ever to achieve creative expression. ...

The crowd usually overestimates the small amount of freedom necessary to guarantee individual expression and genuine creative work. I should like to quote an example from a completely different sphere: "What a simple, circumscribed contrivance is the piano with its always recurring octaves, and how much individual creation it makes possible!"

Photography and its great sisters, television and film, have in fact widened the confines of our optical awareness and opened up hitherto uncharted regions. For this reason every artist who still paints like the masters of the past, however perfect his craftsmanship and skill, is a doubtful artist. The crowd may think his work ever so beautiful and "easy to understand" but his contribution to our age and world has no significance. Colour photography can do his work better.

The real artists have known this for a long time. They also know that painting is a primitive human phenomenon that will still be with us on the Day of Judgment.

Let me repeat: when we take a photograph of a human being in the nude we are acting not only from and for vitality, nostalgia, realism or magic, sublimation and sex, enrichment, study and aesthetic enjoyment. We are also endeavouring to regain in uncharted regions a point of view which is only one form of expression among others. But the principle is vitally important: the subject is Man.

Too high a claim after all? No. Even in our pursuit we listen to the breath of nature, and that is not yesterday's romanticism but a strong and everlasting thing. And for our photography we demand not only optical realism but realism in craftsmanship, strict self-criticism, and modesty.

The nude herself, the subject of our self-expression, is as new to-day as on the first day. Every age finds what it seeks and forms what it sees. Thus our photographic endeavour is also an outstanding expression of our age.

BOOKS ON CAMERA TECHNIQUE

THE PHOTOGRAPHIC PORTRAIT

By O. R. Croy

Shows, with practical examples, how the correct interplay of the subject's physical characteristics with the advantages and limitations of the photographic medium can produce a good portrait.

246 *pp.*, 8 *colour plates*, 91 *photographs*, 34 *diagrams*
Price £2·50

CAMERA PORTRAITURE

By Herbert Williams

Herbert Williams was for 25 years chief instructor in portraiture at Regent Street Polytechnic School of Photography, London. His book will help to produce likenesses which reach beyond the ephemeral effect of snapshots.

164 *pp.*, 105 *photographs* *Price* £2·50

LIGHTING FOR PHOTOGRAPHY

By W. Nurnberg

Goes back to the technical roots of artificial lighting, reveals the advantages and limitations of different light sources, sketches the principles of their practical use and gives countless suggestions as to their individual application.

210 *pp.*, 8 *colour plates*, 137 *photographs*, 149 *diagrams.*
Price £3·00

PICTURE MAKING WITH THE REFLEX

By H. S. Newcombe

If you handle reflex cameras with understanding, knowledge of what can be expected from the film and learn to appreciate how one subject matter differs from another—you cannot help getting winners. All you need is in this book.

256 *pp.*, 32 *photographs*, 58 *diagrams.* *Price* £1·05

VIEW CAMERA TECHNIQUE

By Leslie Stroebel

The various types of view camera and their features are extensively analysed, compared and evaluated. Covers the most modern applications of the view camera in commercial, architectural and fashion photography.

312 *pp.*, 301 *photographs*, 166 *diagrams.* *Price* £3·50

VIEWS ON NUDES

By Bill Jay

This is a picture survey of the whole spectrum of nude photography, largely representing the work of present-day masters and experimentalists, but also including a chronologically arranged selection of classics from the earliest Victorian to the outstanding work of the earlier part of this century.

156 *pp.*, 136 *photographs.* *Price* £1·75

LIGHT ON PEOPLE

By Paul Petzold

This is a book on photographic lighting—with a difference. In the past, indoor lighting had to be contrived and outdoor light just accepted. Light is now a creative tool irrespective of whether you use it indoors or outdoors, for black and white or colour. Paul Petzold's book reflects this new freedom of spirit.

229 × 194 *mm.* 152 *pp.*, 45 *colour plates*, 133 *photographs* *Price* £1·75

LIGHTING FOR PORTRAITURE

By W. Nurnberg

The precision of thought and clarity of system presented here are as unprecedented as is the breadth of the illustrations. A work which will serve for a life time—as a guide and an encyclopaedic source of reference.

186 *pp.*, 20 *colour plates*, 232 *b & w photographs*, 264 *diagrams.* *Price* £3·00

35mm. PHOTO TECHNIQUE

By H. S. Newcombe

The essential factors of the perfect miniature image—delicate negatives, big enlargements, long lengths of film, standardised processing, wide range of equipment—are correlated here into a straightforward system of practical camera work.

326 *pp.*, 116 *photographs*, 33 *diagrams.* *Price* £2·25

PHOTOGRAPHY WITH THE EYE-LEVEL REFLEX

By H. S. Newcombe

Explains how the system works and its all-round versatility. Shows how to use the reflex for black-and-white and colour, how to process film and produce good prints.

248 *pp.*, 4 *colour plates*, 42 *b & w photographs*, 17 *diagrams.* *Price* £1·50